Sport, War and the British

Spanning the colonial campaigns of the Victorian age to the War on Terror after 9/11, this study explores the role sport was perceived to have played in the lives and work of military personnel, and examines how sporting language and imagery were deployed to shape and reconfigure civilian society's understanding of conflict.

From 1850 onwards war reportage – complemented and reinforced by a glut of campaign histories, memoirs, novels and films – helped create an imagined community in which sporting attributes and qualities were employed to give meaning and order to the chaos and misery of warfare. This work explores the evolution of the Victorian notion that playing-field and battlefield were connected and then moves on to investigate the challenges this belief faced in the twentieth century, as combat became, initially, industrialised in the age of total warfare and, subsequently, professionalised in the post-nuclear world. Such a longitudinal study allows, for the first time, new light to be shed on the continuities and shifts in the way the 'reality' of war was captured in the British popular imagination.

Drawing together the disparate fields of sport and warfare, this book serves as a vital point of reference for anyone with an interest in the cultural, social or military history of modern Britain.

Peter Donaldson is Senior Lecturer in modern British history at the University of Kent, UK.

Routledge Research in Sports History

The *Routledge Research in Sports History* series presents leading research in the development and historical significance of modern sport through a collection of historiographical, regional and thematic studies which span a variety of periods, sports and geographical areas. Showcasing ground-breaking, cross-disciplinary work from established and emerging sport historians, the series provides a crucial contribution to the wider study of sport and society.

Available in this series:

The Black Press and Black Baseball, 1915–1955
A Devil's Bargain
Brian Carroll

Football and Literature in South America
David Wood

Cricket: A Political History of the Global Game, 1945–2017
Stephen Wagg

Wrestling in Britain
Sporting Entertainments, Celebrity and Audiences
Benjamin Litherland

A History of Chinese Martial Arts
Edited by Fan Hong and Fuhua Huang

The Early Development of Football
Contemporary Debates
Edited by Graham Curry

Sport, War and the British
1850 to the Present
Peter Donaldson

For more information about this series, please visit: www.routledge.com/sport/series/RRSH

Sport, War and the British
1850 to the Present

Peter Donaldson

LONDON AND NEW YORK

First published 2020
by Routledge
2 Park Square, Milton Park, Abingdon, Oxon OX14 4RN

and by Routledge
605 Third Avenue, New York, NY 10017

Routledge is an imprint of the Taylor & Francis Group, an informa business

First issued in paperback 2021

© 2020 Peter Donaldson

The right of Peter Donaldson to be identified as author of this work has been asserted by him in accordance with sections 77 and 78 of the Copyright, Designs and Patents Act 1988.

All rights reserved. No part of this book may be reprinted or reproduced or utilised in any form or by any electronic, mechanical, or other means, now known or hereafter invented, including photocopying and recording, or in any information storage or retrieval system, without permission in writing from the publishers.

Trademark notice: Product or corporate names may be trademarks or registered trademarks, and are used only for identification and explanation without intent to infringe.

Publisher's Note
The publisher has gone to great lengths to ensure the quality of this reprint but points out that some imperfections in the original copies may be apparent.

British Library Cataloguing-in-Publication Data
A catalogue record for this book is available from the British Library

Library of Congress Cataloging-in-Publication Data
Names: Donaldson, Peter (Peter McIntosh), author. | Routledge (Firm)
Title: Sport, war and the British : 1850 to the present / Peter Donaldson.
Other titles: Routledge research in sports history.
Description: New York : Routledge, 2020. | Series: Routledge research in sports history | Includes bibliographical references and index.
Identifiers: LCCN 2019054037 (print) | LCCN 2019054038 (ebook) | ISBN 9780367340780 (Hardback) | ISBN 9780429323799 (eBook)
Subjects: LCSH: Sports—Political aspects—Great Britain. | Sports and state—Great Britain. | Sports—Social aspects—Great Britain. | Sports—Great Britain—History.
Classification: LCC GV706.35 .D66 2020 (print) | LCC GV706.35 (ebook) | DDC 796.0941—dc23
LC record available at https://lccn.loc.gov/2019054037
LC ebook record available at https://lccn.loc.gov/2019054038

ISBN 13: 978-0-367-34078-0 (hbk)
ISBN 13: 978-1-03-223799-2 (pbk)
ISBN 13: 978-0-429-32379-9 (ebk)

Typeset in Times New Roman
by Apex CoVantage, LLC

For Dr Daniel Donaldson

Contents

List of figures		viii
Acknowledgements		ix
	Introduction	1
1	Victoria's small wars, 1837–1899: 'Hunt, shoot, and fight'	11
2	The South African War, 1899–1902: 'We are having a very enjoyable game'	39
3	The First World War: 'A new and deadly game'	65
4	The Second World War: Winning in the 'ashes of civilisation'	94
5	War in the nuclear age, 1945 to the present: 'Top guns 1, mad dog 0'	125
	Conclusion	154
Bibliography		159
Index		175

Figures

1.1	John Leech, 'Now for It!', *Punch*, 17 January 1855	25
1.2	John Leech, 'The New Alliance', *Punch*, 24 September 1859	26
2.1	H. W. Wilson, *With the Flag to Pretoria: A History of the Boer War of 1899–1900 Volume II* (London: Harmsworth Bros., 1901), p. 493	43
2.2	Bernard Partridge, 'The Last Wicket', *Punch*, 15 May 1901	53
3.1	Samuel Begg, 'In the Wings of the Theatre of War: Behind the Centre of the Fighting Line, Belgium', *Illustrated London News*, 5 December 1914	69
3.2	*The Times*, 8 December 1914	71

Acknowledgements

I would like to thank the staff of the various libraries and archives visited in the course of the research for this book, all of whom fielded my constant questions with patience and professionalism. I am also grateful to the School of History at the University of Kent for the provision of study leave and research grants. The editorial boards for *War and Society* and the *Journal of Military History* provided permission to reprint portions of articles that appeared in their journals. Finally, I would like to thank the staff at Routledge, in particular Simon Whitmore and Rebecca Connor, for their help in preparing the manuscript for publication.

Introduction

In Charlotte Brontë's *Jane Eyre*, published in 1847, Miss Ingram vainly attempts to win over the dashing Mr Rochester by outlining the key attributes she believes all true English gentlemen should exhibit: 'Let them be solicitous to possess only strength and valour: let their motto be – hunt, shoot, and fight.'[1] Although Rochester refuses to conform to such cultural expectations, Miss Ingram's creed would, nonetheless, have struck a chord with the novel's largely middle-class readership. By the accession of Victoria, the belief that the army officer was also a sportsman and a gentleman had become firmly embedded in the popular consciousness. With its roots in the cultural and social traditions of the rural landed gentry, the English officer corps had, unsurprisingly, adopted the leisure pursuits and associated values of that class. Thus, expertise in field sports, in hunting, fishing and shooting, served as one of the defining characteristics of the commissioned soldier. However, the popularly accepted sporting interests of the military were by no means limited to country pursuits. The expansion of the public school system in the second half of the nineteenth century saw the range of sports associated with the idealised sporting warrior extended to embrace team games. Cultivated on the playing-fields of schools such as Eton and Harrow, a cult of athleticism evolved among the burgeoning middle classes and, disseminated to the wider populace by journalists and middle-brow novelists, quickly became rooted in the value system of late Victorian society.[2] The public school–educated British officer was, then, expected to have a passion for, and to be proficient at, a range sporting activities. And this veneration of sport was given the full encouragement of those in authority. As J. D. Campbell has shown in his comprehensive survey of sporting culture and the British military, by the turn of the twentieth century, the army's belief in the moral as well as physical benefits of athletic endeavour matched, if not exceeded, that of the great public schools.[3] Sport, it was assumed, not only promoted fitness, teamwork, stoicism and bravery but also instilled a sense of honour and a respect for the rules of the game.[4] Indeed, for the radical commentator J. A. Hobson, the upper-middle-class officer's fervour for true sport had become so all-consuming by the time of the South African War of 1899–1902 that it could 'only be satisfied by expansion and militarism'. 'The leisured classes in Great Britain', he argued in a searing indictment of the imperial mission, published in 1903,

> having most of their energy liberated from the necessity of work, naturally specialise in sport. . . . As the milder expressions of this passion are alone

permissible in the sham or artificial encounters of domestic sports, where wild game disappears and human conflicts more mortal than football are prohibited, there is an even stronger pressure to the frontiers of civilisation in order that the thwarted 'spirit of adventure' may have strong free play.[5]

And the sporting passions and practices of the British army did not stop when the age of imperial conquest came to an end. In the two total wars of the twentieth century, in the Falklands conflict of 1982, in the Gulf War of the early 1990s and in the War on Terror from 2001 onwards, team games and physical recreation continued to feature prominently in the lives of frontline soldiers.

Yet, the nexus between sport and war was not simply restricted to the military's enduring predilection for games during wartime or to the generally favourable press coverage that such activity attracted. In many ways, even more revealing of the playing-field's conflation with the battlefield was the way in which sporting language and imagery were deployed by both combatants and non-combatants to shape and reconfigure the experience of conflict. As Jenny Seagrove has observed, this use of the sporting world as a frame of reference for military operations had a long history in Western culture.[6] Let two examples serve to illustrate the point. First, from the commemorative practices of the Ancient Greeks: the nine-metre-high statue of Nike abutting the great Temple of Zeus in Olympia, constructed from the spoils of war by the Messenians to celebrate the recapture of Sphacteria from the Spartans in 425 BCE, was symbolically significant as an allusion to not only martial but also sporting victory.[7] Second, from Shakespeare's reimagining of the Wars of the Roses: the courage and determination of Talbot's English troops, when confronted by overwhelming French forces outside the gates of Bordeaux, was emphatically underscored in *Henry VI, Part 1* by the deployment of an extended hunting metaphor:

> How we are park'd and bounded in a pale,
> A little herd of England's timorous deer,
> Maz'd with a yelping kennel of French curs!
> If we be English deer, be then in blood,
> Not rascal-like, but fall down with a pinch,
> But rather, moody-mad; and, desperate stags,
> Turn on the bloody hounds with heads of steel,
> And make cowards stand aloof at bay.
> Sell every man his life as dear as mine,
> And they shall find dear deer of us my friends.[8]

Thus, by the mid-nineteenth century, the practice of using sporting imagery and values to make sense of warfare was firmly rooted in the popular imagination. In particular, as the Shakespearean illustration above intimates, blood sports were seen as possessing rich metaphorical potential. First-hand accounts of military life in Africa and India, in which imperial campaigning was portrayed as little more than an exhilarating sporting adventure, appeared to support the claim of Robert

Surtees' comic Cockney creation, Mr. Jorrocks, that hunting was 'the image of war'.[9] As the twentieth century ushered in an era of industrialised global conflict, however, hunting metaphors no longer seemed so appropriate. Although Jorrocks' epigram was resurrected by Churchill in a Parliamentary speech of November 1944, it was in an amended version that, as far as the *Manchester Guardian* was concerned, merely served to highlight its contemporary irrelevance. By reducing the dangers of fox-hunting relative to war from Jorrocks' original 25 per cent to just half a per cent, all Churchill had done, the paper's editor insisted, was to underline the fact that the world was now confronted by 'a mechanised warfare of which Mr. Jorrocks happily knew nothing'.[10] Yet, this is not to say that sporting metaphors were simply abandoned after 1914. Throughout the two world wars and on into the second-half of the twentieth century, war correspondents, memoirists, novelists and even combatants continued to use the terminology and symbolism of the playing-field to impose a nobility and sense of moral purpose on the barbarities of attritional fighting and mass killing. Indeed, even Mrs Thatcher, hardly renowned as a sports fan, was reputedly not immune to wedding sport and war. On being informed by a despondent minister, after England's defeat in the semi-final of Italia '90, that members of the cabinet were unusually subdued because 'Germany had beaten us again at our national game', she was reported to have briskly directed everyone to 'remember that we have twice this century beaten them at theirs'.[11]

This use of metaphorical language served an important purpose. Although Justin Wren-Lewis and Alan Clarke, in their study of the politics surrounding the FIFA World Cup, may well be correct in arguing that 'the use of sporting metaphors in war and nationalistic/militaristic metaphors in sport doesn't imply a necessary conflation of the two discourses', the blurring of boundaries between the literal and figurative inherent in such language exchange does, nevertheless, have an import beyond that of the purely linguistic.[12] Metaphors, as Jonathan Charteris-Black has astutely observed, are as much about thoughts as they are about words; they have cognitive as well as linguistic significance. By evoking an emotional response, they can help to 'persuade us of certain ways of viewing the world'.[13] An exploration of conceptual metaphors such as war is sport can, therefore, provide a useful window on the values and ideologies that underpin societal belief systems. Undoubtedly, as J. A. Mangan and Callum McKenzie have acknowledged, measuring with any accuracy the impact on popular attitudes of conceptualising war as sport is problematic.[14] Yet, the frequency with which contemporary commentators adopted such metaphorical wordplay does, nevertheless, point to just how deeply embedded in the popular consciousness the sport/war nexus was. And, certainly, for both combatants and non-combatants in Britain's wars since 1850, the sporting metaphor was a powerful conceptual tool. Packaging conflict in the language and imagery of sport helped to promote self-sacrifice on the frontline, sustain bellicosity on the home front and mitigate grief for the bereaved.[15] But, as one might expect, there were also those who considered this reconfiguration of the battlefield as a playing-field the height of bad taste. Indeed, bouts of national soul-searching, prompted typically by crises on the fighting front, frequently led to a questioning of not only the use of sporting terms to portray war but also the place of sport itself in wartime culture. This work will, then, start by exploring the evolution of the Victorian notion that the games pitch and the battle ground could be equated, before moving on to investigate the challenges this belief faced in the twentieth century, as warfare became, initially, industrialised in the age of total warfare and, subsequently, professionalised in the post-nuclear world. Such a longitudinal study will allow, for the first time, new light to be shed on the continuities and shifts in the way war was reconfigured for, and understood by, the wider public.

Although both British sporting life and British military culture in the nineteenth and twentieth centuries have, independently, generated extensive bibliographies, there has been little attempt to explore the overlap between these two important areas of study. Indeed, even when an attempt has been made to explore the intersection between the army and wider society, the role of sport has been largely overlooked. In Edward Spiers' study of military life from Waterloo to the outbreak of the First World War, only two pages are devoted to sporting activity, and those are indexed under 'recreation' for other ranks and 'social life' for officers.[16] The coverage of sport is equally perfunctory in both David French's and Richard Holmes' sweeping surveys of service culture, with just seven pages in the former and two in the latter.[17] More often than not, when sport does warrant a mention in such works, it is in terms of its function as a recruitment tool.[18] Historians are, however, beginning to address this historiographical gap with James D. Campbell's *The Army Isn't All Work: Physical Culture and the Evolution of the British Army, 1860–1920* and Tony Mason's and Eliza Riedi's *Sport and the Military: The British Armed Forces 1880–1960* leading the way.[19] A retired US army officer, Campbell was the first scholar to undertake a serious study of the development of organised sport and physical training in the British army in the late nineteenth and early twentieth centuries.[20] Arguing that the professionalisation of the military that occurred in this period was as much a result of internal doctrinal and institutional transformations as it was of externally imposed political reforms, Campbell concluded, '[I]nstead of detracting from its competence, the Army's sport and physical training programmes were some of its major contributors.'[21] Extending the scope of the analysis to encompass the Second World War and the government's post-war commitment to National Service, Tony Mason and Eliza Riedi arrived at a rather less definitive conclusion. Prepared to concede that the army's fixation with organised games improved general levels of physical fitness and helped build regimental esprit de corps, they felt the evidence was less clear-cut when it came to evaluating the professional benefits, in the age of a new technological warfare, of so much time spent with bat and ball. What was certain, though, according to Mason and Riedi, was that war brought the whole issue of army sport to the forefront of public discourse.[22]

However, despite serving as excellent studies of the evolution of sporting culture within the armed forces, the works of Campbell, Mason and Riedi stop short of exploring in any depth the intersection between the military and civilian worlds and the ways in which sporting language and imagery were used to shape the popular understanding of military service and war. Equally restricted in scope are a number of recently published studies that chart the fortunes of individual sports across the course of a single conflict. Thus, Alexander Jackson's edited volume, *The Greater Game*, on the history of football in the First World War, and Anton Ripon's *Gas Masks for Goal Posts*, which moves the narrative forward to the Second World War, both focus exclusively on the impact hostilities had on the footballing world without making any attempt to delve into the wider ramifications in terms of popular culture.[23] It is this latter theme that is the focus of Michael Paris' *Warrior Nation: Images of War in British Popular Culture, 1850–2000*.[24] Using a wide range of literary and visual sources, Paris traces the evolution of the 'pleasure culture of war' from the Victorian high age to the end of the twentieth century. His work in many ways complements Graham Dawson's earlier examination of war in British popular culture, *Soldier Heroes: British Adventure, Empire and the Imagining of Masculinity*.[25] In both these studies, the notion of the 'sporting warrior' is touched on but only as a small part of the wider public imagining of conflict. Yet, during times of war, the concept of the 'sporting warrior' was a recurring motif in British popular culture and was a central element in the nation's sense of identity. This study will, therefore, advance the theses set out by Dawson and Paris and provide the first in-depth analysis of this critical issue by drawing together the British public's fascination with conflict and its obsession with sporting culture.

From 1850 onwards, with the possible exception of occasional bombing raids during the two world wars, the overwhelming majority of the British public experienced war vicariously. They were, in the words of the media historian Philip Taylor, 'witnesses to history via the media rather than . . . actual participants in it'.[26] It was in the pages of the popular newspapers, in war-related memoirs and works of fiction, and, latterly, through cinema and television screens, that British military operations were conveyed to and discussed by the wider populace. This public image of warfare was, of course, a carefully filtered one. The media did not simply reflect reality but, by a deliberate process of selecting, editing and structuring, shaped and reconstructed it. Although, as Susan Carruthers has pointed out, it would be wrong to regard consumers of wartime media as no more than 'absorbent sponges' stripped of the capacity for critical thought, there were, nevertheless, limits to the public's ability to arrive at independent judgements.[27] Respect for journalistic objectivity and a lack of alternative sources of information, for example, both served to constrain attempts at reinterpretation. Perhaps, even more critically, as Mark Pedelty has observed, the frequent framing of media messages in the language and values of cultural landmarks such as sport had the effect of making counter viewpoints appear irrational and unpatriotic.[28]

It is, therefore, through an investigation of how the idea of warfare was packaged for, and presented to, the consumers of media texts that some sense of the 'reality' of war in the popular imagination can be captured.[29] Newspapers, in particular, are a rich source. In the middle of the nineteenth century, technological improvements in the printing industry combined with a reduction in stamp duty from 4d to 1d sparked an unprecedented growth in the press, with 563 papers in circulation by 1851.[30] At the same time, the publication in *The Times* of William

Howard Russell's despatches from the Crimean front ended the remoteness of war and gave, in Michael Paris' words, 'events an immediacy that made civilians feel a part of the experience'.[31] With a series of Education Acts from the 1870s onwards ensuring Britain was 'a near universally functionally literate society', the burgeoning newspaper industry employed more and more specialist war correspondents to feed the British public an on-going diet of war stories in which combat and the imperial warrior were idealised. The new conservative popular dailies, the *Mirror*, the *Daily Mail* and the *Daily Express*, enjoyed mass readerships among the emerging working and lower-middle classes, while the old press, papers such as *The Times*, the *Telegraph* and the *Guardian*, although unable to compete in terms of circulation, still held sway in the corridors of power.[32] This level of popularity and influence endured for much of the following century. Throughout this period, despite the imposition of censorship during the two world wars, the industry remained, for the most part, commercially acute.[33] The relatively light touch of the censor's hand enabled editors to stay sensitive to the attitudes and cultural reference points of their constituencies and to package war in a manner their readers would find informative, entertaining and sympathetic.[34]

The portrayal of war in newspapers was buttressed by other literary and visual representations. From the middle of the nineteenth century, lending libraries, weekly magazines and low-cost publishers ensured that a broad range of fiction and non-fiction was readily available to, and easily affordable for, the vast majority of the British public. Increased literacy and exposure in the new mass press turned many authors into household names and, from 1850 onwards, afforded them not only a wide readership but also a popular authority.[35] Although Mangan and McKenzie have quite rightly cautioned against approaching these literary texts as a record of historical fact, they have, nevertheless, stressed the value of such works, pointing out that they were not only a notable source of entertainment but also, as Peter Burke and Roy Porter have observed, an important means for the propagation and maintenance of dominant ideologies.[36] Indeed, Mangan and McKenzie have gone so far as to argue that literary depictions were pivotal in teaching modern society 'the "styles" and "forms" of living, dying, fighting and mating'.[37] And, of course, these written sources were supplemented and reinforced by visual art forms. Artists, cinematographers and, latterly, television producers all offered up mirrors to society's concerns and helped to bolster prevailing values and ideas.

This book, then, will explore this range of media texts in a bid to shed light on how far the image of the sporting warrior and the association between the playing-field and the battlefield were employed to give meaning and order to the outside world during the dislocation of war. The first chapter will focus on the colonial campaigning of the second-half of the nineteenth century. In these decades, the British army found itself embroiled in a seemingly continuous series of small wars as it sought to protect and extend the nation's imperial reach. An increasingly literate public, buoyed by its fascination for the Empire, eagerly devoured a ceaseless flood of war reportage and campaign histories, memoirs and novels. With the fighting far removed from British shores, and with the country's vital interests never really under threat, specialist correspondents and authors were, for the most part, released from any obligation to explore complex geo-political contexts and instead free to package military operations in a way that they felt would best appeal to, and resonate with, their readers. The chapter will, therefore, explore how the language and codes of sport were used to represent and reimagine combat in this age of what Anne Summers has called 'popular militarism'.[38]

The second chapter advances the analysis to the South African War of 1899–1902. As Victoria's reign drew to a close, the long-simmering tension between Britain and the two Boer Republics of the Transvaal and Orange Free State finally gave way to outright hostility. The scale and nature of this new war, with the enlistment of tens of thousands of volunteers and the employment of modern technology, captivated civilian society. Indeed, just how deep public interest went can be gauged from the deluge of war-related literature that saturated the market during and in the immediate aftermath of the conflict. It has been estimated that between 1899 and 1914, in the English language alone, over 500 books and pamphlets on the war were published.[39] In these works, organised games and athletic endeavour featured prominently, as journalists and authors mobilised late Victorian society's veneration of the cult of athleticism to present the fighting in the fashion of a glorified sporting contest. Yet, as the war dragged on and British counter-insurgency tactics grew ever more brutal, reservations began to be expressed, most famously by Rudyard Kipling in *The Times*, about the value of an ideology that equated proficiency on the rugby pitch or cricket square with strength of character and military capability. The second chapter will, then, examine how far the war against the Boers was a moment of transition for the role of sport in the British armed forces and for the public's acceptance of the British soldier as a sporting warrior.

The following two chapters advance the analysis to the two world wars of the twentieth century and explore how the intensity and horrors of industrialised total warfare placed a further strain on the sport/war nexus. In Chapter 3, official and unofficial attitudes towards the function of sport during the nation's first experience of total conflict are examined. As the fighting on the Western Front became reduced to an attritional stalemate by the winter of 1914, the conceit that sporting contests and military operations could be somehow connected was stretched to breaking point. But, as Jay Winter has observed in his far-reaching study of European culture and 'collective remembrance' in the opening decades of the twentieth century, so great was public dislocation between 1914 and 1918 that traditional tropes and motifs were frequently resurrected in an effort to impose some meaning on a world in flux.[40] The Victorian idealisation of the sporting warrior was one such coping mechanism. By reimagining the battleground as a playing-field and the soldier as a sportsman, it was possible to impose a sense of nobility and purpose on the slaughter of France and Flanders. Although, in the years following the Armistice, the use of sporting symbolism was a recurring feature in the memorialisation of the fallen, it was, nonetheless, evident that the connection between sport and war was no longer as secure as it had been. Just how secure it was, and whether it could endure the strains of another struggle for national survival, will form the focus of the next chapter

8 *Introduction*

In September 1939, the government, aware that the Home Front would inevitably play a much more prominent part in the war effort than it had between 1914 and 1918, entered hostilities with a greater understanding of the importance of sport in sustaining public morale. Yet, as British forces faced a series of devastating reverses in the first few years of the conflict, old debates about the appropriateness of sport in wartime resurfaced. Chapter 4, therefore, offers a close examination of this public discourse – a discourse in which the focus was disproportionately on what were perceived to be working-class sports: professional football, boxing, greyhound racing – and in the process evaluates the shifting cultural landscape during what was dubbed 'the people's war'. The chapter concludes with an investigation of the extent to which army authorities and military commentators, notwithstanding the experience of the First World War, continued to cling to the belief that sport generally, and amateur sport specifically, fulfilled a moral as well as practical function.

The book concludes by considering the portrayal of war in the nuclear age. When laser-guided missiles fired from RAF Tornadoes destroyed a series of military installations in Colonel Gaddafi's Libya in March 2011, the *Sun*'s lead story screamed: 'Top Guns 1, Mad Dogs 0'.[41] Thus, more than 50 years after the British public had experienced the depredations of total war, the chaos of combat was, once again, being packaged for the front page in the language of the back page. Yet, for most of the population, the half century following the Second World War had been a period in which both the military and warfare had become ever more removed from everyday life. Although conscription, in the form of National Service, had continued until the early 1960s, by the time of the Falklands War in 1982, a whole generation had grown up with no direct experience of the armed forces. Increasingly sophisticated weaponry had served to reinforce the sense of distance between the military and civilian worlds. Precision firepower, accompanied by high-tech intelligence, had apparently delivered a futuristic form of warfare in which the individual heroics of sporting warriors had no place. Yet, as the *Sun* headline of March 2011 reveals, sporting language and imagery continued to be used to reimagine combat for an ever more media-literate domestic population. This final chapter, then, explores the enduring popularity of traditional sporting motifs in the presentation of modern high-tech warfare. The focus falls not only on literary but also televisual and cinematic representations of warfare to uncover the extent to which, just as had been the case in the second half of the nineteenth century, the familiar landscape of sport was employed to sanitise conflict in an age of limited warfare.

Notes

1 Charlotte Brontë, *Jane Eyre* (London: Smith, Elder, and Co., 1847), p. 56.
2 Richard Holt, *Sport and the British: A Modern History* (Oxford: Oxford University Press, 1989), pp. 74–116.
3 J. D. Campbell, *'The Army Isn't All Work': Physical Culture and the Evolution of the British Army, 1860–1920* (Farnham: Ashgate, 2012), chapter 5. Indeed, it has been claimed that sport for the Edwardian officer corps occupied more time than any other

single activity, including military duties, with even those attending Staff College being subjected to an endless round of team games and physical activity. See Tim Bowman and Mark Connelly, *The Edwardian Army: Recruiting, Training and Deploying the British Army, 1902–1914* (Oxford: Oxford University Press, 2012), p. 56.
4 For more on the presumed benefits of the late Victorian/early Edwardian cult of athleticism, see Peter Parker, *The Old Lie: The Great War and the Public-School Ethos* (London: Constable and Company Ltd., 1987), pp. 77–84.
5 J. A. Hobson, *Imperialism: A Study* (London: George Allen and Unwin Ltd., 1902), pp. 213–214.
6 Jenny Seagrove, 'The Sports Metaphor in American Cultural Discourse', *Culture, Sport, Society*, 3/1 (Spring 2000), p. 49.
7 For more on the link between sport and war memorialisation, see Anthony King, 'Sport, War and Commemoration: Football and Remembrance in the Twentieth and Twenty-first Centuries', *European Journal for Sports and Society*, 13/3 (2016), pp. 208–229.
8 *King Henry VI, Part 1*, Act 4, Scene 2, lines 45–54. For more on the role of sport as a metaphor for war in *King Henry VI, Part 1*, see Gregory M. Colón Semenza, 'Sport, War, and Contest in Shakespeare's Henry VI', *Renaissance Quarterly*, 54/4 (Winter 2001), pp. 1251–1272.
9 Robert Smith Surtees, *Handley Cross or, the Spa Hunt: A Sporting Tale* (London: Henry Colburn, 1843), p. 684. Of course, Jorrocks modified his analogy somewhat by adding that hunting was 'without [war's] guilt, and with only five and twenty per cent of its danger'.
10 *Manchester Guardian*, 1 November 1944.
11 John Ramsden, 'England versus Germany, Soccer and War Memory: John Huston's *Escape to Victory* (1981)', *Historical Journal of Film, Radio, and Television*, 26/4 (October 2006), p. 583.
12 Justin Wren-Lewis and Alan Clarke, 'The World Cup – A Political Football: The International Scene: The Play's the Thing . . .', *Theory, Culture and Society*, 1/3 (1983), p. 123.
13 Jonathan Charteris-Black, *Corpus Approaches to Critical Metaphor Analysis* (Basingstoke: Palgrave Macmillan, 2004), p. xii.
14 J. A. Mangan and Callum C. McKenzie, *Militarism, Hunting, Imperialism: "Blooding" the Martial Male* (Abingdon: Routledge, 2009), p. 50.
15 Mangan and McKenzie, *Militarism, Hunting, Imperialism*, p. 51.
16 Edward Spiers, *The Army and Society 1815–1914* (London: Longman, 1980).
17 David French, *Military Identities: The Regimental System, the British Army, and the British People, c. 1870–2000* (Oxford: Oxford University Press, 2005); Richard Holmes, *Soldiers: Army Lives and Loyalties from Redcoats to Dusty Warriors* (London: HarperPress, 2011).
18 See, for example, Spiers, *The Army and Society*, p. 63; A. R. Skelley, *The Victorian Army at Home: The Recruitment and Terms and Conditions of the British Regular 1859–1899* (London: Croom Helm, 1977), pp. 58–60 and 162–165.
19 Campbell, *The Army Isn't All Work*; Tony Mason and Eliza Riedi, *Sport and the Military: The British Armed Forces 1880–1960* (Cambridge: Cambridge University Press, 2007).
20 Campbell first addressed the issue of army sport in an article for the *International Journal of the History of Sport* published in 2000. J. D. Campbell, '"Training for Sport Is Training for War": Sport and the Transformation of the British Army, 1860–1914', *International Journal of the History of Sport*, 17/4 (December 2000), pp. 21–58.
21 Campbell, '"Training for Sport Is Training for War"', p. 52. In diametric opposition, Laura Kriegel, in a detailed survey of the influence the public school games cult had on military culture, has argued that 'the idea that what happened on playing fields influenced battlefields . . . would face its dissolution during the First World War'. Laura Kriegel, 'The Strange Career of Fair Play, or, Warfare and Gamesmanship in the Time

of Victoria', in Juliet John (ed.), *The Oxford Handbook of Victorian Literary Culture* (Oxford: Oxford University Press, 2016), p. 270.
22. Mason and Riedi, *Sport and the Military*, pp. 38–42.
23. Alexander Jackson (ed.), *The Greater Game: A History of Football in World War 1* (London: Shire Publications, 2014); Anton Ripon, *Gas Masks for Goal Posts: Football in Britain During the Second World War* (Stroud: Sutton Publishing Ltd., 2005).
24. Michael Paris, *Warrior Nation: Images of War in British Popular Culture, 1850–2000* (London: Reaktion Books, 2000).
25. Graham Dawson, *Soldier Heroes: British Adventure, Empire and the Imagining of Masculinity* (London: Routledge, 1994).
26. Philip M. Taylor, *Global Communications, International Affairs and the Media Since 1945* (London: Routledge, 1997), p. 99.
27. Susan L. Carruthers, *The Media at War: Communication and Conflict in the Twentieth Century* (Basingstoke: Macmillan, 2000), p. 8. See also Sonia Livingstone, 'Relationships Between Media and Audiences: Prospects for Audience Reception Studies', in Tamar Liebes and James Curran (eds.), *Media, Ritual and Identity* (London: Routledge, 1998), pp. 237–255.
28. Mark Pedelty, *War Stories: The Culture of Foreign Correspondents* (London: Routledge, 1995), pp. 7–8.
29. For an example of this approach, see Glenn R. Wilkinson, '"The Blessings of War": The Depiction of Military Force in Edwardian Newspapers', *Journal of Contemporary History*, 33/1 (January 1998), p. 97.
30. Philip M. Taylor, *Munitions of the Mind: A History of Propaganda from the Ancient World to the Present Day* (Manchester: Manchester University Press, 1995), pp. 149–153.
31. Paris, *Warrior Nation*, p. 33.
32. Adrian Gregory, 'A Clash of Cultures: The British Press and the Opening of the Great War', in Troy R. E. Paddock (ed.), *A Call to Arms: Propaganda, Public Opinion, and Newspapers in the Great War* (Westport, CT: Praeger, 2004), p. 15.
33. John Osbourne, '"To Keep the Life of the Nation in the Old Line": *The Athletic News* and the First World War', *Journal of Sport History*, 14/2 (Summer 1987), p. 141.
34. Troy R. E. Paddock, 'Introduction,' in Paddock (ed.), *A Call to Arms: Propaganda, Public Opinion, and Newspapers in the Great War* (Westport, CT: Praeger, 2004), p. 15.
35. Richard Altick, *English Common Reader: A Social History of the Mass reading public, 1800–1900* (Chicago: University of Chicago Press, 1957), p. 299. See also, Paula M. Krebs, *Gender, Race, and the Writing of Empire: Public Discourse and the Boer War* (Cambridge: Cambridge University Press, 1999), pp. 143–178.
36. Mangan and McKenzie, *Militarism, Hunting, Imperialism*, p. 39; Peter Burke and Roy Porter, *Language, Self, and Society: A Social History of Language* (Cambridge: Polity Press, 1991), p. 12.
37. Mangan and McKenzie, *Militarism, Hunting, Imperialism*, p. 50.
38. Anne Summers, 'Militarism in Britain Before the Great War', *History Workshop Journal*, 2 (Autumn 1976), pp. 104–123.
39. Fred R. Van Hartesveldt, *The Boer War: Historiography and Annotated Bibliography* (Westport, CT: Greenwood, 2000).
40. Jay Winter, *Sites of Memory, Sites of Mourning: The Great War in European Cultural History* (Cambridge: Cambridge University Press, 1995), pp. 78–116.
41. *Sun*, 21 March 2011.

1 Victoria's small wars, 1837–1899

'Hunt, shoot, and fight'

In April 1901, just three months into the reign of Edward VII, Hamish Stuart used an essay on the evolution of association football in *Blackwood's Edinburgh Review* to reflect on the accomplishments of what he presciently called 'the Victorian era'. In the opening paragraphs he set out some of the challenges facing a modern industrial society like Britain. 'Manliness', he warned, would have to be encouraged if a nation was, 'in a commercial age', to continue to 'hold dominion'. Britain must, therefore, maintain its leading position in the ever-expanding community of soccer nations. 'For football above all games', according to Stuart, not only promoted 'physical and moral strength' but also stimulated 'the realisation and the sinking of self'. To press home the truth of this observation, playing-field and battlefield were then neatly yoked to provide an explanation for Britain's rise to imperial pre-eminence over the course of Victoria's reign. 'The Historian', Stuart asserted:

> when he comes to deal with the Victorian era, will hail it as not only the golden age of football, but the age also during which the citizen soldier, trained to manliness in the playing-fields, first voluntarily abandoned the shop for the sword, to show how fields were won in the grim game of war.[1]

In an age when, for football at least, professionalism was in the ascendancy, this paean to amateur sporting ideals serves as a fascinating indication of just how deeply embedded the Victorian public school games ethic was in the public consciousness.

Certainly, Britain, over the course of the second-half of the nineteenth century, became a nation obsessed by sport. From the 1860s onwards the codification of games resulted in the development of a truly national sporting life and gave rise to an all-pervading cult of athleticism.[2] For the emerging middle classes especially sport was, in J. A. Mangan's phrase, elevated 'to the status of a moral discipline'.[3] Educated in a burgeoning public school system where athletic endeavour was regarded as more important than intellectual achievement, Victorian polite society valued character above all else.[4] And sport was regarded as the major medium for developing character. Courage, discipline, teamwork and, that ill-defined yet catch-all term used by Stuart, 'manliness' were all thought to be cultivated through regular and intensive participation in games.⁵ This view was given an official stamp of approval in 1864 when the Clarendon Commission reported, '[T]he cricket and football fields . . . are not merely places of exercise and amusement: they help form some of the most valuable social qualities and manly virtues.'⁶ Although propagated in the public schools, the belief that sport cultivated moral as well as physical strength quickly filtered out into wider society. As both Michael Paris and Geoffrey Best have noted, the public schools enjoyed something of a cultural hegemony in the Victorian period. Citing as evidence the popularity of public school fiction in state elementary and secondary schools, Best and Paris have argued that there was a widespread acceptance in the non-public school world of the elite's cultural ideals and that these ideals, in the words of Best, 'filtered downwards and outwards until they permeated the whole of society'.⁷

Sport also lay at the heart of late Victorian society's attachment to Empire. Notwithstanding the economic imperatives that underpinned neo-imperialism, Britain's imperial drive was presented to the public as a moral crusade, a force for good in which salvation for indigenous populations lay in their assimilation of British values. Central to this cultural transmission was sport. The *Daily Telegraph* was commenting on more than just a national predilection for bat and ball when, in an editorial of September 1888, it proudly declared:

> Wherever we go, whatever land we conquer, we found the great national instinct of playing games. Plant a dozen Englishmen anywhere – on an island, in a backwoods clearing or in the Indian hills – and in a wonderfully short time . . . the level sward is turned into a cricket field in summer and a football arena in winter.⁸

For the readers of the *Telegraph*, and indeed for the wider public, cricket and rugby were distinctively British and encapsulated many of the qualities that made up their imagined national identity. Thus, the colonialist's commitment to the propagation of these games could serve as shorthand for the civilising mission at the heart of British imperial expansion.⁹ Versed in the poetry of Henry Newbolt, it was taken for granted by the British middle classes in the late nineteenth century that the nation's imperial warriors and sportsmen would, without hesitation, transfer the lessons they had learned facing 'a bumping pitch and a blinding light' to the perils of rallying 'the wreck of a square that broke'.¹⁰

The veneration of sport, however, was not restricted to the civilian and imperial worlds. As J. D. Campbell revealed in his pioneering study on sport and the army, the military also indulged in games to an almost fanatical degree. With the establishment of the Army Gymnastics Staff in 1860, organised sport quickly assumed a central position in the professional and social lives of officers and men.¹¹ From the 1870s, according to Edward Spiers, sporting opportunities no longer depended on the actions of a few enthusiastic officers but instead became institutionalised.¹² Athletic endeavour, the authorities felt, not only improved physical fitness but also helped to build regimental esprit de corps by offering a rare chance for officers and men to mix, at least temporarily, on an even footing. Indeed, the games field was considered to be so central to the creation of regimental identity and cross-rank harmony that the editor of the *Manchester Guardian* was moved to suggest that the introduction of sporting opportunities for the armies of the East India Company might have even warded off the horrors of the Mutiny. 'In the English army', he lectured the paper's readers a month after news of the massacre at Cawnpore had broken,

> pleasure brings the regimental officer continually in contact with his men.... [H]e joins in their sports. On the cricket field Colonel Parade is bowled out by Private Pipeclay, and my Lord Viscount Sabretache gains undying honour for the manner in which he stopped the slashing hits of Corporal Trim. At sport in which they do not actually take part, such as boating, foot racing, jumping and wrestling, they are present, providing stakes for competition, backing the chances of their favourites, and feeling that the credit of the regiment depends upon the wind and sinews of Jones and Smith, who would be bad fellows indeed if they did not take some interest in their officers in return.... The good feeling begotten this way in times of peace finds expression under the fire of the enemy, in the deadly trade, in the weary march, in the hospital.... But as for mutinying and murdering [their officers] in cold blood, the thing is moral impossible.[13]

However, as David French has pointed out, sharing games fields did not necessarily lead to sharing cultural values. For other ranks, the public school spirit of sportsmanship generally took a poor second place to the more primal spur of winning.[14] Whatever the differences in individual motivation though, it was still the case that by the end of Victoria's reign, the army's adherence to, and passion for, organised sport had become all-consuming. Campbell noted that by the late nineteenth century the average officer spent more time on sport than any other single pursuit, including military duties; even students attending Staff College had their time filled up with a never-ending diet of physical activity and team games.[15]

This explosion in military sport was, in no small part, driven by fears of national degeneration. There was widespread concern from the 1850s onwards that rapid industrialisation and urbanisation were undermining the health and martial vitality of the nation.[16] Shocking reports during the Crimean War about the poor physical condition of the troops and their susceptibility to disease led to demands for government action. Sport and exercise appeared to be the best way forward.[17] The military authorities took as a model of good practice the military training programmes of the French and Prussian armies, where physical drill and gymnastics had been part of compulsory fitness regimes for a number of years.[18] Yet, as Jeffrey Richards has astutely observed, the appeal of establishing military sport in Britain in the late 1850s and 1860s went beyond the purely physical. With the Crimean War, Indian Mutiny and Jamaican Revolt all throwing into high relief the vulnerability of Britain's overseas possessions, military preparedness and the defence of Empire quickly assumed a moral purpose.[19] Team games, with their roots in the amateur sporting creed of the public schools, seemed, therefore, a perfect fit for this new-found belief in the morality of what J. A. Mangan has termed 'militaristic imperialism'.[20] Henry Brackenbury, a future director of Military Intelligence, was of the opinion that Britain already had at its disposal a vast reserve of amateur sporting warriors who could secure the Empire; the real challenge was how this resource was to be exploited. In a review of a report by the Royal Commission into Army Recruitment in 1866, he tacitly acknowledged the degenerative effect of urbanisation by insisting that the maintenance of Britain's imperial supremacy depended on untapping the potential of its rapidly shrinking rural communities. 'There is no country in the world', he informed readers of *Fraser's Magazine*,

> which possesses finer material for soldiers than Great Britain, but it is certain that the men with whom she is now supplying the ranks of her army are not those whom she ought to have and might have as her protectors. We have a race of hardy villagers and stalwart country lads fond of sport, of all games that require pluck and skill, a quick eye, a strong hand, and a fleet foot, to whom the spice of danger enhances the pleasure of such games as football and cricket, and who are ready to join in anything promising a chance of adventure.[21]

The racehorse breeder Henry Strickland Constable, writing in the wake of the Cardwell-Childers army reforms of the 1870s and 1880s, was equally certain that city-dwelling sapped martial vigour. The product of 'exclusive industrialism', he claimed in a passionate polemic, *Something About Horses*, published in 1891, was 'cowardice'. Salvation was to be found in sport, which, by cultivating 'manliness', served as 'one of the antidotes to the effeminacy that ruined nations'. Thus, for Strickland Constable, it was the duty of the military authorities and the nation at large to 'do what [they] can to impart useful ideas about sporting as about all other matters'.[22]

Sport as an agent of moral as well as physical well-being was a belief that enjoyed wide currency in the second-half of the nineteenth century.[23] It was assumed that the development of a sporting ethos within the armed services promoted efficiency by not only substituting the excitement of the games field for the lure of the public house or brothel but also ensuring that men, or more particularly officers, were made of the right stuff.[24] Most famously, the case for the playing-field as a training ground for the battlefield was made by Henry Newbolt. Described, by J. A. Mangan, as the 'media voice of his era', Newbolt unapologetically propagated the image of the sacrificial sporting warrior, for whom games had served as a prelude to war. *Vitaï Lampada* might have stood as the 'triumphalist anthem' of this vision, but it was by no means the only one.[25] In *He Fell Among Thieves*, for example, published in 1898, just a year after *Vitaï Lampada*, the last thoughts of a young subaltern condemned to death by his captors on the North-West Frontier are for the school and college sports that had shaped his character:

> He saw the School Close, sunny and green,
> The runner beside him, the stand by the parapet wall,

The distant tape, and the crowd roaring between
His own name over all.

He saw the dark wainscot and timbered roof,
The long tables, and the faces merry and keen;
The College Eight and their trainer dining aloof,
The Dons on the dais serene.[26]

Newbolt's poetry may have been the most celebrated articulation of the sport-war nexus for the late Victorian, but the link between games field and battlefield had been taking shape since the first half of the nineteenth century. As Mark Girouard has pointed out, the legend that the Duke of Wellington had attributed victory at Waterloo to the playing-fields of Eton was firmly embedded in the popular consciousness by 1850 and was given formal recognition by the reformist journalist Samuel Smiles at the end of the decade.[27] It was, argued Smiles, in his best-selling work of 1859, *Self-Help*,

> in no slight degree to the boating and cricketing sports still cultivated at our best public schools and universities, that they produce so many specimens of healthy, manly, and vigorous men, of the true Hodson stamp. It is said that the Duke of Wellington, when once looking at boys engaged in their sports in the play-ground at Eton, where he had spent his juvenile days, made the pregnant remark, 'It was here that the battle of Waterloo was won!'[28]

In fiction, the idea of armed conflict being the natural extension of athletic competition had been broached a decade earlier by William Thackeray in his viciously satirical work *Vanity Fair*. On the eve of Waterloo, the novel's dashing but flawed hero, Lieutenant George Osborne, 'famous in field-sports . . . and the best batter and bowler, out and out, of the regimental club', is seen eagerly abandoning his new bride to rush to the colours.[29] The young lieutenant's whole life, Thackeray suggested, had been spent preparing for this moment. 'The champion of his school and regiment', he had 'flung himself with all his might' into 'all contests requiring athletic skill and courage'. Now, at last, he was to be 'one of the players' in the 'great game of war'. Although, unsurprisingly, the scene concludes on a sardonic note, with Thackeray mockingly reflecting, 'I wonder is it because men are cowards in heart that they admire bravery so much', the very fact, as Michael Paris has noted, that such thinking could be so successfully lampooned revealed just how deeply entrenched it was.[30]

The novel that, perhaps, did most to give form to the concept of future imperial warriors honing their martial prowess on cricket squares and football pitches was Thomas Hughes' hugely influential paean to his *alma mater*, *Tom Brown's School Days*. Published at a time of national self-doubt in the wake of the Crimean War, the story presented an idealised vision of the reformed public school system in which the Muscular Christian sporting hero was held up as a martial role model. Sport – be it the School-house football game, when Tom first arrives as a new boy, or the closing cricket match against MCC, by which time he has assumed the captaincy of the First Eleven – was portrayed as the essential heartbeat of school life and the defining factor in shaping the pupils' characters. As Laura Kriegel observed, it was on the games field of Hughes' fictionalised Rugby that pupils were 'prepared for larger eventualities of greater consequence'.[31] An 'Old Boy' saw fit to stress this very point in a glowing critique of the book that appeared in the *Edinburgh Review* in January 1858. Games, he asserted, far from being 'mere amusements', helped develop that 'special form of courage (once most absurdly deprecated as a merely animal quality) which consists in readiness to brave obvious and immediate danger, and to which this country owes a very large proportion of its greatness'.[32]

Thus, by the age of new imperialism in the late nineteenth century, the playing-field-battlefield paradigm had become securely fixed in the nation's cultural landscape. Evidence of this can be found in the juvenile literature of the period. Children's magazines, or more specifically boys' magazines, which frequently took colonial wars and imperial adventurers as their subject matter, were enormously popular by the 1890s, with titles like *Chums* and *Boy's Own Paper* achieving circulation figures in excess of 200,000.[33] Lavishly illustrated with heroic imagery steeped in 'aggressive virility', such publications, according to Robert McDonald, reinforced the cult of the martial athlete by 'linking the battles of the playing field to the glamorous sport of war, repeating the familiar theme of Newbolt's *Vitaï Lampada* with its twinned scenes of the cricket match and the last stand in the desert'.[34]

The doyen of the boy's adventure story was G. A. Henty. Described by the contemporary journal *Young England* as 'the most popular writer of boys' books', he was a regular contributor to *Boy's Own Paper* and produced, in a publishing career spanning the late 1860s to early 1900s, over 120 children's novels, with total sales in the region of 20 million.[35] His stories, with their formulaic structure and didactic tone, both reflected and reinforced the accepted mores and dominant values of the high imperialist age.[36] Indeed, Henty was unashamedly a propagandist, stating that his twin objectives when writing were to teach history and inculcate moral character.[37] Although, as Gail Clark has observed, it is impossible to assess whether juvenile readers really did absorb the values Henty wished to instil, what is certain is that they 'learned what they were meant to believe'.[38] And, at the heart of Henty's belief system was the message that the Empire was a sphere of action where imperial conquest, just like school sport, served as a rite of passage to manhood, a crucible in which the young hero could be tested and proved. Steeped in the anti-intellectualism of the public school system, the stories presented the English devotion to the cult of athleticism as the root of imperial power. Victory in small colonial wars was attributed to an innate sporting courage, to what Victorians often termed 'pluck'.[39] Thus, in *The Dash to Khartoum*, published at the turn of the twentieth century, an injured young officer's exceptional bravery in the face of an overwhelming Dervish force is taken for granted by the novel's hero: ' "I should think so," Rupert said. "A fellow who could play an uphill game of football as he could can be trusted to keep his courage up under any circumstances." '[40]

Using a love and aptitude for games and sporting activity to signal a hero's possession of pluck was a device that Henty repeatedly employed. Prowess at cricket, in particular, was seen as significant. In *By Sheer Pluck: A Tale of the Ashanti War*, the main character's heroic credentials are established in the opening scene when, as 'the best bat among the home boarders', he saves the day during the annual House-versus-Town cricket match.[41] Both Thomas Ripon and Edgar Smith, the heroes of *For Name and Fame; or, Through Afghan Passes* and *The Dash to Khartoum* respectively, are expert cricketers, with the latter being assured by his commanding officer that his skill on the cricket square 'is not a bad thing . . . as it brings you into notice . . . as a man who does his regiment credit'.[42] The sub-text of such proficiency with bat and ball would have been clear to Henty's readers. The game was widely thought to symbolise all that was good about Anglo-Saxon culture.[43] Lord Harris, a Test cricketer and the president of MCC in 1895, spoke for the majority of Britons when he stated that cricket was 'not only a game, but a school of the greatest social importance'.[44] The sport, it was assumed, fostered discipline, self-abnegation, a sense of fair play and teamwork: all the essential attributes that went to make up what, in late-nineteenth-century Britain, was termed 'character'. And, as J. A. Mangan has noted, 'Late Victorians were committed to the Empire *primarily* [italics in the original] because of the close association that it came to have with the inculcation, demonstration and transmission of valued "Anglo-Saxon" qualities embodied in the concept of "character".'[45]

Although cricket may have been pre-eminent, all sports, for Henty, that required 'activity and endurance rather than weight and strength', in other words those that relied on innate skill and moral fortitude as opposed to brute force and raw power, formed the foundations upon which success in colonial warfare was built.[46] This viewpoint is explicitly articulated in one of his later novels, *At the Point of a Bayonet*, published in 1902. Opening on the eve of the Second Anglo-Maratha War at the turn of the nineteenth century, two stock characters, the loyal native retainer and the orphaned English hero, are employed to deliver a sermon on the natural superiority of the imperialist. Love of sport, a doting ayah instructs her bereaved young charge, sets the coloniser apart:

> Yes, [the Marathas] can stand great fatigues, living as they do, so constantly on horseback, but, like all the people of India, they are not fond of exercise save when at war; that is the difference between us and the English. . . . Exercise to them is a pleasure, and we in the service of the English have often wondered at the way in which they willingly endure fatigues when they might pass their time sitting quietly on their verandahs [*sic*]. But I came to understand that it was to this love of theirs for outdoor exercise that they owed their strength and the firmness of their courage. None can say that the Mahrattas are not brave, but although they will charge gallantly, they soon disperse if the day goes against them. So also with the soldiers of Tipoo.[47]

This devotion to the cult of athleticism, the ayah concludes, by staving off physical and moral degeneration, has enabled the English to become 'masters of southern India and half of Bengal'.[48]

Critically, though, games were thought not only to supply the courage and character required for military victory but also, as was meant to be implied by a Henty hero's passion for cricket, to infuse warfare and imperial conquest with an element of fair play. Throughout the era of Victoria's small wars, playing in the spirit of the game was viewed by the British as something of a national characteristic. In the sporting arena and on the battlefield, Britons were expected to abide by the rules and, whenever necessary, ensure others followed suit. Thus, the code of the 'good sport', which was, as Michael Paris has noted, 'just another iteration of the chivalric ideal', by calling for the taming of cheats and bullies, provided a further moral rationale for the nation's colonial conquests.[49] Both Thomas Hughes, on the eve of new imperialism, and Henry Newbolt, at its height, reflected and reinforced this imperial sporting creed. In *Tom Brown's School Days*, the eponymous hero's decision to confront the bully Slogger Williams in the boxing ring was used as an excuse by Hughes to furnish his young readers with a homily on manly duty and the justness of physical force:

> After all, what would life be without fighting, I should like to know? From the cradle to the grave, fighting, rightly understood, is the business, the real highest, honestest business of every son of man. Every one who is worth his salt has enemies, who must be beaten, be they . . . Russians, or Border-ruffians, or Bill, Tom, or Harry, who will not let him live in quiet till he has thrashed them.[50]

Forty years later, conflict was still being presented as the 'honestest business' by Newbolt. In *Clifton Chapel*, his famous salute to his old school, published in 1898, the brutality inherent in a father's advice to his son is made more acceptable by applying a balm of fair play:

> To set the Cause above renown,
> To love the game beyond the prize,
> To honour, while you strike him down,
> The foe that comes with fearless eyes;[51]

From 1850 onwards, such was the importance attached to sport as an ethical and practical cornerstone of warfare that it came to be valued by many military leaders more highly than intellectual ability or professional expertise. In many ways this should come as no surprise. Senior officers were, almost exclusively, the products of a public school system where, as Thomas Hughes astutely observed, the aim was 'not to ram Latin and Greek into the boys but to make them good English boys, good future citizens, and by far the most important part of that work [was] done, or not done, out of school hours'.[52] And, of course, the sporting arena was widely acknowledged as the principal site for this extra-curricular instruction. Just occasionally dissenting voices were heard. The mismanagement of the Crimean War and shock of the Indian Rebellion, for example, did result in some calls for sport's primacy in military training to be addressed. In January 1860, the editor of the *Observer* expressed concern that although potential recruits from the middle-classes possessed 'unrivalled proficiency in the sports of the field, and [the] practice of all athletic pursuits', that did not make up for the fact that they were 'comparatively ignorant' in the 'use of firearms in war'.[53] Just over a decade later, as discussions about army reform assumed even greater urgency in the light of Napoleon III's defeat in the Franco-Prussian War, an editorial in the *Manchester Guardian* complained that the army was 'not a profession in the sense in which other occupations are professions'. 'To the mass of officers', the piece continued, 'military service means sport. . . . Poor merit is nowhere'.[54] The following month, the *Guardian* once again focused on the army's obsession with upper-middle-class accomplishment rather than military proficiency. Appalled at the 'affectation common to British officers of giving themselves out as gentlemen and nothing more', the paper demanded a more professional approach to training:

> We fully believe the British Army contains possibly a larger proportion than any other army of high-spirited, dashing young officers. . . . But it is also unfortunately true that there are comparatively few of our officers who make the duties of their profession the study of their lives. . . . Late events, however, have shown that war has ceased to be a sport for men of honour, and is now a trade in which knowledge of business is the only guarantee of success.[55]

However, such criticism was relatively rare, and the army remained firmly wedded to a robust sporting culture. Even a reform as moderate as the introduction of an entrance exam for the Royal Military College at Sandhurst was enough to provoke General Sir John Burgoyne, the colonel commandant of the Royal Engineers, into picking up his pen in protest. In a pamphlet entitled *Army Reform*, published in 1857, he railed against the idea that candidates for a commission should be judged on their academic ability:

> At a public school will be found one set of boys who apply to their studies, and make the greater progress in them, another set take to cricket, boating, fives, swimming etc. Now, of the two, I should decidedly prefer the latter, as much more likely to make good officers, but they are to be absolutely rejected, and for ever, unless they can come up to the mark in other matters which are of no absolute use to them in their profession.[56]

On the eve of the Cardwell Reforms, this anti-intellectual stance was still being endorsed by no less a figure than Colonel Garnet Wolseley, a renowned moderniser and future commander-in-chief of the forces. In his highly influential 1869 publication, *The Soldier's Pocket Book for Field Service*, he made abundantly clear how the ambitious officer should expend his energy: 'Being a good sportsman, a good cricketer, good at rackets or any other manly game, is no mean recommendation for staff employment. Such a man, without book lore, is preferable to the most deeply-read one of lethargic habits.'[57] Unsurprisingly, this viewpoint percolated into wider society through the works of popular novelists like G. A. Henty. In *Through the Sikh Wars*, a veteran of British rule in India explains to his fellow passengers on board a steamer bound for Calcutta why 'book-worms' will not help the imperial cause:

> Give me a lad with pluck and spirit, and I don't care a snap of the fingers whether he can construe Euripides or solve a problem in higher mathematics. What we want for India are men who can ride and shoot. . . . What do natives care for learning? It is our pluck and fighting prowess that have made us their masters.[58]

Blood-sports, in particular, were considered the perfect preparation for warfare. For Robert Baden-Powell, a captain in the 13th Hussars and future founder of the scouting movement, a natural aptitude for hunting rather than a detailed acquaintance with drill regulations served as the best indicator of martial potential. This viewpoint was most forcefully articulated in his passionate defence of wild boar hunting in India, *Pigsticking*, published in 1889. In a passage redolent with the cavalry officer's innate antipathy towards the Mounted Infantry, sporting flair was held up as the essential mark of a true warrior:

> Not infrequently does it happen that . . . one of that rapidly increasing 'arm' – mounted rifles – wins for himself the reputation of being a smart leader on a field-day ground, and yet completely and conspicuously fails when put to the real test of actual campaigning in a strange country. He is capable of putting bodies of troops through most intricate movements in good order on a level parade, but once on unknown, wild, or broken country he is all at sea. He does not possess by nature, or has not developed by practice, the power of taking in at a glance the peculiarities of the terrain and making the best uses of them, nor of recognising his opportunities and seizing them; just two of the most useful acquirements in a cavalry leader. These are the two faculties that are particularly developed in pig-sticking.[59]

To validate his argument, Baden-Powell cited the case of Lieutenant-General Sir James Outram, a hero of the Indian Rebellion, who, as 'one of the best pig-stickers' on the sub-continent, had brought the 'same dash' to war as he had shown in the 'hog-hunting field'.[60] In fact, the connection between Outram's brilliance as a pig-sticker and his distinction as a commander had first been made by the military historian Sir John Kaye, in a gushing potted biography that appeared in the *Cornhill Magazine* in January 1861. Commissioned to produce the piece to mark Outram's recent retirement from active service, Kaye maintained that his subject's triumphs as a sportsman were proof that '[t]he jungle is the battle-field of play hours; it leads straight up to the red ribbon and the Victoria Cross'. Outram, Kaye insisted, should act, therefore, as a beacon of hope for the parents of the academically disinclined:

> Do not fret yourselves if you find that [your son] takes more kindly to the stable and the rabbit warren than to Euclid and Eutropius. When the struggle comes, as come some day it will, for dear life, what will it avail him that he can demonstrate the *Pons Asinorum* or recount the labours of Hercules? But that true eye, that steady hand, that firm seat in the saddle, with all the cool courage of the hunting-field – these are the aids which will find him out in the hour of trial, and help him to the front in the grand Indian career.[61]

It was not only in an imperial setting that the martial benefits of blood sports were acclaimed. During the Crimean War, *The Field*, the self-proclaimed 'country gentleman's newspaper', attributed the courage and stoicism of the British Expeditionary Force (BEF) to the 'occupations and amusements to which this journal is devoted'. 'The daring, dashing deeds of heroism done by our troops', it was asserted in an editorial written a month after the Battle of Balaclava,

> [are] mainly due to the field sports and manly country occupations, which are so marked a characteristic of the life of the English gentleman. He is taught to ride as soon as he can walk; he spends the greatest portion of his days in the open air, in healthy and manly occupations; he is accustomed to imperil his life in the hunt ... he exercises his limbs in long days of shooting; he invokes his ingenuity with the fly-rod; he strengthens his muscles with the oar. . . . These were the training of our gentlemen, who have proved, on the heights of the Crimea, the value of the lessons they have learned in the field at home.[62]

The value of a hunting pedigree to the Crimean combatant was also appreciated by A. W. Kinglake in his monumental history of the conflict. Singling out Colonel Lacy Yea's refusal to allow 'his cherished regiment', the Royal Fusiliers, to yield to Russian pressure during the Battle of the Alma as a prime example, Kinglake drew a direct line between the hunting ground and the battlefield:

> To [Lacy Yea] this left bank of the Alma crowned with Russian troops was very like the wayside acclivity which often enough in his boyhood had threatened to well him back and keep him down in the depths of a Somersetshire lane whilst the hounds were running high up in the field some ten or fifteen feet above. His practised eye soon showed him a fit shord or break in the scarped face of the bank, and then, shouting out to his people, 'Never mind forming! Come on, men! Come on, anyhow!', he put his cob to the task and quickly gained the top.[63]

The extent to which not just field-sports but all sports assumed a central role in the culture of the armed forces from 1850 onwards can be seen in the enthusiasm with which military personnel on active duty continued to pursue games and physical activity. Predictably, for the officer corps, hunting took precedence, with campaigning in Africa being particularly rich in opportunity. Thus, during the expedition to Abyssinia to rescue captured British missionaries in 1868, *The Times'* special correspondent noted that rock grouse, hyenas and jackals all provided 'good sport', while, as a full-page illustration in the *Graphic* revealed, antelope and eland performed the same function during the second invasion of Zululand eleven years later.[64] Indeed, blood-sports were so deeply ingrained in the narrative of colonial warfare that accounts of operations could, as Hew Strachan has observed, often appear to be little more than 'a combination of travelogue, big-game hunting, and exploration, with a little fighting to spice up the tale'.[65] This was perfectly illustrated in Lieutenant-Colonel Edwin Alderson's stirring, though somewhat prosaically titled, memoir *With the Mounted Infantry and the Mashonaland Field Force, 1896*. As preparations were being made to take the troops up the Pungwe River into enemy territory, Alderson was struck by 'a certain indescribable sense of sport being in the air'. 'Was it', he speculated,

> because the little that we had read about the river was in books on big game shooting, or was it that one knew it to be one of the few remaining wild and little used rivers, and that it led one through a country which had not been shot out by so-called 'sportsmen'? Whatever the reason, we were all on the *qui vive*, and those who had brought their sporting rifles got them out, and were very soon popping away at the numerous crocodiles who were basking in the sun on a strip of mud below the bank.

Seven months later, with the pacification of the rebellious tribes successfully accomplished, Anderson contentedly observed that he had 'hunted hounds in June, fought until the end of November, and then taken hounds again. What more could a soldier possibly want?'[66] Even in theatres of war less blessed with potential game than the plains and bush of Africa, some semblance of a sporting life could still be maintained. Duck in the Crimea and sandgrouse in Afghanistan, as was pointed out by the *Manchester Guardian* and *The Times* respectively, offered the sporting officer a chance to keep his eye in.[67]

The pursuit of sport in the combat zone was, however, by no means confined to the commissioned ranks. The newspapers frequently contained reports on the ordinary soldiers' propensity to engage in sporting activity. The *Manchester Guardian* was impressed by the fact that 'all the divisional generals and a great number of staff officers' attended a day of athletics for the men held at the camp outside Sebastopol in March 1855, while the *Scotsman* noted the Cameron Highlanders' attempts to make the best of trying conditions during the expedition to relieve Gordon in Khartoum by playing games of cricket and football.[68] When an Anglo-Egyptian force under Kitchener returned to the Sudan in 1896, both *The Times* and the *Daily Mail* provided their readers with details of camp life in which tug-of-war contests, hockey matches, tent-pegging competitions and rounders games featured prominently.[69] Indeed, so fervent was the military's commitment to team games and physical activity during Victoria's small wars that the sporting paper *Bell's Life* felt able to conclude a review of 'three pleasant days' sport . . . at the Camp Hurnai, South Afghanistan, on March 9th, 10th, and 11th, 1881' with the proud claim that 'the Englishman carries sport with him into whatever out of the way region the call of duty may take him'.[70]

Reports on the sporting endeavours of troops on campaign not only helped to portray the colonial soldier as a true Englishman in the best traditions of the great public schools but also had the effect of distancing from public view the harsh realities of imperial warfare.[71] As the combatant assumed the form of the athlete, the battlefield could be recast as a playing-field. This process of transformation was aided by the packaging of warfare in the language and imagery of sport. Again and again, in press reports, veterans' memoirs and popular fiction, combat was presented as a game. *The Times* described both an assault on a Russian position at Sebastopol in January 1855 and the defeat of a Zulu impi at the Battle of Gingindlovu in April 1879 as 'fine sport'.[72] Indeed, so common was this practice of reconfiguring conflict as a game that, as early as February 1858, *The Times*' editor felt obliged to address it directly. The occupation of Canton and the capture of its anti-imperial governor, Ye Mingchen, may be considered little more than 'excellent sport', he reprimanded the paper's readers during the Second Opium War, but that should not be allowed to mask what was 'really a brilliant achievement'.[73] In their memoirs, both the historian Ésme Wingfield-Stratford and the career cavalry officer General Sir James Hope Grant emphasised the composure of men on the eve of battle by representing hostilities in terms of the country's national game. Wingfield-Stratford remembered war being 'regarded almost in the light of a glorified test match – a thrill of all thrills, more to be looked forward to than feared', while Hope Grant reminisced that 'on the eve of the storming of Delhi [in 1857], men seemed to regard the coming struggle as if it were a cricket-match, in which every one felt comfortable his side would win.'[74] Winston Churchill, who could include active service at the Battle of Omdurman in a life full of achievement, provided an explanation for this poise in his 1930 autobiography, *My Early Life*. During colonial campaigning, he recalled,

> [N]obody expected to be killed. Here and there in every regiment or battalion, half a dozen, a score, at worst thirty or forty, would pay the forfeit; but to the great mass of those who took part in the little wars of Britain in those vanished light-hearted days, this was only a sporting element in a splendid game.[75]

Yet, even when the prospect of death was acknowledged as a reality of fighting, war could still be presented as a little more than an exceptionally thrilling sporting encounter. A case in point was the storming of the fortress of Secunderbagh by the 93rd Highlanders and 4th Punjab Infantry during the relief of Lucknow in November 1857. One of the most celebrated events of the Indian Rebellion, it was, as Heather Streets has remarked, refashioned for a domestic audience as a 'friendly competition' between Sikh and Highlander, in which the 'the gory details of death were kept in the background'.[76] Thus, a stirring account that appeared in

Blackwood's Magazine in 1858 read more like an account of a particularly vigorous inter-house paperchase than a deadly assault:

> It was a glorious rush. On went, in generous rivalry, the turban of the Sikh and the dark plume of the Highlander. A native officer of the Sikhs, waving his tulwar above his head, dashed on a full five yards in front of his men. The Highlanders, determined not to be left behind, strained nerve and limb in the race. Their officers led like gallant gentlemen, shaking their broadswords in the air.[77]

Nearly 40 years later, this vision of the taking of Lucknow as the ultimate sporting contest was echoed by Field Marshal Lord Roberts in his best-selling autobiography, *Forty-One Years in India*. The assault on Secunderbagh was, he enthused, 'a magnificent sight, a sight never to be forgotten – that glorious struggle to be the first to enter the deadly breach, the prize to the winner of the race being certain death! Highlanders and Sikhs, Punjabi Mahomedans, Dogras and Pathans, all vied with each other in a generous competition'.[78]

One sport that lent itself most readily as a metaphor for war was boxing. The carefully choreographed violence of the ring provided the perfect framework within which the chaotic brutality of battle could be infused with structure and meaning.[79] Cartoonists, in particular, regularly looked to boxing as a way of making sense of complex and, not infrequently, contentious military expeditions. When Aberdeen's coalition government fell as a result of growing disquiet at the Allies' halting progress in the Crimea, John Leech reassured the largely middle-class subscribers to *Punch* magazine that a speedy end to hostilities could now be expected by depicting the new prime minister, Lord Palmerston, fearlessly preparing to take on an anxious-looking Tsar in a bare-knuckle fight.[80]

The disastrous first invasion of Zululand was all but forgotten when Gordon Thompson, in *Punch*'s short-lived liberal competitor, *Fun*, celebrated victory at the battle of Ulundi, in July 1879, with a cartoon of the British commander, Lord Chelmsford, manfully delivering a firm left hook to a crestfallen Cetywayo, the Zulu chief.[81] Fifteen years later, Thompson used exactly the same imagery to mark the defeat of the Mahdi's followers by an Anglo-Egyptian force at the Battle of Tamai. This time it was Gladstone, in the guise of a British lion, who was shown supplying the knock-out blow.[82] Not only did these representations of armed conflict as a boxing bout help to sanitise the horrors of combat but they also managed to buttress the conceit that colonial warfare somehow adhered to the English creed of fair play. The implication was that engagements were even matches, governed by the Marquess of Queensbury's rules, in which success depended on skill and courage rather than money and materiel.[83]

It was, however, to the language and imagery of field sports rather than boxing contests that commentators on warfare most frequently resorted. As Mark Cocker noted in his biography of the controversial imperial adventurer Colonel Richard Meinertzhagen, colonial wars against the indigenous populations of Africa and India in the late nineteenth century were generally viewed as 'little more

Victoria's small wars, 1837–1899 25

Figure 1.1 John Leech, 'Now for It!', *Punch*, 17 January 1855

than a challenging form of blood sport'.[84] The cartoons of John Leech and Gordon Thompson once again provide some supporting evidence. The Anglo-French onslaught against Chinese positions outside Peking during the Third Opium War in 1859 and General Frederick Roberts' defeat of the Afghan leader, Ayub Khan, at the Battle of Kandahar on 1 September 1880 were both portrayed, by Leech and

Thompson respectively, as shooting expeditions, while Thompson reimagined the capture of the Egyptian nationalist Colonel Ahmed 'Urabi after the surrender of Cairo in 1882 as the reeling in of a prize salmon.[85]

That imperial campaigning was really no more than hunting writ large was explicitly articulated in the pages of the sporting magazine *County Gentleman* in January 1881. In the 'broken regions which lie contiguous to India, South Africa, and elsewhere', it was asserted in an editorial entitled 'The Relation of Sport to War', 'the enemies are stealthy savages, whose habits, movements, and mode of attack more resemble those of wild beasts of the forests than any other animate beings'.[86]

The Indian Rebellion of 1857–1858 and the Zulu War of 1879 provide clear evidence of this mindset. During the Indian Rebellion the press repeatedly presented the pursuit and suppression of enemy forces as a hunt with the mutinous sepoys as the prey. Typical was *The Times*' description of operations in Northern India in January 1858. As the rebel armies fell back on Oudh, the paper insisted British forces under Sir Colin Campbell would now be able to 'wend towards the province, and gradually hunt the game towards Lucknow'.[87] The Rebellion's leaders, in particular, were singled out as sub-human. Repeatedly branded as beasts

Figure 1.2 John Leech, 'The New Alliance', *Punch*, 24 September 1859

in reports from the front, animalistic associations were buttressed by the labelling of strongholds as lairs or dens. Thus, as the search for Nana Sahib, 'the beast' who had orchestrated the seizure of Cawnpore in 1857, intensified in the winter of 1859, *The Times* urged caution lest he be 'startled from his lair . . . amid the jungles where his nature must be at home'.[88] The widespread conviction that the rebel sepoy had revealed his true base character by betraying British trust heightened passions and charged the use of hunting imagery with a potent shot of vitriol. Even the Archbishop of Canterbury, The Right Reverend Dr. John Bird Summer, fell victim to this press-induced public frenzy as his belief in the essential human decency of the subjugated peoples of the Empire's outposts was tested to breaking point by events on the subcontinent in the summer of 1857. In Charles Ball's contemporaneous *History of the Indian Mutiny*, Summer was reported to have informed a meeting of the Society for the Propagation of the Gospel in India that the massacre of the British garrison at Cawnpore had revealed the superficiality of Britain's civilising mission:

> We have seen what heathenism is. Many of us have been brought up with such an admiration of the old classical heathen, that we had almost got to think that a refined heathen was not such a bad sort of man after all. But we now know what a refined heathen is: we know that in a moment he can be transformed into a raging beast.[89]

This rendering of the enemy as little more than quarry had far-reaching repercussions. Stripped of their humanity, rebel sepoys could be portrayed as insensate beings with no claims to fair treatment. So, a *Times*' editorial in January 1858 could unapologetically declare that 'no punishment is too severe for the vile traitors who have betrayed their trust amid circumstances of cruelty so revolting that one can but think of them as wild beasts to be exterminated from the surface of the earth'.[90] And, as was graphically revealed in a tribute to Major Anson of the 9th Lancers, who died in January 1859 while recuperating from the strains of active service during the Rebellion, such uncompromising exhortations were acted on. In a posthumously published letter dated 4 January 1858, Anson recalled a captured rebel leader being 'brought into camp bound hand and foot [like a] wild beast . . . before he was well flogged . . . and then hung'.[91]

Just over 20 years later, the British invasion of Zululand was couched in similar terminology. Thus, native levies were described as 'beating the bush' as they endeavoured to drive the fugitive Zulu chief, Cetywayo, from his 'lair'.[92] Although enemy warriors were yet again dubbed beasts, this time, with accusations of treachery absent, the label was simply used to imply brute essence rather than innate evil. For the editor of the *Manchester Guardian*, the term was used to invoke the Zulus' want of any sense of agency. 'Like the beasts of the field', he argued in a review of the campaign on Wolseley's assumption of command during the second invasion, '[the Zulu] are not aware of their power to do mischief.'[93] The reading was the same for the editor of *The Times*. The Zulu warrior may be courageous, he observed in an editorial marking the capture of Cetywayo, but he was, still, 'a savage, and the savage like the wild beast, however daring in his first spring, has no power of organised and persistent effort . . . or moral strength'.[94] However, in a letter to the *The Times* demanding the establishment of a permanent military presence in the region, a former settler warned against underestimating the threat the defeated enemy still posed. The indigenous population may lack the higher understanding and sensibilities of the white coloniser, 'one who lived several years in Zululand' cautioned the paper's editor in January 1881, but it should not be dismissed as unthinkingly docile. 'The wild beast that has tasted human blood', he chillingly concluded, 'is ever a difficult beast to control'.[95]

Occasionally, dissenting voices from the margins were raised in opposition to this vision of war as a glorified hunt. In 1896, as an Anglo-Egyptian force prepared to confront the Mahdist army in Africa, *The Times* reported on the Russian press' widespread condemnation of English 'arrogance' in the colonies. British imperialism was so 'hypocritical, selfish and immoral', claimed the editor of the St Petersburg paper *Petersburgskiya Viedomosti*, that 'the Sudanese and other half-civilised defenceless tribes' functioned solely 'to furnish sport for British soldiers and aristocrats'.[96] Two years later, the socialist journalist Robert Buchanan, in the preface to an impassioned polemic against blood-sports by Jim Connell, addressed the same issue in the same terms, arguing that British actions overseas revealed the full extent of the imperial sporting warrior's brutish contempt for the lives of others:

> The Englishman, both as a soldier and colonist, is a typical sportsman; he seizes his prey wherever he finds it with the hunter's privilege. He is lost in amazement when men speak of the rights of inferior races, just as the sportsman at home is lost in amazement when we talk of the rights of the lower orders. Here, as yonder, he is kindly, blatant, good-humoured, aggressive, selfish, and fundamentally *savage* [emphasis in original].[97]

Another journalist, Ernest Bennett, who in his capacity as a war correspondent for the Liberal *Westminster Gazette* had witnessed appalling scenes on the battlefield of Omdurman on 2 September 1898, also looked to recast the imperial 'huntsman', rather than his prey, as the insensate being. 'Any Man', he seethed in a piece for another Liberal publication, *Contemporary Review*, 'who, after killing and wounding 26,000 Dervishes, with the total loss to his own side of some 500 casualties all told, was still unsatisfied and lusted after the blood of wounded men must be little better than a brute beast'. What was worse, Bennett noted in a concluding flourish that placed him firmly in the racial zeitgeist of the late Victorian, 'This unsoldierly work was not even left to the exclusive control of the black troops; our own British troops took part in it.'[98] However, such criticism remained relatively muted and certainly brought little weight to bear on the actions or attitudes of the military through the course of the imperial wars of conquest from the 1850s onwards. As Lieutenant-Colonel H. C. Lowther of the 1st Scots Guards noted when reflecting on his early career in the last years of the nineteenth century, the thrill of the chase remained unchallenged as, perhaps, the defining feature of army life. The key draw for recruits, he claimed in his 1912 memoir, *From Pillar to Post*, was the 'possibility of taking part in the greatest sport the world has to offer – hunting man and being hunted by man'.[99]

As Victoria's reign drew to a close, then, the nexus between sport and war was still firmly in place. Evidence of this can be found in the art world. There was, to use the art historian Joan Hichberger's phrase, 'an unarticulated equation' between sporting and military art in the 1890s, with the subject matters of both being regarded as exclusively masculine preserves, in which 'manly attributes of courage, energy and aggression' could be celebrated.[100] Indeed, manliness, that all-encompassing quality of the late-Victorian athlete, became a standard leitmotif at Royal Academy exhibitions in the last decade of the nineteenth century, with many sporting pictures, according to Paul Usherwood, carrying 'the unspoken assumption that sport [was] the best preparation for war'.[101] One of the first battlefield paintings to establish a direct link between the sports arena and the fighting front was Elizabeth Thompson's *Floreat Etona!*.[102] Exhibited at the Royal Academy in the summer of 1882, the painting focuses on the last moments of Lieutenant Robert Elwes at the Battle of Liang's Nek in the First Boer War. As a fellow Old Etonian has his horse shot from beneath him, Elwes is seen urging him on with, we are to assume, the eponymous sporting rallying cry of their *alma mater*. The painting's implicit sporting associations were made explicit by the literary editor Wilfred Meynell in a review of Thompson's career that appeared in *The Art Annual* in 1898:

> Poor Elwes fell among the 58th. He shouted to another Eton boy (adjutant of the 58th), whose horse had been shot, 'Come along Monck – *Floreat Etona!* – we must be in the first rank,' and he was shot immediately. The cry, which was the last uttered by the young soldier eager for glory, is significant of the spirit of enterprise with which the English man and boy alike enter upon war – which is, in part, the spirit of sport. . . . Sport and battle each have a share in the aspiration, gravity, and happiness of a worthy fight, as an Englishman understands it. If there is evident joy in the serious affair of war, is there not an equal seriousness in the trivial affairs of the cricket-ground and the hunting-field?[103]

By the end of the nineteenth century, this image of the dashing young officer, imbued with the public school games ethic, treating war as if it were a chivalric sporting competition had become a staple of celebrated military artists such as John Charlton, Thomas Baker and William Wollen, all of whom were also well-known for their sporting works.[104]

Such art, of course, did not operate in a cultural vacuum but rather reflected the prevailing values of wider society. In *Floreat Etona!*, Elwes' actions at Laing's Nek were removed from any professional judgements on the military's performance in the First Boer War or moral assessments of the rights and wrongs of British annexation of the Transvaal and, instead, valued for their individual worth. Elwes, viewers of the painting were being informed, should be admired not because of the outcome of his actions but simply because he had played the game as it should have been played. In the age of high imperialism, this approach became the norm. As Bradley Deane pointed out in his study of late Victorian popular literature, by the 1890s the imperial warrior was being judged solely by his adherence to an individual code of honour and not by his subservience to questions of utilitarian merit or universal morality.[105] Thus, the moral bankruptcy and military incompetence of Jameson's botched raid on the Transvaal Republic in December 1895 did nothing to discourage the editor of the *Nottinghamshire Guardian* from praising two local men who had taken part.[106] Not only, he argued in an editorial under the tag-line 'Sport the Image of War', had the men 'put in practice so gallantly' the lessons they had 'learnt not least well in a Leicestershire hunting field' but, despite having 'no earthly business there', they had also remained true to 'the belief that courage and chivalry are real things still'.[107] Robert Baden-Powell was equally devoted to this Newboltian precept of putting 'the game beyond the prize'. The Englishman, he loftily declared in his 1897 reminiscences of the Matabele campaign,

> is endowed by nature with the spirit of practical discipline, which is deeper than the surface veneer of discipline of Continental armies. Whether this has been instilled into him by his public-school training, by his football . . . or whether it is inbred . . . one cannot say; but, at any rate, the goodly precepts of the game remain as best of guides: 'keep in your place,' and 'play, not for yourself, but for your side.' It is thus that our leaders find themselves backed by their officers playing up to them; not . . . because it may bring them crosses and rewards, but simply – *because it is the game* [emphasis in original].[108]

As relations between the two Boer Republics and Britain deteriorated in the aftermath of the Jameson Raid, sport continued to be advanced as one of the best ways for the Empire to ready itself for any coming conflict. Concerned that the British military presence in South Africa would be found wanting in the event of an invasion, the editor of the *Daily Mail* was convinced that the nation's sporting heritage could be exploited to save the day. 'By our athletic enthusiasm, our football and rowing and cricket', he argued in an editorial entitled 'To Strengthen the Empire', 'we are creating a body of admirable fighting material which will serve us well in time of war'. The government should, he therefore suggested, ensure supremacy in the Cape and Natal, by financially backing the emigration of 'a large number of these Englishmen, so well fitted for military service'.[109] Three years later, in the wake of an unsuccessful arbitration conference at Bloemfontein, the same paper's military expert, Ian McAllan, was in no doubt that the appointment of Lieutenant-General Sir George White as commander of the forces in Natal was the right move. The fact, McAllan maintained, that White was 'a fine horseman, devoted to sport and never happier than when in the saddle', should be enough to reassure readers that 'he no doubt knows the game of war by heart'.[110] Earlier the same year, the importance of equestrianism in military proficiency had also been addressed by William Elliott Cairns, a captain in the Royal Irish Fusiliers.

In his highly popular study, *Social Life in the British Army*, he explained why the sporting exploits of serving officers at professional race meets should continue to receive both official and public backing:

> In some societies feats of this kind would be regarded with an attitude of mild condemnation, or of doubtful approbation at best; but those who know the courage, readiness of resource, self-denial, and continuous hard work necessary before a success of this kind can be hoped for, are little likely to undervalue the steeplechase course as a training school for the young soldier. The gallant Roddy Owen, who, by-the-bye, was an infantry officer, proved that the coolness and courage which had gained him such high honours on the race-course, making his name in very deed a household word, were equally available when the opportunity came for employing them in the service of his country, and eminent soldiers and statesmen soon recognised a kindred spirit in the hero of Aintree and Sandown. On active service, in the moment of imminent danger and great and sudden emergency, the self-reliance and quickness of resolution which are indispensable to the successful steeplechase rider cannot fail to be of the utmost value to the soldier; consequently, I hope the day is far distant when the amateur jock will be looked upon with disfavour by his military superiors.[111]

Even as late as 1900, with the humiliations of the opening stages of the South African War fresh in the memory, hunting was still being held out as a prerequisite for military success. In *Pink and Scarlet*, an in-depth tactical treatise on the relationship between field-sports and the cavalry, Lieutenant-Colonel Edwin Alderson echoed Kinglake a quarter of a century earlier when he argued, 'if we had not sport, and above all sport – fox-hunting', the nation would be unable 'to train our future Lacy Yeas'. Improvements in military hardware since the Crimean War had, Alderson continued, merely reinforced his case: 'the better the weapons . . . the more essential it is that troops be mobile, and that Officers who lead the troops should be . . . able *to use the accidents of the ground* [emphasis in the original].' However, he concluded on a note of caution. 'Too many of us', he warned, 'forget to combine sport, which we take to so readily, with the necessary study to make us soldiers in every sense of the word'.[112] As the struggle against the Transvaal and Orange Free State dragged on, at ever greater financial and human cost, this tension between the professionalism of the instruction hall and the amateurism of the sports ground was, as shall be seen in the following chapter, to be thrown into high relief.

Notes

1 Hamish Stuart, 'The Football Nations', *Blackwood's, Edinburgh Magazine*, 169/1026 (April 1901), p. 489.
2 Richard Holt, *Sport and the British: A Modern History* (Oxford: Oxford University Press, 1989), chapter 2.

3 J. A. Mangan (ed.), *The Cultural Bond: Sport, Empire and Society* (Abingdon: Routledge, 1992), p. 2.
4 H. John Field, *Toward a Programme of Imperial Life: The British Empire at the Turn of the Century* (Oxford: Clio Press, 1982), pp. 26–30.
5 Ric Sissons and Brian Stoddart, *Cricket and Empire* (Sydney: Allen & Unwin, 1984), p. 34.
6 Mark Girouard, *The Return to Camelot: Chivalry and the English Gentleman* (New Haven: Yale University Press, 1991), p. 233. Set up by the government in 1861, the Clarendon Commission, or, more formally, the Royal Commission on the Public Schools, was tasked with investigating the widespread ill-discipline affecting a number of leading public schools. See Colin Shrosbree, *Public Schools and Private Education: The Clarendon Commission, 1861–64, and the Public Schools Acts* (Manchester: Manchester University Press, 1988).
7 Geoffrey Best, 'Militarism in the Victorian Public School', in Brian Simon and Ian Bradley (eds.), *The Victorian Public School: Studies in the Development of an Educational Institution* (Dublin: Gill and Macmillan, 1975), p. 130; Michael Paris, *Warrior Nation: Images of War in British Popular Culture, 1850–2000* (London: Reaktion Books Ltd., 2000), pp. 50–51.
8 *Daily Telegraph*, 28 September 1888. For readers of the *Daily Telegraph* at the end of the nineteenth century, 'football' meant rugby union.
9 In fact, the cricketing authorities displayed scant interest in the colonies for the majority of Victoria's reign. It wasn't until the arrival, in the 1890s, of Lords Harris and Hawke as the controlling voices in the MCC, the sport's governing body, that the game assumed its imperial duty with the fervour of the convert. See James Bradley, 'The MCC, Society and Empire: A portrait of cricket's ruling body, 1860–1914', *International Journal of the History of Sport*, 17/1 (1990), pp. 3–22. Harris, a former governor of Bombay (1890–1895), became president of the MCC in 1895. Hawke, who captained Yorkshire and England in the 1890s, was an influential committee member at MCC throughout the late Victorian and Edwardian period, eventually becoming president in 1914.
10 Henry Newbolt, 'Vitaï Lampada', *Admirals All and Other Verses* (London: Elkin Mathews, 1897), pp. 23–24.
11 J. D. Campbell, '"Training for Sport Is Training for War"': Sport and the Transformation of the British Army, 1860–1914', *International Journal of the History of Sport*, 17/4 (December 2000), pp. 21–58.
12 Edward Spiers, *The Army and Society, 1815–1914* (London: Longman, 1980), p. 63.
13 *Manchester Guardian*, 13 October 1857.
14 David French, *Military Identities: The Regimental System, the British Army, and the British People, c. 1870–2000* (Oxford: Oxford University Press, 2005), p. 120.
15 Campbell, '"Training for Sport Is Training for War"', p. 23; Tim Bowman and Mark Connelly, *The Edwardian Army: Recruiting, Training and Deploying the British Army, 1902–1914* (Oxford: Oxford University Press, 2012), p. 56.
16 Certainly, there appeared to be evidence to support such fears. As the traditional rural recruiting grounds began to disappear and the army had to turn to the urban and industrial areas to meet its targets, the minimum physical requirements for enlistees were progressively lowered. Thus, in 1869 the minimum height requirement was 5 feet 6 inches; by 1900 this had fallen to 5 feet 3 inches. Edward Spiers, *The Late Victorian Army, 1868–1902* (Manchester: Manchester University Press, 1992), p. 122.
17 In 1858, for example, the Royal Commission on the Health of the Army called for some form of physical training to be introduced for all troops. See Nikolai Bogdanovic, *Fit to Fight: A History of the Royal Army Physical Training Corps, 1860–2012* (Oxford: Osprey Publishing, 2017), pp. 11–12. See also Vanessa Heggie, 'Bodies, Sport and Science in the Nineteenth Century', *Past and Present*, 231/1 (May 2016), pp. 175–177.

18 Alan Skelley, *The Victorian Army at Home: The Recruitment and Terms and Conditions of the British Regular, 1859–1899* (London: Croom Helm, 1977), pp. 58–61.
19 Jeffrey Richards, 'Popular Imperialism and the Image of the Army in Juvenile Literature', in John M. Mackenzie, (ed.), *Popular Imperialism and the Military, 1850–1950* (Manchester: Manchester University Press, 1992), p. 85.
20 J. A. Mangan, *Manufactured Masculinity: Making Imperial Manliness, Morality and Militarism* (London: Routledge, 2012), p. 26.
21 Henry Brackenbury, 'Military Reforms', *Fraser's Magazine for Town and Country*, 74/144 (December 1866), p. 692.
22 Henry Strickland Constable, *Something About Horses: Sport and War* (London: Eden, Remington and Co., 1891), pp. 138, 291–292.
23 David French may be less sure than J. D. Campbell that sport had a beneficial impact on the military's performance but nonetheless concurs that contemporaries assumed this was the case. French, *Military Identities*, p. 117; J. D. Campbell, *The Army Isn't All Work: Physical Culture and the Evolution of the British Army, 1860–1920* (Farnham: Ashgate, 2012), pp. 3–22.
24 Mason and Riedi, *Sport and the Military*, p. 37.
25 Mangan, *Manufactured Masculinity*, p. 158.
26 Henry Newbolt, 'He Fell Among Thieves', *The Island Race* (London: Elkin Mathews, 1898), p. 69. The poem was loosely based on the death of Lieutenant George W. Hayward, who was captured and killed during an expedition to the Pamir Mountains in Central Asia in 1878. See J. A. Mangan, 'Tragic Symbiosis: Distinctive "Anglo-Saxon" Visions and Voices', in J. A. Mangan and Thierry Tenet (eds.), *Sport, Militarism and the Great War: Martial Manliness and Armageddon* (London: Routledge, 2012), p. 192.
27 Girouard, *The Return to Camelot*, p. 233.
28 Samuel Smiles, *Self-Help: With Illustrations of Character and Conduct* (London: John Murray, 1859), p. 242. Brevet Major William Hodson famously raised a cavalry regiment (Hodson's Horse) during the Indian Rebellion. Smiles was reputed to have got the story from the French politician and historian the Count of Montalembert, who, in 1855, claimed that Wellington, on returning to his *alma mater*, declared, "C'est ici qu'a été gagné la bataille de Waterloo". Elizabeth Longford, *Wellington: The Years of the Sword* (London: HarperCollins Publishers Ltd., 1971), p. 16.
29 William Makepeace Thackeray, *Vanity Fair: A Novel Without a Hero* (London: Bradbury and Evans, 1848), p. 104.
30 Thackeray, *Vanity Fair*, p. 264. Paris, *Warrior Nation*, p. 27.
31 Laura Kriegel, 'The Strange Career of Fair Play, or, Warfare and Gamesmanship in the time of Victoria', in Juliet John (ed.), *The Oxford Handbook of Victorian Literary Culture* (Oxford: Oxford University Press, 2016), p. 278.
32 An Old Boy, 'Tom Brown's Schooldays', *Edinburgh Review*, 107/217 (January 1858), p. 173, p. 177.
33 J. A. Mangan and Callum C. McKenzie, *Militarism, Hunting, Imperialism: 'Blooding' the Martial Male* (London: Routledge, 2010), p. 15.
34 Robert H. McDonald, 'Signs from the Imperial Quarter: Illustrations in Chums, 1892–1914', *Children's Literature*, 16 (1998), p. 31.
35 Half hours with some of our writers: Mr George A. Henty', *Young England*, 14/144 (1893), p. 414; Ralph Crane and Lisa Fletcher, 'Picturing the Empire in India: Illustrating Henty', *ELT Journal*, 55/2 (2012), p. 160.
36 Dennis Butts, 'Exploiting a formula: the adventure stories of G. A. Henty (1832–1902)', in Julia Briggs, Dennis Butts and M. O. Grenby (eds.), *Popular Children's Literature in Britain* (Aldershot: Ashgate, 2008), p. 149.
37 Godfrey Davies has suggested that Henty was less than successful when it came to the first of these objectives. In a detailed examination of four Henty novels set during

the Napoleonic Wars, Davies uncovered numerous factual errors. Godfrey Davies, 'G. A. Henty and History', *Huntingdon Library Quarterly*, 18/2 (February 1955), pp. 159–167.
38 Gail S. Clark, 'Imperial Stereotypes: G. A. Henty and the *Boys' Own Empire*', *Journal of Popular Culture*, 18/4 (Spring 1985), pp. 49–50.
39 Crane and Fletcher, 'Picturing the Empire', p. 161. Brooke Allen has noted that although the majority of Henty's novels were not set in contemporary times, the protagonists, nonetheless, were never 'anything but a Victorian gentleman'. Brooke Allen, 'G. A. Henty and the Vision of Empire', *New Criterion* (April 2002), p. 22. In a similar vein, Gail Clark has argued that all the heroes in the 23 novels with an explicit imperial setting seem to uphold public school values despite the fact that only four of them are actually shown to have had the benefit of such a privileged education. Clark, 'Imperial Stereotypes', pp. 43–45.
40 G. A. Henty, *The Dash for Khartoum: A Tale of the Nile Expedition* (New York: Charles Scribner's Sons, 1902), p. 225.
41 G. A. Henty, *By Sheer Pluck: A Tale of the Ashanti War* (London: Blackie and Son Ltd., 1883), pp. 10–14.
42 G. A. Henty, *For Name and Fame: Or, Through Afghan Passes* (New York: Scribner and Welford, 1880), p. 275; Henty, *The Dash for Khartoum*, p. 99.
43 Brian Stoddart, 'Sport, Cultural Imperialism, and Colonial Response in the British Empire', *Comparative Studies in Society and History*, 30/4 (October 1988), pp. 658–659.
44 Quoted in James D. Coldham, *Lord Harris* (Sydney: Allen & Unwin, 1983), p. 109.
45 Mangan, *The Cultural Bond*, p. 2.
46 G. A. Henty, *With Clive in India: Or the Beginnings of an Empire* (New York: Charles Scribner's Sons, 1894), p. 9.
47 G. A. Henty, *At the Point of a Bayonet: A Tale of the Mahratta War* (London: Blackie and Son Ltd., 1902), p. 32.
48 Henty, *At the Point of a Bayonet*, p. 33.
49 Paris, *Warrior Nation*, p. 77.
50 Hughes, *Tom Brown*, p. 277.
51 Henry Newbolt, 'Clifton Chapel', *Island Race*, p. 76.
52 Hughes, *Tom Brown*, p. 60. For more on the social composition of the officers corps, see P. E. Razzell, 'Social Origins of Officers in the Indian and British Home Army, 1758–1962', *British Journal of Sociology*, 14 (1963), pp. 248–260.
53 *Observer*, 16 January 1860.
54 *Manchester Guardian*, 19 February 1871.
55 *Manchester Guardian*, 17 March 1871.
56 Sir John Burgoyne, *Army Reform* (n.p, 1857), p. 10, quoted in Colin Veitch, 'Sport and War in the British Literature of the First World War' (unpublished MA diss., University of Alberta, Edmonton, 1983), p. 26.
57 Quoted in Byron Farwell, *Eminent Victorian Soldiers: Seekers of Glory* (New York: W. W. Norton and Co., 1985), p. 206.
58 G. A. Henty, *Through Sikh Wars: A Tale of the Conquest of the Punjaub* (New York: Charles Scribner's Sons, 1902), p. 30.
59 Captain R. S. S. Baden Powell, *Pigsticking; or Hoghunting: A Complete Account for Sportsmen, and Others* (London: Harrison and Sons, 1889), pp. 8–9. A similar case against the parade-ground martinet had been presented by John Colquhoun almost half a century earlier in the introduction to his widely read manual on field-sports, *The Moor and the Loch*. 'Although a man who devotes all his time and energy to military duty', Colquhoun had argued, 'may be an excellent and valuable parade officer, yet in actual service, when anything dashing was done, it was, in nine cases out of ten, by those who loved the hunting-field . . . these were generally the most efficient officers

in an arduous campaign'. John Colquhoun, *The Moor and the Loch* (Edinburgh: William Blackwood and Sons, 1840), pp. 37–38. For more on the brief history of the Mounted Infantry, see Andrew Philip Winrow, 'The British Regular Mounted Infantry, 1880–1913: Cavalry of Poverty or Victorian Paradigm?' (unpublished D.Phil. thesis, University of Buckingham, 2014).
60 Baden-Powell, *Pigsticking*, p. 168.
61 Sir John Kaye, 'The Career of an Indian Officer', *Cornhill Magazine*, 3/13 (January 1861), pp. 73–74. In fact, Outram rejected his nomination by the volunteer cavalry regiment for the Victoria Cross after the battle of Alambagh 'on the ground that he was ineligible as the general under whom they served'. Hugh Chisholm (ed.), *The Encyclopaedia Britannica, Volume XX* (New York: The Encyclopaedia Britannica Company, 1911), p. 382.
62 'Field Sports and the War', *The Field*, 4/100 (25 November 1854), p. 1108.
63 A. W. Kinglake, *The Invasion of the Crimea: Its Origin, and an Account of Its Progress Down to the Death of Lord Raglan Volume III* (Edinburgh: William Blackwood and Sons, 1874), p. 111. Even Lord Cardigan's exploits in the Crimea could be hailed as proof of the martial qualities latent in the huntsman. In 1869, without a hint of irony, the Master of the Horse, informed the assembled officers of the Household Brigade, 'He thought the hunting-field a good training ground for soldiers, and any who had ever witnessed the straight way the late Lord Cardigan was in the habit of going over the Leicestershire country could not have been surprised at his performance in the famous Balaklava charge.' 'The Journal of the Household Brigade for the year 1869', quoted in French, *Military Identities*, p. 117.
64 *The Times*, 31 March 1868; 'The Zulu War – with General Wood: A Buck-Hunt on the March', *Graphic*, 30 August 1879.
65 Hew Strachan, 'The Idea of War', in Kate McLoughlin (ed.), *The Cambridge Companion to War Writing* (Cambridge: Cambridge University Press, 2009), p. 10.
66 E. A. H. Alderson, *With the Mounted Infantry and the Mashonaland Field Force, 1896* (London: Methuen & Co., 1898), pp. 47–48, 248.
67 *Manchester Guardian*, 18 March 1855; *The Times*, 28 January 1879. The British officer's propensity to hunt during the Crimean campaign was also alluded to by Henty. In *Jack Archer: A Tale of the Crimea*, he noted that outside the Light Brigade's camp, 'game abounded and the officers who had brought guns with them found for a time capital sport'. G. A. Henty, *Jack Archer: A Tale of the Crimea* (New York: Mershon Company, 1880), p. 43.
68 *Manchester Guardian*, 14 April 1855; *Scotsman*, 18 April 1885.
69 *The Times*, 18 May 1896; *Daily Mail*, 11 August 1896.
70 'Sport in Afghanistan', *Bell's Life in London and Sporting Chronicle*, 16 April 1881, p. 8.
71 See Paris, *Warrior Nation*, pp. 70–78.
72 *The Times*, 2 February 1855; 10 May 1879.
73 *The Times*, 27 February 1858.
74 Ésme Wingfield-Stratford, *Before the Lamps Went Out* (London: Hodder & Stoughton, 1945), p. 78; General Sir Hope Grant, *Incidents in the Sepoy War, 1857–58* (London: William Blackwood and Sons, 1873), p. 120. Wingfield-Stratford did go on to concede that '[t]o anyone born in the twentieth century [this view] must seem incredible'. Wingfield-Stratford, *Before the Lamps Went Out*, p. 78.
75 Winston Churchill, *My Early Life: A Roving Commission* (London: Odhams Press Ltd., 1930), p. 179.
76 Heather Streets, *Martial Races: The Military, Race and Masculinity in British Imperial Culture, 1857–1914* (Manchester: Manchester University Press, 2004, p. 71.
77 'Lord Clyde's Campaign in India', *Blackwood's Edinburgh Magazine*, 84/156 (October 1858), p. 492.

78 Field-Marshal Lord Roberts of Kandahar, *Forty-One Years in India: From Subaltern to Commander-in-Chief, Volume 1* (London: Richard Bentley and Son, 1898), p. 325.
79 See Steven W. Pope, 'An Army of Athletes: Playing-Fields, Battlefields, and the American Military Sporting Experience, 1890–1920', *Journal of Military History*, 59/3 (1995), pp. 435–438.
80 John Leech, 'Now for It!' *Punch*, 17 January 1855. And this despite the fact that Palmerston was seventy-years-old.
81 Gordon Thompson, 'Bravo, Chelmsford!' *Fun*, 30 July 1879.
82 Gordon Thompson, 'Science Versus Pluck; or Too Much for the Mahdi', *Fun*, 12 March 1884.
83 Of course, as Michael Paris has noted, the technological imbalance in imperial wars made a mockery of the Victorians' professed love of fair play. Paris, *Warrior Nation*, p. 78. Indeed, the mismatch between opposing forces was hinted at in Thompson's use of the title 'Science versus Pluck' for his cartoon of the Battle of Tamai. The science referred to the 14 field-guns deployed by the Anglo-Egyptian force against the numerically superior but relatively poorly equipped Mahdist army. See Mark Bryant, *Wars of Empire in Cartoons* (London: Grub Street Publishing, 2008), p. 101.
84 Mark Cocker, *Richard Meinertzhagen: Soldier, Scientist and Spy* (London: Secker and Warburg, 1989), p. 48.
85 John Leech, 'The New Alliance', *Punch*, 24 September 1859; Gordon Thompson, 'Sport', *Fun*, 15 September 1880; 'Fishing for Arabi – Catching a Big 'Un', 6 September 1882.
86 'The Relation of Sport to War', *County Gentleman, Sporting Gazette and Agricultural Journal*, 2 January 1881. John Richardson has noted that in the drinking songs of the eighteenth century, the Marquess of Granby's campaigns on the European mainland during the Seven Years' War (1756–1763) were often compared to fox-hunts. John Richardson, 'Imagining Military Conflict During the Seven Years' War', *Studies in English Literature, 1500–1600*, 48/3 (Summer 2008), p. 587. However, by the time of the wars of Italian and German Unification in the second-half of the nineteenth century, the repackaging of war as a hunt seems to have become largely the preserve of colonial campaigning.
87 *The Times*, 28 January 1858. For other examples of hunting imagery, see *The Times*, 26 February 1858; *Manchester Guardian*, 18 October 1857; 3 January 1858; 3 May 1858.
88 *The Times*, 11 February 1859. For further examples of rebel leaders being branded with similar language, see *The Times*, 25 September 1857; 3 September 1858; *Illustrated London News*, 21 August 1858; 1 January 1859; *Manchester Guardian*, 9 August 1858.
89 Charles Ball, *History of the Indian Mutiny* (London: London Printing and Publishing Company, 1859), p. 453. An interesting departure from the orthodoxy of portraying rebellious sepoys as savage beasts appeared in the *Illustrated London News* on 23 January 1858. In a letter to the paper's editor, an anonymous British officer noted that the enemy were 'very shy in showing fight – firing a few shots, and then off like deer'. *Illustrated London News*, 23 January 1858. Of course, although the imagery may have been a little more benign, the analogy of a hunt was just as strong.
90 *The Times*, 17 January 1858.
91 Harcourt S. Anson, *With H. M. 9th Lancers During the Indian Mutiny. The Letters of Brevet-Major O. H. S. G. Anson* (London: W. H. Allen, 1896), pp. 225–226.
92 A. Winton, *A History of the Zulu War* (London: Richardson and Best, 1880), p. 209; *The Times*, 23 August 1879. The impression that operations against the Zulu were similar to hunting expeditions was reinforced by the British troops' habit of taking trophies to validate kills. According to Michael Lieven, as well as shields and assegais, 'the hardened sole from the foot of a dead Zulu and the skull of a warrior' also featured as collectible objects. Michael Lieven, 'A Victorian Military Genre: Military Memoirs and the Anglo-Zulu War', *Journal of the Society of Army Historical Research*, 77/310 (1999), p. 119.

93 *Manchester Guardian*, 4 September 1879.
94 *The Times*, 28 May 1879. In fact, the Zulu were a highly militarised society with relatively sophisticated battle tactics. See Adrian Greaves, *Crossing the Buffalo: The Zulu War of 1879* (London: Weidenfeld and Nicolson, 2005), especially chapter 3, 'The Zulu Military and their Tactics'.
95 *The Times*, 31 January 1881.
96 *The Times*, 1 February 1896.
97 J. Connell, *The Truth About the Game Laws: A Record of Cruelty, Selfishness and Oppression* (London: William Reeves, 1898), p. vii.
98 Ernest N. Bennett, 'After Omdurman', *Contemporary Review*, LXXV (January 1899), p. 25. The sense that the scale of slaughter at Omdurman was out of all proportion to the risk posed by the Dervish army was, no doubt inadvertently, hinted at in *The Times*' use of a rather more bucolic animal analogy when establishing the pre-battle scene for its readers: 'The Sirdar used his cavalry with great skill, sending the Egyptians to the right and the lancers to the left to keep the Dervishes away from Omdurman, very much in the manner that a well-trained sheep-dog keeps in hand a flock of sheep.' *The Times*, 6 September 1898.
99 Lieutenant-Colonel H. C. Lowther, *From Pillar to Post* (London: Edward Arnold, 1912), p. 162.
100 Joan Hichberger, 'Military Themes in British Painting, 1815–1914' (unpublished PhD thesis, University College London, 1985), p. 151.
101 Paul Usherwood, 'Officer Material: Representations of Leadership in Late Nineteenth Century British Battle Painting', in Mackenzie (ed.), *Popular Imperialism and the Military, 1850–1950* (Manchester: Manchester University Press, 1992), p. 173. Usherwood cited William Barnes Wollen's rugby painting, *The Battle of the Roses; Yorkshire v Lancashire* (1896), as a good example of this 'unspoken assumption'.
102 Usherwood, 'Officer Material', p. 173. *Floreat Etona* roughly translates as 'May Eton Flourish'.
103 Wilfred Meynell, 'The Life and Work of Lady Butler (Miss Elizabeth Thompson)', *The Art Annual* (London: The Art Journal Office, 1898), p. 14.
104 Hichberger, 'Military Themes in British Painting', p. 150.
105 Bradley Deane, 'Imperial Boyhood: Piracy and the Play Ethic', *Victorian Studies*, 53/4 (2011), pp. 692–693.
106 In late December 1895, Leander Starr Jameson, with, it is generally thought, the tacit consent of the Colonial Office, attempted to instigate an anti-government uprising in the Transvaal Republic. The scheme ended in ignominious failure at the battle of Doornkop on 2 January 1896, with Jameson himself, much to the embarrassment of Whitehall, briefly imprisoned in Johannesburg. See Chris Ash, *The If Man: Leander Starr Jameson, the Inspiration for Kipling's Masterpiece* (Solihull: Helion and Co., 2012), pp. 246–251.
107 *Nottinghamshire Guardian*, 1 February 1896.
108 Colonel R. S. S. Baden-Powell, *The Matabele Campaign 1896: Being a Narrative of the Campaign in Suppressing the Native Rising in Matabeleland and Mashonaland* (London: Methuen & Co., 1897), pp. 466–467.
109 *Daily Mail*, 13 October 1896.
110 *Daily Mail*, 22 September 1899. Sir George White, despite his sporting credentials, proved unable to live up to McAllan's billing. Refusing to countenance a retreat south of the river Tugela, White allowed the bulk of the British forces in Natal to become trapped in the garrison town of Ladysmith, where they remained under siege until February 1900. See Thomas Pakenham, *The Boer War* (London: George Weidenfeld and Nicolson Ltd., 1979), pp. 148–153.
111 "A British Officer", *Social Life in the British Army* (London: Harper and Brothers, 1899), pp. 38–39. As a serving soldier, Cairns, understandably perhaps, chose to be published anonymously. In 1892, Roddy Owen, a captain in the Lancashire Fusiliers,

achieved a remarkable double of winning the Distinguished Service Order in West Africa and the Grand National at Aintree. Joe Eastwood, 'Major E. R. (Roddy) Owen DSO The XXth The Lancashire Fusiliers' (17 October 2006), XXth Lancashire Fusiliers website, <www.lancs-fusiliers.co.uk/featre/roddyowen/RoddyOwen.htm> [accessed 17 March 2017].

112 Lieutenant-Colonel E. A. H. Alderson, *Pink and Scarlet or Hunting as a School for Soldiering* (London: William Heinemann, 1900), p. 166, pp. 116–117, p. 213. David French has also noted that the army's tactical doctrine after 1880 placed greater emphasis on mobility and initiative, the very qualities that sports were thought to develop. French, *Military Identities*, p. 115.

2 The South African War, 1899–1902

'We are having a very enjoyable game'

In January 1902, a heated debate erupted in the letters columns of *The Times* on the back of the paper's publication of Rudyard Kipling's poem *The Islanders*.[1] Kipling's cutting criticism that a national preoccupation with 'muddied oafs' and 'flannelled fools' had detracted from the successful prosecution of the war against the Boers touched a nerve with *The Times*' largely privileged middle-class readership, many of whom, undoubtedly, retained a deep affection for the sports teams of their schooldays.[2] The impact of this poetic assault on sport, however, went beyond the confines of a narrow stratum of former public schoolboys. An editorial in the leading French newspaper *Le Temps*, quoted at length in *The Times*, linked *The Islanders*' condemnation of organised team games with a wider socio-economic revolution that Britain was experiencing:

> [B]etween the ideals of sport and the barracks there is an utter antagonism. The England of Liberalism, of trade unions, of peace, and of commercial activity demanded the former. The new Imperialism, with its dreams of conquests, its love of military glory, its scorn of the constitutional law, demands the second. The *Temps* fancies it has discovered that while the partisans of sport are in general robust and healthy men who are or have been sportsmen themselves, the neo-Imperialists school is composed of literary men with excitable nerves and morbid temperaments. . . . [T]he fact that the artists and men of letters have taken this idea up is, thinks the *Temps*, a most significant sign of the times, for the practical campaign to alter the whole basis of military organisation in England is a parallel movement, which, if carried out will, in the opinion of this journal, make a revolution in England involving the whole social and economic structure.[3]

That Kipling's dismissal of football and cricket should excite such passions not only provides further evidence of the central role sport played in both the civilian and the military culture of late Victorian and early Edwardian Britain but also points to the challenge the South African War posed to the public school games cult. What made this questioning of the primacy of the playing-field all the more remarkable was that it came just as sport was assuming an ever-stronger hold on the military world.

As the fragile peace between the two Boer Republics and the British Empire collapsed in October 1899, the army's fixation with games and physical endeavour was reinforced by the flood of volunteers who swelled the ranks of the British army in the aftermath of three early reverses at the battles of Stormberg, Magersfontein and Colenso in December 1899. A significant proportion of these new recruits came from the middle classes, the very stratum of society at the forefront of the cult of athleticism, and they brought to the barrack room and parade ground a civilian fervour for games.[4] As will be seen, however, this coalescing of the civilian and military world's fascination for sport directed a spotlight towards the on-going conflict between the amateur and the professional sporting ideal. For the military, this had implications that went far beyond the boundaries of the cricket square or the rugby pitch. If the army, in general, and the officer corps, in particular, adhered to the gentleman-amateur's creed of valuing sport for sport's sake rather than the winning, then it raised questions about the efficacy of the amateur-military tradition as a whole and the attitude towards war that it engendered.[5] As British forces struggled to defeat the numerically inferior militias of the Boer Republics, these tensions were going to be thrown into high relief.

As has already been shown, by the time of the South African War, the connection between sport, the military and the imperial battlefield was firmly embedded in the popular consciousness. The conflict, however, proved to be more protracted and more costly, in both financial and human terms, than anyone anticipated.[6] Sir Redvers Buller's early reverses culminating in the disasters of Black Week in December 1899, the Boer *bitterenders*' stubborn resistance during the lengthy guerrilla endgame of 1901–1902 and Roberts' and Kitchener's fierce counterinsurgency measures, including the establishment of concentration camps, all triggered a period of intensive national soul-searching.[7] This public introspection was heightened by blanket press coverage of the fighting. As Stephen Badsey has noted, the South African War captured the public's imagination as no previous conflict had done. Although, as we have already seen, the war correspondent had been a fixture of campaigning since the 1850s, the quantity and variety of news items and images emanating from the battlefields of South Africa gave truth to Badsey's claim that this was the 'first media war'.[8] Improved literacy levels on the back of the Education Acts of 1870, 1876 and 1880; lower production costs stemming from the abolition of Stamp Duty in 1855 and Excise Duty on paper in 1861; and the introduction of new print technologies all resulted in a new mass newspaper readership by the end of the nineteenth century. The rush of volunteers to the colours in late 1899 and early 1900, which gave the army, albeit for a very short time, a demographic much more akin to its parent population further fuelled the public's impatience for information from the frontline. Press magnates, such as Alfred Harmsworth of the *Daily Mail* and Arthur Walter of *The Times*, in an effort to boost their circulation figures, fed the civilian world's fascination with all things khaki by despatching scores of war correspondents to South Africa. Coeval with this all-consuming appetite for war stories was a growing demand for sports reporting. In 1861 there were less than a dozen dedicated sporting journals, by 1881 there were over 30, and by 1901 there were 158.[9] Perhaps more significantly, by the outbreak of the South African War, the non-specialist press was giving extensive coverage to sport. Fourteen per cent of the total space of the *News of the World*, one of the best-selling weeklies catering for the newly literate working classes, was being devoted to sport by 1900.[10] Even an establishment institution like *The Times* was prepared to bend to this trend acknowledging that sport had become 'a positive passion, thanks to the publicity given by the sporting press'.[11]

This thriving press interest in organised games served to disseminate the cult of athleticism throughout late Victorian society and created an imagined community in which sporting values and characteristics were employed to give meaning and order to the outside world. Glenn Wilkinson has shown, in his study of the depiction of military force in Edwardian newspapers, that sporting imagery was frequently used to portray warfare as both beneficial and desirable. In this reading, even the early reverses against the Boers could be given a positive spin. Black Week had, so the readers of *Lloyd's Weekly Newspaper* were told, provided the country with a salutary lesson by demonstrating that the 'great heart' of the Empire had been suffering 'from fatty degeneration'.[12] Further evidence of the role of sport as an essential frame of reference for society at the turn of the twentieth century, and of the importance of the press in developing this phenomenon, can be found in the language exchange between the sporting and military worlds that became an increasing feature of popular journalism of the period. According to Dean Allen, it was the conflict in South Africa that made this transmission of sporting jargon to military reporting an acceptable tool of the war correspondent.[13]

Most obviously, though, the grip the games' cult had on the public imagination can be gleaned from the newspapers' insistence on covering sport in the combat zone. The press regularly made a point of remarking on the continuing sporting activities of the British army during the war in South Africa. The *Manchester Guardian* noted that Lord Roberts' troops in Bloemfontein in the spring of 1900 enjoyed 'daily cricket and athletic contests', while at Chieveley camp, near the besieged garrison town of Ladysmith, football and cricket filled most of the daylight hours 'unless the stern requirements of war necessitated a call to duty'.[14] On the Modder River, so the readers of the *Observer* were informed, a lull in the fighting allowed Lord Methuen's men to engage in boxing contests 'every evening' with the presentation of 'handsome cups for the winners of the heavyweight and middleweight competitions'.[15] The army's penchant for marking public holidays with sporting events was a constant feature of war reports in the first year of the conflict. The endless round of gymkhanas and inter-regimental football and cricket matches with which Sir Redvers Buller's troops at Chieveley, Lord Methuen's on the Modder River and General Gatacre's in Sterkstroom greeted Christmas of 1899 was given full coverage in the pages of the daily newspapers.[16] Indeed, Julian Ralph, special war correspondent with the *Daily Mail*, rather wearily observed in his collected despatches that 'with the approaching festivities [British officers] get up an uncommon strong interest in a new subject – sports for New Year's Day. That, I take it, is a topic that never fell flat in a British company'.[17]

However, it was the predilection for organised games shown by the besieged garrisons in Kimberley, Mafeking and Ladysmith that really captured the attention of the press. The *Manchester Guardian* told its readers that they would be wrong to think that life in Kimberley was 'all work and no play'. Although there were three parades a day, there were also 'two very good cricket grounds' where matches 'between teams representing the regulars and volunteers' were held.[18] The *Daily Mail* noted that the beleaguered population of Mafeking had celebrated the eighteenth Sunday of the siege with 'a cricket match in the morning and cycle sports in the afternoon'.[19] *The Times* was particularly fascinated by the difficulties that Colonel Robert Baden-Powell, the commandant at Mafeking, had to overcome in order to implement his 'big programme of sporting events'. An article published in February 1900 recounted the reluctance of the Boer commander, General Snyman, to observe the traditional Sunday truce because of the British propensity to 'indulge in "unholy practices" such as sports and cricket'. This 'unctuous announcement', the correspondent witheringly noted, effectively proscribed 'all those pastimes by which the garrison could gain some relief from the week's siege'.[20] Sport was also a feature of the reports coming out of Ladysmith. A recently escaped resident detailed for the readers of the *Manchester Guardian* not only the remarkable range of sports available to the besieged troops but also the sang-froid shown by some of the participants:

> Every day there is cricket and football and the officers play polo quite regularly, joking if Boer shell-fire interferes with the game. On Tuesday there was an athletic meeting of the soldiers. There were numerous prizes. The sports included foot-racing as well as the usual contests – jumping, tug-of-war etc. There was quite a large attendance of spectators.[21]

The dismissive attitude of the town's hard-pressed population towards Boer military operations was also acclaimed by the *Daily Mail* in its regular campaign briefing, 'War Notes': 'At a cricket match in Ladysmith', the paper pithily observed, 'bowling and batting were both so dangerous to the spectators that they remarked it was much worse than Boer shells, and all solemnly retired to their caves.'[22]

Far from being viewed as evidence of foolhardiness, the insistence on the part of British soldiers to engage in sporting contests, no matter what the risks were, was invariably portrayed in a positive light. Typical was an illustration, which appeared in H. W. Wilson's hugely popular part-history, *With the Flag to Pretoria*, of the Gordons determinedly playing football in Ladysmith despite Boer shellfire.[23] Supposedly drawn from a true incident, the troopers' composed continuation of their game clearly signalled to the reader that these men were made of the right stuff. Cricket, in particular, had a powerful symbolic significance.[24] When an account of the Battle of Colenso, which featured in the *Manchester Guardian*, described men from the Durham Light Infantry fielding low-velocity Boer shells 'like cricket balls', it was the moral fibre of the British soldier rather than the shortcomings of the enemy artillery that was being stressed.[25] A similar

The South African War, 1899–1902 43

Figure 2.1 H. W. Wilson, *With the Flag to Pretoria: A History of the Boer War of 1899–1900 Volume II* (London: Harmsworth Bros., 1901), p. 493

line was adopted by the *Observer*. 'So little was thought of the Boer bombardment [of Kimberley]', the paper's readers were informed, 'that the alarm was not even sounded and business was carried on just the same . . . the men in the redoubts were actually playing cricket while it was going on.'[26] Most famously, Colonel Robert Baden-Powell was depicted as the archetypal cricketing hero; although, in an ironic twist, it was his refusal to indulge in his passion for the game that excited the interest of the press. In a widely reported anecdote, a Boer challenge to a cricket match during one of the regular Sunday truces in Mafeking was rejected by Baden-Powell with the cutting rebuke: 'Just now we are having our innings and have so far scored 200 days not out, against the bowling of Cronje, Snijman [*sic*], Botha and Eloff: and we are having a very enjoyable game.'[27] The newspapers had a field-day. The *Daily Graphic* caught the general mood with a cartoon in which Baden-Powell defended his 'Mafeking' wicket wielding a bat labelled 'British Pluck'.[28] Even a year after the siege had been lifted, Baden-Powell's scoreboard analogy was still being used to celebrate the garrison's resistance. In *The Romance of the Boer War*, a compendium of reflections on the conflict from the perspective of the ordinary soldier, published in 1901, Mafeking's refusal to capitulate was honoured with a piece of painfully cricket-themed doggerel:

> 218 Not Out!
> Ah, 'Captain' Baden-Powell! You
> Have given them 'tit for tat';
> You've won the game for Mafeking
> And 'carried out your bat'.
> The while they served 'straight, byes and wides'
> To storm your 'cute redoubt,
> You 'held the wicket' till the score
> Was 'two-eighteen, not out'.
> So give three cheers for Baden-Powell,
> Who, answering every 'ball'
> With 'no surrender!' proudly kept
> The old flag over all[29]

For the British public this love of sport was an important cultural signifier. The committed sportsman was thought to embody all the qualities, moral as well as physical, required by those destined to see through the imperial mission. At the outbreak of war, Arthur Conan Doyle was certain that, should the crisis in South Africa deepen, the military's ability to draw on a vast reservoir of amateur sportsmen would be enough to guarantee the Empire victory. A week after the Conservative government had mobilised the militia, he reassured the audience at Victoria Park Cricket Association's awards evening:

> In time of national excitement like the present they were proud of the love of manly games which coursed through the veins of British subjects. Although they had been informed of the calling out of the Reserves in this country, he ventured to say that the real reserves had not yet been called upon, for the latter were to be found among the athletes, the sportsmen, the yachtsmen, the men who rode to hounds, and the footballers of the country.... The manliness which such recreations produced, taught them to stand little inconveniences, and to be warlike – a spirit which all well-wishers of the Empire loved.[30]

Even the staunchly anti-war *Manchester Guardian* agreed that team games served as a valuable apprenticeship for soldiering. It reported approvingly Baden-Powell's advice to a young admirer that to be a good soldier, 'you must be obedient to the captain of your cricket or football team'.[31] In addition to obedience, the 'qualities engendered by games', according to the sports correspondent of the *Daily Mail* in a lengthy feature entitled 'Football: Its History, Traditions and Present Standing', included 'determination, perseverance, and patience'.[32] For Charles Waldstein, Slade Professor of fine art at Cambridge University and a member of Baron de Coubertin's founding Olympic Committee, a sense of fair play was the key attribute that distinguished the Anglo-Saxon sporting warrior from his Continental rivals.[33] Responding to criticism in the German press about British conduct during the conflict with the Boers, he vigorously argued:

> [T]he chief agent in producing and spreading this national virtue in England and America is athleticism in the best sense of the term. Cricket, football, rowing and hunting etc. have trained the people of this country, from childhood upwards, from the yokel to the greatest in the land, in the laws and the spirit of fairplay until they have entered *in succum et sanguinem* of the whole people, and have become a general national characteristic.[34]

To underline further the sporting probity of the British officer corps, Waldstein recounted the story of a friend, 'a distinguished scholar and public servant', who refused a commission while serving in South Africa because of his lack of sporting experience. ' "You see" ', Waldstein recalled his friend saying, ' "if I had been a hunting man I should not have hesitated; for the experience in the hunting-field produces the qualities which I consider most important in an officer of any grade." '[35]

In fiction too sport could be used as an indicator of a man's true character. One of the most popular fictional figures of the late Victorian period was E. W. Hornung's amoral gentleman thief, Athur J. Raffles. The reading public was, in equal measure, entertained and scandalised by this new anti-hero, who seemed the antithesis of Conan Doyle's Sherlock Holmes.[36] *The Spectator*, reviewing the first volume of Raffles' short stories, *The Amateur Cracksman*, a few months before the outbreak of the South African War, reflected this ambivalence with the rather prim observation that the work was 'a feat of virtuosity rather than a tribute to virtue'.[37] Yet, Raffles was also a sportsman. Not only had he been 'the fastest man in the fifteen and athletic champion' at Uppingham School but he was also a first-class cricketer, having played for Middlesex and England.[38] For Hornung, such a sporting pedigree, especially the gift for cricket, implied integrity and hinted at a character underpinned by an essential decency. In the final story of the second volume, published two years into the war, this was brought to the fore through the deployment of cricketing metaphors to signal Raffles' redemption from a life of crime.[39] Compelled by sporting instinct to 'do his bit' when news arrives that Sir Redvers Buller has been bowled 'neck-and-crop, neck-and-crop' at Colenso, Raffles volunteers and eventually finds himself pinned down by a Boer sniper as he attempts to assist a gravely wounded companion. With time running out, the cricketer in him takes control: 'another over . . . scoring's slow . . . I wonder if he's sportsman enough to take a hint? Will he show his face if I show mine?'[40] The inevitable happens and Raffles is shot dead. Hornung's message was clear. By dying a sportsman's death in battle, Raffles had adhered to the public school code of manliness and had thus been deemed to have atoned for his earlier misdemeanours.

It was not just in the ranks of the military but also in civilian life that a passion for sport (and, again, particularly a passion for cricket) could be used as the acid test of true character. In the spring of 1900, a concerted attack by some of the more jingoistic elements of the British press on what were deemed the disloyal policies of the Afrikaner Bond, the majority party in the Cape Parliament, prompted a spirited retort from Francis Dormer, the former editor of the *Cape Argus* newspaper.[41] In a detailed letter to *The Times*, Dormer provided a potted history of the evolution of the Bond, stressing its moderate, imperialist credentials. To underline the validity of his analysis, he concluded with a reassuring pen portrait of the Bond's leader, Jan Hofmeyr:

> Strange as it may appear to those who have been taught to regard the Afrikander statesman as the embodiment of everything that is anti-English, he is passionately devoted to every form of manly sport, and more particularly to the essentially English game of cricket. The interest he takes in the pursuit of that game by young Afrikanders is the one relaxation that he has always permitted himself.[42]

The *Manchester Guardian* was equally certain that proof of Hofmeyer's loyalty could be found in the impossibility of cricket and treason ever being bedfellows:

> One has but to consider the personal aspect to realise the absurdity of the notion that Mr Hofmeyr is an anti-English conspirator. He is passionately fond of cricket and, as like as not, if one calls upon him at night one finds him studying the cricket news.[43]

For the advocates of sport, physical exercise and organised games were not just character-forming but also helped to cultivate important transferrable skills for the battlefield. Addressing a Conservative Party meeting in his home constituency of Penrith, Mr. J. W. Lowther, the deputy speaker of the House of Commons, insisted 'that the training which came from games' was eminently 'suitable for war'. Among the skills developed were 'pertinacity, perseverance and courage'. To rally his audience to his viewpoint, Lowther cited the example of a local war hero, Colonel Rimington, 'who excelled on the polo grounds before going to South Africa'.[44] The hunting correspondent of the *Manchester Guardian* was also keen to celebrate the military benefits of field sports. Reviewing the 1899/1900 season, he proudly noted,

> When the crisis came, right well did fox-hunting justify its existence as a national sport. A list of the masters of hounds, past and present, of men well known with various packs who volunteered for active service would fill the rest of this column.

It was, though, the martial aptitude of these volunteers rather than their patriotic enthusiasm that the piece emphasised: 'if we learned anything from the Boer War it should be that the precision and niceties of drill rank second in modern warfare to mobility and straight shooting'.[45] Another admirer of the rural sportsman was Arthur Conan Doyle. In his populist history of the early stages of the conflict in

South Africa, *The Great Boer War*, published in 1900, a charge by the Imperial Yeomanry at Lindley was said to have revealed that 'there are few more high-mettled troops in South Africa than these good sportsmen of the shires'. Yet, the passage concluded on a note of caution. Hinting at a lack of military professionalism, Conan Doyle observed that the men 'showed a trace of their origin in their irresistible inclination to burst into "tally-ho" when ordered to attack'.[46]

The question over the extent to which the army's adherence to equestrian sports undermined professionalism by perpetuating the amateur military tradition came to a head early on in the war. The disasters of Black Week and, in particular, the lacklustre performance of the cavalry in the first few months of the war ignited a simmering debate over the cost and efficacy of officer sport.[47] This dispute coalesced around the issue of polo. Concerned that both the inordinate amount of time spent playing polo detracted from military training and the exorbitant expense of maintaining polo ponies restricted the pool of potential officers, the Army Council issued a draft order in January 1900 to curb the activities of regimental polo clubs.[48] *The Times*, ever grateful for an opportunity to advance its campaign for army reform, was quick to bring the perceived scandal to the public's attention. In an editorial of February 1900, the paper railed against the 'expensive habits, mostly connected with amusements', which effectively 'made the Army a close corporation just as in the old purchase days'.[49] The next day a letter from Lieutenant-Colonel Mark Lockwood, formerly of the Coldstream Guards and Conservative MP for Epping, fully endorsed the editor's stance. The cost involved, he argued, in pursuing the sporting lifestyle demanded of an officer meant that 'the sons of country gentlemen, the men above all others you want to attract, are unable to join the cavalry'. He supported his case by carefully locating the rural gentry's exclusion from army life within pervading fears about racial degeneration:

> These are men used to the ordinary standard of country house living, brought up to hunt and shoot from boyhood, not gamblers or fond of spending money for show. What do we get instead in many regiments of the cavalry of the line? Sons of a certain class, reared in the towns, taught as children the habits of self-indulgence and luxury, that once acquired are difficult to eradicate.[50]

Lockwood's belief in the deteriorating social composition of the officer corps was echoed the following week by another, this time anonymous, correspondent to *The Times*. However, for 'C. O.', any move to discourage the recruitment of young men with an interest in field sports would only serve to exacerbate rather than resolve the problem:

> Restrict the sporting instincts of our cavalry officers, forbid them to hunt or to play polo . . . and in a very short time I venture to predict a very different class of person will offer himself for cavalry commissions: whether this will be to the advantage of the service remains to be seen.

The solution lay, the letter concluded, not in tampering with 'the pleasant social life' of cavalry officers but rather in addressing the 'falling incomes of country gentlemen'.[51] As these letters suggest, more was at stake here than the fate of regimental polo. With the future direction of the cavalry under discussion as the reverses in South Africa threw into high relief the *arme blanche* versus mounted infantry debate, the equestrian leisure pursuits of a privileged set of officers came to assume a symbolic importance out of all proportion to the time actually spent on them.[52] Polo and hunting were employed as convenient shorthand for an unreformed army culture, in which amateur military ideals stood in diametric opposition to the modernising agenda of meritocratic restructuring.[53]

Although it was the value of equestrian sport as a preparation for war that generated the most heated exchanges, the deleterious impact of organised games on the professionalism of the army as a whole was also subjected to close scrutiny as the fighting against the Boers revealed serious shortcomings in the military's performance. In the immediate aftermath of the shock of Black Week, the *Manchester Guardian* reported on the German press's ambivalent assessment of British officers' enthusiasm for the games field. The *Post*, it was noted, while full of admiration for the courage exhibited in South Africa by British forces, was, nonetheless, appalled 'that this valiant army, skilled in all branches of sport, should be decimated through circumstances connected with difficulties of climate and territory'. The military correspondent of *Berliner Neueste Nachrichten* was more direct. The sporting instincts displayed by British soldiers when faced by adversity, he declared, couldn't disguise the fact that the nation's reverses were 'due to the disregard of the Boer mode of fighting, which requires special study'.[54] This theme was developed further by Charles Savile Roundell, Liberal MP for Skipton until 1895 and former first-class cricketer, in a speech to the Macclesfield branch of the Christian Social Union that appeared in the *Observer* in February 1900. Having made an unfavourable comparison between the 'application to systematised knowledge' that underpinned Germany's recent military success and the 'mental and material decay' that afflicted Britain's armed forces, Roundell set out clearly both problem and solution as revealed by the reverses in South Africa:

> We prided ourselves upon our national love of sport, and we attributed their good qualities to the theory that distinction in games at school and in the sports of after life was the sure passport to military excellence. But was that so? . . . War, like politics, was not a game, but a serious business demanding scientific training and scientific direction.[55]

For one anonymous correspondent to the *Daily Mail*, the lack of professionalism shown by commanders in the initial engagements against the Boers had been so egregious that only a root-and-branch reform of the public school culture of athleticism would do:

> Among the causes which have contributed to the recent military disasters in South Africa ought we to include the devotion which our officers have so

long been in the habit of paying to sport (football, cricket, tennis, polo, racing etc), with its natural, if not necessary, sequel, the omission to study seriously and continuously the art and science of war? If the answer to this question be in the affirmative, ought we not at once to ask ourselves whether it is advisable that the youth of this country should any longer be encouraged, from the beginning of their schooldays onwards, to give their best energies to football, cricket, and the like, to neglect military exercise, and to hold all science in contempt? If 'righteousness exalteth a nation', so does knowledge; but ignorance as certainly degrades it.[56]

As the war rumbled on, the press continued to lament the lack of professionalism within the British officer corps. A disastrous army exercise at Aldershot in the summer of 1900 roused the reforming zeal of *The Times*. 'The question of questions for the country in the immediate future is', the paper's editor stated in a heartfelt rhetorical flourish, 'How can we change all this? How can we prevent incompetent officers from entering the Army, and how can we develop the intelligence and the skill of those who enter it?' The answer, he continued, was to be found by embracing a new professional age in which the amateur games ethos had no place:

> The Duke's old saying (if he really said it) about the Playing Fields of Eton has done its work, and should be relegated to limbo. Athletics, cricket, and the like are an admirable half-school for the modern officer, but they are not the whole school. One feels tempted to say that if the battle of Waterloo was won on these playing fields, the battle of Colenso was lost there, and the battle of Sedan was won in the study, the laboratory, and the Kriegakademie.[57]

The military correspondent of the *Daily Express*, similarly appalled by the fiasco at Aldershot, placed the blame squarely on the shoulders of a sports-obsessed senior command. Under the tagline 'Too Much Cricket and Polo', he argued that the country's poor military showing in South Africa was due to the

> disinclination of higher staff to take field-days seriously and to stop to correct errors, tactical and strategic. . . . In a word, they 'sit about' in offices too much and see far too little of the tactical battlefield, while the rest of their time is spent in the cricket-field or the polo camp.[58]

The *Daily Mail*'s American-born war correspondent, Julian Ralph, was equally convinced that the British officer's fixation with sport hindered his professional development. Despite having just witnessed Roberts' victorious army raise the Union Jack in the Transvaal capital, Pretoria, he still felt it his duty to reveal for his readers 'some truths about the war':

> As a man the British officer is superb. He will do his duty. He does not fear the Boers or death. He sets the finest example of unwavering patience and

manly courage to a body of privates already richer in those qualities than any others in Europe; but he is thinking of the hounds, of polo, of cricket, or Goodwood and Ascot, of anything except of making soldiering his life-work and the ladder to a career.[59]

The publication, in October 1900, of *An Absent-Minded War* by William Elliot Cairns, soon-to-be-secretary to the post-war Committee on the Education and Training of Officers, further fuelled the furore surrounding the role of sport in army instruction. In a tightly argued treatise advancing the case for systemic army reform, Cairns lambasted what he considered to be the anti-intellectual, anti-professional culture that enveloped the military. The new recruit, he bemoaned, quickly realises that 'keenness is "bad form" and will soon openly manifest his impatience to throw off his uniform – the uniform he was so proud to put on for the first time – and will devote himself to sport'. At the root of the problem, according to Cairns, lay a daily routine of monotonous duties, 'not one tenth of which formed any useful training for war' and that, inevitably, persuaded officers to spend 'most of [their] time in the hunting-field, on the polo or cricket ground'.[60] Although Cairns, as a serving soldier himself, was at pains not to impugn the courage of his fellow officers by stressing their eagerness to engage in active service, even this apparent virtue was construed as evidence 'that the officer cares for nothing but sport and scorns – as a rule – the serious study of his profession':

Active service is regarded rather as a new and most exciting kind of sport, a feeling which has been heightened by our numerous campaigns against savages, than as a deadly serious business where the stakes are the lives of men and the safety of the empire.[61]

Although a review in the *Spectator* welcomed the work as 'a sane and judicious piece of criticism', there was, predictably, a backlash in the letters columns of the popular press.[62] Typical was the sentiment expressed by Colonel Lonsdale Hale in *The Times*. Attacks on the army, he fumed, had 'reached the lowest level' when 'a "British officer", under the safe shelter of anonymity, is not ashamed to describe the regimental officer as one who "cares for nothing but sport"'.[63] Cairns, however, was quick to defend himself. Far from 'vilifying his brother officers', he pointed out in a carefully reasoned response to Lonsdale Hale, he had simply been highlighting the army's structural weaknesses, for he had 'attributed every military shortcoming of the British officer to the faults of the system'.[64]

Cairns' belief that the army officer's preoccupation with sport was simply a symptom rather than cause of a wider malaise received the support of both Leopold Amery of *The Times* and Colonel G. F. R. Henderson, director of Intelligence under Roberts during the South African War. In volume II of his hugely influential *Times History of the War in South Africa*, Amery, a relentless campaigner for army reform, was scathing about the standard of officer training. With drill and tests of a 'mechanical character', which served 'only to dull the wits and discourage the zeal', the response of young officers was, he felt, no more than one could expect:

> It need hardly be cause for surprise that the common sense of many officers made them feel that playing cricket and polo, or hunting and shooting were quite as good military training, and infinitely more pleasant, than the ordinary routine duties of their profession.[65]

Henderson went even further. Sport was, it was asserted in a posthumously published collection of his writings, not just a consequence of, but a compensation for, the inadequacy of the training regime:

> Nauseated by dull theory, cramped by want of responsibility, his energy unawakened by appeals to his intelligence, with no opening offered to him to acquire that higher knowledge which would have aroused his interest and kindled his ambition, and with abundant leisure at his command, it is no wonder [the British officer] sought distraction in other fields. If he was a mere barrack square soldier, he was generally a sportsman; and in his cricket and in his football, in his hunting, his polo, and his shikar, he was at least hardening his nerve and learning the great lessons of self-control, improving his power of observation, training his eye to country, and acquiring to some extent those qualities which make the Boer so formidable an enemy.[66]

For other commentators, however, the shortcomings of the military were no more than a reflection of a wider cultural failing. *A Handbook of the Boer War*, written by an anonymous veteran of the conflict and published in 1910, contended that the security provided by Britain's island status had afforded the public the luxury of viewing '[w]ar as a branch of Sport or Athletics'.[67] Consequently, it was claimed, the country's priorities had become inverted and sporting endeavour, rather than patriotic duty, had assumed primacy in the national consciousness:

> Thousands of loafers, idlers, and work shirkers live upon the anticipations and recollections of outdoor sports when not actually present at them, and are ready to spend their last shilling at the turnstile of the ground on which a handful of football gladiators are at play: and are more exasperated by the defeat of the team which they patronise in a Cup Tie match than they would be by the loss of a battle by the British Army.[68]

The same note had been struck by *The Times* when reviewing the lessons of the war in an editorial of January 1902. Having decried the 'British passion for sport', which meant 'that a great part of the energy which might be turned to better use is diverted to mere play', the piece had concluded with a stinging criticism of the sporting spectator: 'a great deal too much of the interest in cricket and football is bestowed upon those games by those who do not take any part whatever in them, and who, therefore, derive no physical advantage from the training.'[69]

Such criticisms reveal much about the inherent class bias in British sporting life at the turn of the twentieth century. Lack of space, time and finance restricted the sporting opportunities of a large proportion of the urban unskilled workforce to those of the passive consumer. Thus, with the emergence of sport as a mass spectacle, there was a rapid growth in the number of professional leagues and competitions in the years leading up to the South African War.[70] For many from the middle and upper classes, who had been or still remained amateur players, the professionalisation of the games they loved undermined the very essence of the cult of athleticism. At a dinner held in his honour at the Authors' Club, Lord Alfred Lyttleton, one of the great all-round amateur sportsmen of his generation and soon-to-be colonial secretary, told those assembled how gratified he had been to find that soldiers on active service in South Africa could 'indulge in a game of cricket, and he trusted that cricket would now become a national game with the Boers'. It was, of course, the intrinsic worth of the amateur game that Lyttleton was extolling. Sporting pursuits, he made clear for his privileged audience, were a means to an end and not an end in their own right:

> The intention of sport was to make men fitter, stronger, and better served for the main work of life. It was a misfortune that young men should be tempted from the main work of life to make a profession of any game.[71]

The concern for the quality press was that it was not only the participant in professional sport who had his moral compass distorted but also the spectator. In January 1902, a *Times* editorial was critical of the passions aroused by the English cricket team's collapse in the second test match against Australia. 'It is surely out of proportion to the importance of the matter at stake', the editor despaired, 'when we see the streets filled with placards about these athletic contests as if issues depended upon them as vital to our race as those decided at Trafalgar and Waterloo.'[72] The editor of the *Manchester Guardian* was similarly bewildered by the precedence that sport seemed to take over any other matter. As the death toll in the refugee camps mounted in October 1901, he attempted to prick the conscience of his readers by noting, 'We are keen on sport; cannot we be keen on this question . . . so that the fair name of England at least may remain.'[73] The public's interest in sporting trivia rather than events on the veldt was also noted by P. T. Ross in his often satirical but nonetheless perspicacious reminiscences of his active service in South Africa. A poetic entry dated 27 October 1900 lamented:

> At home first China, then elections,
> Have claimed their keen attention,
> Now football, crimes and other things –
> The war they seldom mention.[74]

Once again, just how deeply the culture of athleticism and games was entrenched in the public consciousness can be gleaned from the frequency with which sporting language and imagery was used to portray the war in South Africa. The British

The South African War, 1899–1902   53

army's defeat at the battle of Stormberg on 10 December 1899 was explained away in a J. M. Staniforth cartoon, which appeared in the *Western Mail* on 12 December 1899, as nothing more than one lost round in a protracted boxing match.[75] Later in the war a *Punch* cartoon made light of the Boer *bittereinders*' persistent evasion of Kitchener's massed forces by framing it in terms of the last stand by the eleventh man in a cricket match.[76]

Even combatants were prone to reimagining their experiences of battle in sporting terms. For J. Barclay Lloyd, a lance-corporal in the City of London Volunteers, cricket and football served as the best comparators for combat. The shelling of Boer positions during the battle of Vaal Krantz in February 1900 was, he enthused in his hastily published memoir *One Thousand Miles with the C. I. V.*, 'sport with a vengeance, better than seeing Aston Villa's left forward scoring the

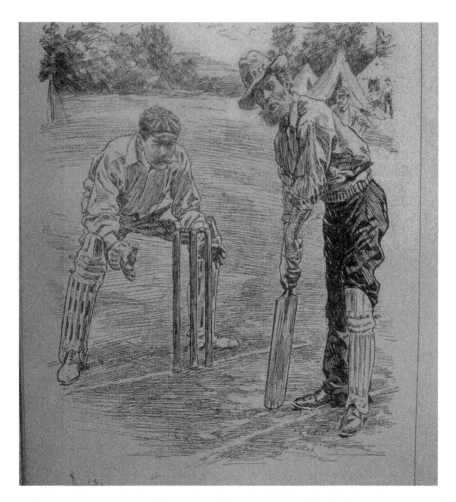

Figure 2.2 Bernard Partridge, 'The Last Wicket', *Punch*, 15 May 1901

winning goal, or W. G. hitting three successive boundaries from the best Australian bowling'.[77] Private W. C. Hilbourne of the 2nd Gloucester Regiment, in a widely syndicated article for the regional press, reframed the first nine months of the war as an international football match:

> *Final Tie for the Championship of South Africa*
>
> Baden Powell and White were playing grandly, and although the home forwards were in the visitors' territory, they failed to score. The 'Empire' forwards now began to get into their stride and French, working like a machine round his opponents, completely beat Cronje, and with a swift lightening shot, he found the net with a beauty (Kimberley). Soon after Cronje was dismissed from the field (Paardeburg).

The occupation of Pretoria in June 1900 signalled, for Hilbourne, the end of the game with the score standing at 'British Empire 5, Transvaal and Orange Free State 0'.[78]

Yet again though, as had been the case during the earlier colonial conflicts of Victoria's reign, commentators frequently looked to blood sports as a handy frame of reference. Subscribers to the monthly equestrian journal *Baily's Magazine* were treated to a piece of stirringly patriotic doggerel that celebrated the sacrifices of the Imperial Yeomanry using the familiar language of the hunt:

> They'd a clinking seat, and were hard to beat,
> Like many of Britain's sons,
> They were yeomen free, and a treat to see
> In the best of Midland runs.
> Through burst and check, they were neck and neck,
> Right straight away from the find;
> If Jack, with a rush, secured the brush,
> Joe wasn't a stride behind.
>
> So, when the game of war became
> Young Britain's latest tip,
> Said Jack to Joe: 'To the war we go!
> It's a breakneck sort of hunt, Joe,
> A devil-me-carish chase;
> If we fall we'll fall *in the front*, Joe,
> Straight in the foeman's face!'
>
> Said Joe, on the way to an outpost fray,
> As the squadron lobbed along;
> 'We shall see some sport of a stiffish sort
> And the going will be strong.
> But never mind, it's a *certain find*

No *blank* shall we draw today;
And behind those rocks there's a Transvaal fox
That can show some awkward play.'

A flash and a bang! A rattle and a clang!
And – Jack lay stretched on the veldt;
Ere his spirit fled, with a smile he said
As Joe beside him knelt:
'I'm fairly out of the hunt, Joe,
Jostled out of the chase;
Tell 'em I died *in the front*, Joe,
Straight in the foeman's face.'[79]

The *Daily Mail*'s veteran war correspondent, Charles Eustace Hands, also chose to portray as a particularly invigorating hunt the first taste of action of the 3rd and 10th Battalions of the Imperial Yeomanry at the Battle of Boshof in April 1901. Under the heading 'The Blooding of the Yeomen', Hands noted,

> It was a sporting affair from the first. Colonel Eric Smith, of the 10th Battalion, went ahead waving on his men with his helmet in his single hand with jubilant hunting cries. The men from the Aylesbury County made a hunting business of it, and went ahead to be in at the death.

Yet, despite taking over 50 prisoners, there was, the account concluded, some dissatisfaction with the catch: 'This little bag of Frenchmen gave a fair morning's sport. But cub-hunting is not the real thing. We want Boers, real Boers, and plenty of them.'[80] The only disappointment for one officer at the Battle of Elandslaagte in November 1899 was that the 'chase' was curtailed by fading light. In a graphic letter to the editor of *The Times*, he breathlessly recalled:

> After the enemy were driven out, one of our squadrons (not mine) pursued and got right in among them in the twilight, and the most excellent pig-sticking ensued for about ten minutes, the bag being about sixty. One of our men, seeing two Boers riding away on one horse, stuck his lance through the two, killing both with one thrust. Had it not been getting dark we should have killed many more.[81]

Eighteen months later, *The Times* switched to a different blood sport and presented operations in Middleberg in May 1901 as a grouse shoot. 'The situation is best understood', wrote a special correspondent, 'if we characterize the Lyndenberg and Middleberg columns as beaters driving the game up to the butts – the drifts, held by General Plumer's Bushmen and New Zealanders.'[82] Even government communications were not immune from the deployment of sporting jargon and imagery. Typical was an official despatch issued by Kitchener's headquarters on 11 September 1901 and quoted in the *Manchester Guardian*: 'Since 2 September the columns have again got good results, the total bag, including all separately reported, being 681, composed of 67 Boers killed, 67 wounded, 381 prisoners, 43 surrenders.'[83]

Such usage was thought by some to detract from the seriousness of war. The anonymous author of *A Handbook of the Boer War* worried that 'there are metaphors which impair the dignity of a cause and degrade it in the eyes of those whose duty is to maintain that cause'. The professionalism of the army would, he felt sure, suffer as a result:

> When the advances of a British Division at a critical period in the operations is frivolously termed a 'drive', and when the men extended at ten paces' interval over a wide front are called 'beaters', it is natural that the leaders should look upon their work as analogous to the duties of a gamekeeper; and when an artillery officer is instructed to 'pitch his shells well up', he is encouraged to regard failure as no worse than the loss of a cricket match.[84]

Of greater concern for two correspondents to the *Manchester Guardian* was the effect this language exchange would have on the nation's reputation. In a letter published under the heading 'The "Total Bag"', 'Indignant' condemned 'the treatment of the [war] in the language of sport when the issue is the making of widows and orphans', before concluding, 'It is only another step in the degradation of the honour of our country'. In the same issue, a pro-Boer sympathiser expressed relief at being informed that it was a subordinate of Kitchener, and not Kitchener himself, who had been responsible for the wording of recent despatches in which hunting terminology had been used. He was, nonetheless, appalled that 'any Englishman should use such expressions about brave men fighting and dying for the independence of their country'.[85] Lord Rosebery, the Liberal prime minister between March 1894 and June 1895, placed the blame for 'the detestable impression' aroused by the use of such hunting metaphors squarely at the door of the Conservative government. In a much anticipated speech to the Chesterfield Liberal Association in December 1901, he told members of the audience that it was fine for Kitchener to use 'as a telegraphic abbreviation the word "bagged"', but what was 'insane folly [was] that the War Office, instead of interpreting this, as it were, as a code, delivered in its nakedness to the world that our "bag" of Boers for the week was so much'.[86]

The national angst surrounding the public's passion for sport generally, and the merit of sport as a preparation for war specifically, was propelled to the forefront of the national consciousness with the publication of Rudyard Kipling's *The Islanders* in *The Times* on 4 January 1902. Having witnessed first-hand the fighting in South Africa, Kipling felt compelled to voice publicly his disgust at what he regarded as the nation's failure to respond appropriately to the call of duty. Never an admirer of the public school cult of athleticism, he reserved his most stinging criticism for those whom he felt disregarded the value of the military and continued to place sport above the security of the country:

> Ye hindered and hampered and crippled; ye thrust out of sight and away
> Those that would serve you for honour and those that served you for pay.

> Then were the judgments loosened; then was your shame revealed,
> At the hands of a little people, few but apt in the field.
> Yet ye were saved by a remnant (and your land's long-suffering star),
> When your strong men cheered in their millions while your striplings went to the war.
> Sons of the sheltered city – unmade, unhandled, unmeet –
> Ye pushed them raw to the battle as ye picked them raw from the street.
> And what did ye look they should compass? Warcraft learned in a breath,
> Knowledge unto occasion at the first far view of Death?
> So? And ye train your horses and the dogs ye feed and prize?
> How are the beasts more worthy than the souls, your sacrifice?
> But ye said, 'Their valour shall show them'; but ye said, 'The end is close.'
> And ye sent them comfts and pictures to help them harry your foes:
> And ye vaunted your fathomless power, and ye flaunted your iron pride,
> Ere – ye fawned on the Younger Nations for the men who could shoot and ride!
> Then ye returned to your trinkets; then ye contented your souls
> With the flannelled fools at the wicket or the muddied oafs at the goals.[87]

This poetic reproof was buttressed by an editorial on the same page, which, while maintaining that conscription was 'ill-suited to our needs', was in agreement with the broader call for a realignment of educational priorities. This 'thrilling trumpet-call', the piece insisted, was correct to demand that 'the proportion of time now spent, practically under compulsion, in games might well be utilized for military training'.[88]

As both Kipling and *The Times* anticipated, a heated debate ensued.[89] The editor of the *Observer* was quick to marshal the sentiments expressed in *The Islanders* to launch an attack on what he regarded as a privileged elite who refused to acknowledge their duties to the nation. In an editorial of 5 January 1902, he derided 'England's Idol, the Juggernaut of athleticism and sport which insatiably demanded more and more of her sons' best years and brightest energies' by promoting the 'exaltation of the running path, the playing field and the river as the true . . . be all and end all of public school and university careers'. The paper's readers were urged to make a stand against the received view that 'the rich, the lazy and the otherwise minded need not concern themselves with the problems and duties of national defence, so long as others can be paid and got to do it'.[90] In a letter to the editor of *The Times* on 9 January 1902, George Pragnell, the acting president of the largely working-class London Athletic Association, was also keen to use Kipling's verse to admonish the complacency of the middle-class sports supporter.[91] Thankful that *The Islanders* had brought into the open the shortcomings in the nation's treatment of its reserve forces, he carefully selected the archetypal game of the public school to support the main thrust of his argument: 'The millions of people who are keenly interested in cricket do not take the slightest interest in Volunteering during peacetime, and in times like the present shelter themselves behind a small percentage of their fellows who have gone to the front.' Transferring to the reserve forces the attention currently paid to the sporting world was, he concluded, 'the only way to stave off conscription'.[92] The great C. B. Fry, who gained international honours at both cricket and football, also felt there was 'something in what Mr Kipling says, or rather insinuates'. Although he felt it was 'scarcely fair or gentlemanly to call cricketers flannelled fools or footballers muddied oafs', he, nonetheless, informed the editor of the *Daily Express* in a letter dated 6 January 1902 that it was still undoubtedly the case that 'the youth of England does not devote itself as it should to military exercises'.[93] The following day, the paper's letters page was again used to voice support for Kipling's position. However, this time 'a well-known traveller and athlete' argued that both the nature of war and the customs of England had undergone such dramatic changes that it was necessary to look to ex-patriot communities abroad for a way forward:

> In the days of old, when fighting was at close quarters, the hard and trained frame of the athlete gave him a great advantage. But in these days of telescopic sights and pom-poms, things are very different. . . . [T]he finest schools for soldiers are now such places as the back blocks of Australia, the ranches of the Bad Lands of Canada, and the estuaries of the Argentine Republic. Here men learn to do without most things, to ride anything, and to observe without being observed. The fact is, civilisation has made us artificial. Our English artificiality no doubt tends towards manliness, but a nation of good cricketers will not win battles while a nation of rough riders can do.[94]

For the headmaster of Rossall School, Dr Way, the outcry caused by the poem's publication was such that he clearly felt it warranted an immediate response. Having first admitted to a speech day audience on 17 January 1902 that because of their 'many defects' public schools had been 'freely criticised' over the past few days, he proceeded to set his institution apart from its competitors with a vigorous defence of its sporting ethos:

> The latest cry was about the excess of athletics, which had been put tersely in a phrase by Rudyard Kipling in his reference to 'flannelled fools' and 'muddied oafs'. Of course, they agreed with Kipling that it was suicidal folly to spend time upon athletics which ought to be devoted to preparation for the defence of one's country. At Rossall they were fully alive to this fact, and they not only won both their cricket matches this year but had a fine rifle corps numbering nearly 200. Indeed, one of their number had beaten all the other public school corps in shooting.[95]

Unsurprisingly, however, the clamour stirred up by *The Islanders*, with its accompanying frisson of class criticism, offended many. The football correspondent of the *Manchester Guardian* leapt to the defence of his sport. Just two days after the publication of the poem, he opened his weekly column for the paper with the dismissive suggestion that the poem must have been written 'after a heavy nightmare' before citing a series of famous football-playing officers whose 'devotion to the game of the country has not prevented their doing a man's part in the South

African War'.[96] On the same day, the former Middlesex county cricketer W. J. Ford adopted a similar line of argument for the readers of *The Times*' letters columns, although this time the sporting warriors listed came, naturally, from the summer rather than winter game. 'Mr. Kipling's poetry may be above reproach', Ford tersely concluded, 'but he might easily mend his manners without spoiling his rhymes.'[97] The following day the *Daily Mail* devoted the best part of a page to the responses of 'cricketers and footballers to Mr Kipling's poem'. Typical of the views expressed was that of Jack Cameron, the former Everton and Scotland centre forward and club secretary of Tottenham Hotspur. 'Mr. Kipling', he protested, 'has gone too far in calling us "muddied oafs"! He ought to know that football has given many good men to the war, and that some will never return.'[98] One of the most detailed retorts to *The Islanders* was presented by Hely Hutchinson Almond, the proprietor and long-serving headmaster of Loretto School near Edinburgh. Almond, a pioneer of the belief that physical hardiness underpinned personal as well as national health, viewed Britain's imperial mission as a force for good that could only be achieved by robust and disciplined young men free from the enervating influence of an overly literary or artistic culture.[99] In a letter to the editor of *The Times*, published on 9 January 1902, he treated the paper's readers to a reprise of his lengthy article on the physical degeneration of the nation, which had appeared in the journal *The Nineteenth Century* in the autumn of 1900.[100] More emphasis on physical exercise and organised games, Almond claimed, would serve to reinvigorate the country and furnish the army with the sort of recruits it required. By way of support, he pointed out that not only had sportsmen volunteered for the war 'out of all proportion to their numbers' but, because of the nature of their training, which developed strength, courage and, critically, initiative, they had also proven to be exceptionally effective recruits. Interestingly, though, Almond was at odds with his fellow champions of sport on one critical issue. Cricket, he argued, with its focus on 'personal scores and drawn matches', no longer had any 'educative qualities'. Indeed, in an acidic aside suffused with a superciliousness borne of class, he asserted that the game 'fostered selfishness nearly as much as golf'.[101]

The South African War saw a coming together of civilian society's fascination with athletic pursuits and its idealisation of the imperial warrior. The press willingly fed the public's appetite for the romanticised sporting warrior with an on-going diet of war reports featuring athletic endeavour in the combat zone. In this imagining, the army's love of sport and organised games was invested with a moral as well as practical worth. Yet, as the war dragged on, so doubts began to surface. The superior mobility and field-craft shown by Boer commandoes caused many in Britain to question the high Victorian cult of athleticism, which equated sporting achievement with strength of character and military prowess. In the immediate aftermath of the war, damning reports by the Committee on the Education and Training of Officers and the Committee to Enquire into the Experiences incurred by Officers prompted the War Office to introduce measures to rein in the scope of army sport.[102] As it was for so many aspects of civilian and military life, the South African War was, then, a moment of transition for the role of sport in the British armed forces. This is not to say, however, that sporting endeavour completely lost its importance as a cultural signifier in the national consciousness. Although, as will be shown in the next chapter, the advent of hostilities in 1914 quickly brought an end to domestic professional football and cricket, organised games and athletic contests continued a pace at the fighting front.[103] More significantly, perhaps, as Simon John has shown, sporting imagery and terminology were once again used by combatants and non-combatants to make sense of what was happening to them.[104] The South African War may have delivered a serious, even fatal, blow to the sporting ethos that underpinned Britain's amateur-military tradition, but the mechanised slaughter of 1914–1918 was to be the real test of the durability of sport in the wartime imagination.

Notes

1. *The Islanders* was published in *The Times* on 4 January 1902.
2. See *The Times*, 7–10 January 1902.
3. *The Times*, 9 January 1902.
4. M. D. Blanch, 'British Society and the War', in Peter Warwick (ed.), *The South African War. The Anglo-Boer War, 1899–1902* (Harlow: Longman, 1980), pp. 186–209.
5. Tim Travers, 'The Hidden Army: Structural Problems in the British Officers Corps, 1900–1919', *Journal of Contemporary History*, 17/3 (July 1982), pp. 523–544.
6. The war cost Britain £200 million, with 22,000 British and imperial troops dying. Thomas Pakenham, *The Boer War* (London: Weidenfeld and Nicolson, 1979), p. 572.
7. Black Week was the name given to the period covering the three defeats of Stormberg, Magersfontein and Colenso, all of which occurred between 10 and 15 December 1899.
8. Stephen Badsey, 'The Boer War as a Media War', in P. Dennis and J. Grey (eds.), *The Boer War: Army Nation and Empire* (Canberra: Army History Unit, 1999), pp. 70–83. See also, Roger T. Stearn, 'War Correspondents and Colonial War, c1870–1900', in John M. Mackenzie (ed.), *Popular Imperialism and the Military, 1850–1950* (Manchester: Manchester University Press, 1992), pp. 140–157.
9. Mike Huggins, *The Victorians and Sport* (London: Hambledon Continuum, 2004), p. 152.
10. Tony Mason, 'Introduction', in Tony Mason (ed.), *Sport in Britain: A Social History* (Cambridge: Cambridge University Press, 1989), p. 3.
11. *The Times*, 17 June 1895.
12. Glenn R. Wilkinson, '"The Blessings of War": The Depiction of Military Force in Edwardian Newspapers', *Journal of Contemporary History*, 3/1 (January 1998), pp. 97–115; *Lloyd's Weekly Newspaper*, 28 January 1900.
13. Dean Allen, '"Bats and Bayonets": Cricket and the Anglo-Boer War, 1899–1902', *Sport in History*, 25/1 (2005), pp. 31–32. See also J. D. Campbell, '"Training for Sport Is Training for War": Sport and the Transformation of the British Army, 1860–1914', *International Journal of the History of Sport*, 17/4 (December 2000), pp. 21–22.
14. *Manchester Guardian*, 29 March 1900; 28 December 1899.
15. *Observer*, 4 February 1900.
16. *Manchester Guardian* 27 December 1899; 2 January 1900; 1 January 1900.
17. Julian Ralph, *Towards Pretoria: A Record of the War Between Briton and Boer to the Hoisting of the British Flag in Bloemfontein* (London: C. Arthur Pearson Ltd., 1900), p. 249.
18. *Manchester Guardian*, 9 November 1899.
19. *Daily Mail*, 21 February 1900.

20 *The Times*, 27 February 1900. By the following month the Boers had clearly relented. *The Times* noted on 20 March 1900, 'Sunday, as usual, was observed as a day of truce.' Adding, with not a little relish one imagines, 'Cricket was played on the recreation ground.' *The Times*, 6 April 1900.
21 *Manchester Guardian*, 1 January 1900.
22 *Daily Mail*, 8 January 1900.
23 H. W. Wilson, *With the Flag to Pretoria: A History of the Boer War of 1899–1900 Volume II* (London: Harmsworth Bros., 1901), p. 493. Notwithstanding his admiration of the British soldier's sporting pluck, Wilson, assistant editor of the *Daily Mail*, was not one to equate war and sport. In volume I of *With the Flag to Pretoria* he had noted that on the march to Belmont in November 1899, Lord Methuen's men 'were to learn what war was. It was not play. It was not pleasure. It was not sport under the greenwood tree, but a savage encounter with desperate adversaries, who dealt death and grievous wounds with impartial hands'. H. W. Wilson, *With the Flag to Pretoria a History of the Boer War Volume I* (London: Harmsworth Bros., 1900), p. 138.
24 Dean Allen, 'England's "Golden Age": Imperial Cricket and Late Victorian Society', *Sport in Society: Cultures, Commerce, Media, Politics*, 15/2 (March 2012), pp. 209–226.
25 *Manchester Guardian*, 18 January 1900.
26 *Observer*, 27 December 1899.
27 Tim Jeal, *Baden-Powell: Founder of the Boy Scouts* (London: Hutchinson & Co. Ltd., 1989), p. 289.
28 *Daily Graphic*, 19 May 1900.
29 R. MacCarthy and R. O'Moore, *The Romance of the Boer War: Humours and Chivalry of the Campaign* (London: Elliot Stock, 1901), p. 10.
30 *Daily Mail*, 27 October 1899. Conan Doyle, a keen cricketer, played ten first-class matches for MCC. Christopher Redmond, *Sherlock Holmes Handbook*, 2nd Edition (Toronto: Dundurn Press, 2009), pp. 116–117.
31 *Manchester Guardian*, 13 September 1900.
32 *Daily Mail*, 29 January 1900.
33 Nigel Spivey, 'Walston, Sir Charles (1856–1927)', in H. C. G. Matthews and Brian Harrison (eds.), *Oxford Dictionary of National Biography* (Oxford, Oxford University Press, 2004); online edition, Lawrence Goldman (ed.), May 2008, <www.oxorddnb.com/article/48709>. Waldstein changed his name to Walston in the aftermath of the First World War.
34 *The Times*, 16 January 1902.
35 *The Times*, 16 January 1902.
36 Malcolm Tozer, 'Cricket, School and Empire: E. W. Hornung and His Young Guard', *International Journal of the History of Sport*, 6/2 (1989), pp. 156–171.
37 *The Spectator*, 18 May 1899, p. 20.
38 E. W. Hornung, *Mr. Justice Raffles* (New York: Charles Scribner's Sons, 1909), p. 17.
39 The second volume of stories, *The Black Mask*, was published in 1901; the final story being 'The Knees of the Gods'.
40 Hornung, *Mr. Justice Raffles*, pp. 16, 56.
41 For more on the Bond see Fransjohan Pretorius, *Historical Dictionary of the Anglo-Boer War* (Lanham: Scarecrow Press, 2009), pp. 3–4.
42 *The Times*, 12 April 1900. The Liberal leader, Henry Campbell-Bannerman, was not convinced by Dormer's line of reasoning. In a reply published in *The Times* the following week, he insisted that 'Mr. Hofmeyr's loyalty must be gauged by his actions, not by his emotions on Newlands Cricket Ground'. *The Times*, 17 April 1900.
43 *Manchester Guardian*, 4 September 1900. That the *Manchester Guardian* should take issue with anti-Bond sentiments was hardly surprising given its unswerving pro-Boer stance. See M. Hampton, 'The Press, Patriotism and Public Discussion: C. P. Scott,

the *Manchester Guardian,* and the Boer War, 1899–1902', *Historical Journal,* 44/1 (March 2001), pp. 177–197.
44 *Manchester Guardian*, 14 January 1902. During the war, Rimington had come to the public's attention as the commander of Rimington's Guides, an irregular cavalry unit, distinctive for the leopard skin bands they wore on their slouch hats. Before that Rimington had been chiefly known for his prowess on the polo field, as evidenced by that well-established Victorian seal of approval, a G. A. Fothergill lithograph in *Vanity Fair*, in which he was portrayed in full polo gear.
45 *Manchester Guardian*, 11 April 1900.
46 Arthur Conan Doyle, *The Great Boer War* (London: Smith Elder and Co, 1900), p. 434.
47 Edward Spiers, 'The British Cavalry 1902–1914', *Journal of the Society of Army Historical Research*, 57/230 (1979), pp. 72–73.
48 Tony Mason and Eliza Riedi, *Sport and the Military: The British Armed Forces 1880–1960* (Cambridge: Cambridge University Press, 2007), pp. 60–65.
49 *The Times*, 14 February 1900.
50 *The Times*, 15 February 1900; Heather Streets, *Martial Races: The Military, Race and Masculinity in British Imperial Culture, 1857–1914* (Manchester: Manchester University Press, 2004), pp. 106–108.
51 *The Times*, 22 February 1900.
52 Stephen Badsey, 'The Boer War (1899–1902) and British Cavalry Doctrine: A Reevaluation', *Journal of Military History*, 71/1 (2006), pp. 75–97.
53 Tim Travers, 'The Hidden Army: Structural Problems in the British Officer Corps, 1900–1918', *Journal of Contemporary History,* 17 (1982), pp. 523–544. In the aftermath of the war, despite the Committee on the Education and Training of Army Officers recommending that inter-regimental polo tournaments should be banned, Field Marshal Frederick Roberts, by then commander-in-chief of the forces and a great advocate of equestrian sport, permitted the 1903 season to proceed with only a few minor revisions. Mason and Riedi, *Sport and the Military*, pp. 74–76.
54 *Manchester Guardian*, 19 December 1899.
55 *Observer*, 15 February 1900.
56 *Daily Mail*, 19 December 1899. An editorial in the *Daily Mail* three months earlier indicated that the press was fully aware that the use of such language was not entirely appropriate. Under the heading, 'Lord Kitchener's Bag', it was noted that the regular weekly report of prisoner numbers was 'expressed on this occasion in somewhat homely English'. *Daily Mail*, 11 September 1901. In the speech at Chesterfield, Rosebery was expected to announce his return to front-bench politics but instead chose to deliver a scathing attack on the current state of the Liberal Party. See Roy Jenkins, *Asquith* (London: William Collins Sons and Co. Ltd., 1964), p. 130.
57 *The Times*, 18 August 1900. On 11 June 1900, poor preparation and organisation during a field-day at Aldershot resulted in 28 men having to be admitted to hospital with heat-stroke, of whom four died. For further details of the disastrous manoeuvres, see *Hansard*, HC Deb. Vol. 84 col. 15 June 1900. [Online]. www.parliament.uk/ [accessed 31 July 2019].
58 *Daily Express*, 30 August 1900.
59 *Daily Mail*, 9 June 1900. Ralph subsequently published two volumes of memoirs covering his experiences as a war correspondent with Lord Roberts' forces in South Africa. *Towards Pretoria: A Record of the War between Briton and Boer to the Relief of Kimberley* (New York: Frederick A. Stokes Co., 1900) and *An American with Lord Roberts* (New York: Frederick A. Stokes Co., 1901).
60 W. E. Cairns, *An Absent-Minded War: Being Some Reflections on Our Reverses and the Causes Which Have Led to Them* (London: John Milne, 1900), p. 32.
61 Cairns, *An Absent-Minded War,* p. 37.
62 *The Spectator*, 1 September 1900.

63 *The Times*, 29 December 1900. As had been the case for his earlier publication, *Social Life in the British Army*, Cairns chose to withhold his name when *An Absent-Minded War* was published.
64 *The Times*, 4 January 1901.
65 Leopold Amery, *The Times History of the War in South Africa, Volume II* (London: Sampson Low, 1902), p. 36.
66 Sir Neill Malcolm, *The Science of War: A Collection of Essays and Lectures 1892–1903 by the Late Colonel G. F. R. Henderson CB* (London: Longmans, Green and Co., 1912), p. 407.
67 Anonymous, *A Handbook of the Boer War* (London and Aldershot, Gale and Polden Ltd., 1910), p. 26.
68 Anonymous, *Handbook of the Boer War*, p. 33.
69 *The Times*, 7 January 1902.
70 Huggins, *The Victorians and Sport*, pp. 14–15; Richard Holt, *Sport and the British: A Modern History* (Oxford: Oxford University Press, 1989), pp. 144–147.
71 *The Times*, 17 June 1902.
72 *The Times*, 4 January 1902.
73 *Manchester Guardian*, 23 October 1901.
74 P. T. Ross, *A Yeoman's Letters* (London: Simpkin, Marshall, Hamilton, Kent, 1901), p. 109.
75 J. M. Staniforth, 'A Round in Favour of Kruger', *Western Mail*, 12 December 1899.
76 Bernard Partridge, 'The Last Wicket', *Punch*, 15 May 1901. *Bittereinders* was the name given to Boers who fought on until peace was signed in May 1902.
77 J. Barclay Lloyd, *One Thousand Miles with the C. I. V.* (London: Methuen & Co., 1901), p. 154.
78 Hilbourne's 'humorous composition' appeared in the *Bucks Herald*, 24 November 1900, the *Derby Mercury*, 5 December 1900, the *Western Gazette*, 28 December 1900, and the *Sunderland Daily Echo*, 19 June 1901. In the latter, for some unexplained reason, authorship was attributed to Private S. Mawhinney of the Buffs, South African Field Force. Of course, unknown to Hilbourne/Mawhinney, there was to be a protracted period of additional time, with hostilities not in fact concluding until the Treaty of Vereeniging on 31 May 1902.
79 'Jack and Joe – Brothers – of the Imperial Yeomanry', *Baily's Magazine of Sports and Pastimes, Volume 78 July -December 1902* (London: Vinton and Co., 1902), pp. 67–69.
80 *Daily Mail*, 10 May 1900. The 'Boer' forces at Boshof, led by the Comte de Villebois-Mareuil, were comprised of foreign volunteers, most of whom were French. See Stephen M. Miller, *Lord Methuen and the British Army: Failure and Redemption in South Africa* (Abingdon: Frank Cass Publishers, 1999), pp. 184–186.
81 *The Times*, 13 November 1899.
82 *The Times*, 29 May 1901.
83 *Manchester Guardian*, 11 September 1901.
84 Anonymous, *Handbook of the Boer War*, p. 32.
85 *Manchester Guardian*, 16 September 1901. In fact, the correspondent's faith in Kitchener was ill-founded. In private communications with Schomberg MacDonnell, the principal private secretary of Lord Salisbury, and St John Broderick, the secretary of state for war, in May and September 1901 respectively, the commander-in-chief referred to captured and killed Boers as 'the bag'. Andre Wessels, *Lord Kitchener and the War in South Africa, 1899–1902* (Stroud: Sutton Publishing Ltd., 2006), p. 111, p. 153.
86 *Daily Mail*, 17 December 1901.
87 Rudyard Kipling, 'The Islanders', *The Times*, 4 January 1902. For more on Kipling's dislike of sport see William B. Dillingham, *Rudyard Kipling: Hell and Heroism* (London: Palgrave Macmillan, 2005), pp. 207–208.

88 *The Times*, 4 January 1902.
89 Paula M. Krebs, *Gender, Race, and the Writing of Empire: Public Discourse and the Boer War* (Cambridge: Cambridge University Press, 1999), pp. 160–162.
90 *Observer*, 5 January 1902.
91 Bill Mallon and Ian Buchanan, *The 1908 Olympic Games* (Jefferson, NC: McFarland and Co., 2000), p. 7.
92 *The Times*, 9 January 1902.
93 *Daily Express*, 7 January 1902.
94 *Daily Express*, 8 January 1902.
95 *Manchester Guardian*, 18 January 1901. The clothing firm Jaeger also felt that the response to Kipling's charge lay in the shooting range. As 'a quiet answer to Mr Kipling's *The Islanders*', it was noted in the *Manchester Guardian*, the firm set up for its employees a rifle range at Lower Sydenham. *Manchester Guardian*, 4 August 1902.
96 *Manchester Guardian*, 6 January 1902.
97 *The Times*, 6 January 1902.
98 *Daily Mail*, 7 January 1902.
99 J. A. Mangan, *The Games Ethic and Imperialism: Aspects of Diffusion of an Ideal* (Harmondsworth: Penguin, 1986), pp. 25–27.
100 H. H. Almond, 'The Breed of Man', *The Nineteenth Century*, 48 (October 1900), pp. 656–669.
101 *The Times*, 9 January 1902. Golf, which by the early twentieth century had become the game of the aspiring middle-class, was regarded with disdain by many contemporary social commentators. Playing the game obsessively had, they argued, accelerated the fall in the moral fibre of the nation as evidenced by the reverses of the Boer War. See Mason, *Sport in Britain*, p. 190.
102 Mason and Riedi, *Sport and the Military*, pp. 61–65.
103 Colin Veitch, '"Play Up! Play Up! And Win the War!" Football, the Nation and the First World War 1914–1915', *Journal of Contemporary History*, 20/3 (July 1985), pp. 363–378; Christopher Sandford, *The Final Over: The Cricketers of Summer 1914* (Stroud: Spellmont, 2014).
104 Simon John, '"A Different Kind of Test Match": Cricket, English Society and the First World War', *Sport in History*, 33/1 (March 2013), pp. 19–48.

3 The First World War
'A new and deadly game'

The frenzy in the letters pages and editorial columns of the regional and national press aroused by the publication of Kipling's *The Islanders* revealed the extent to which the Boer War had brought the issue of sport and the military to the forefront of public discourse. Certainly, as Mason and Riedi have shown, the British army's ineptitude in the face of Boer guerrillas led to a protracted debate on the professional efficacy of officer sport being played out in the public arena over the next decade, and a series of damning parliamentary reports in the immediate aftermath of hostilities prompted the War Office to rein in, albeit temporarily, the scope of army sport.[1] Yet, as has already been seen, the conflict in South Africa also firmly planted in the public consciousness the idea that sport and war were wedded. It was in this period that the transmission of sporting jargon to military reporting, and vice versa, became a regular feature of popular journalism.[2] The press seized on the language and culture of sport to provide its readers with an easily comprehensible frame of reference for the complexities, both operational and moral, of military action on the veldt. In this imagining, the ideal of the sporting warrior not only survived but flourished both during and in the immediate aftermath of the war. In a paper presented to the Royal Commission on the War in South Africa in 1903, Lieutenant-General Sir Ian Hamilton, who was to oversee the disastrous Gallipoli Campaign of 1915, was still certain, notwithstanding his experience as chief of staff to Lord Kitchener during the brutal campaign against Boer *Bittereinders*, that

> [t]he fondness of our officers for sports ... assists them a good deal in war for it must be remembered that war itself is, after all, a game, just like any other game, only that the stakes are the most important we can conceive. Whether on horse or foot, 50 sporting officers would prove a match for 300 average young soldiers, although the soldiers may be just as brave as the officers.[3]

That the perceived sporting characteristics of modern warfare should come to be a regular feature of the public discourse surrounding the war in South Africa was hardly surprising. The civil and military world's fascination with sport, in general, and organised team games, in particular, had intensified as Victoria's reign had drawn to a close. Indeed, J. D. Campbell paints a picture of an Edwardian army obsessed by the cult of athleticism. Sport was deemed to be essential, both professionally, as a preparation for war, and personally, as a networking activity that oiled the wheels of promotion.[4] Team games, Peter Parker has argued, became 'invested with spiritual qualities' in the late nineteenth and early twentieth centuries, with this process reaching 'a crescendo as the First World War provided the muddiest games pitch in history'.[5] Although Robert Hands has pointed out that not all products of the public school system bought into the ideology of the cult of athleticism, and Wray Vamplew has questioned the extent to which middle-class sporting values were absorbed by the working class, they have both still acknowledged the critical role sport played in military life in the years immediately preceding the First World War. The perceived practical benefits of team games and organised physical activity were enough to keep the army authorities devoted to an all-embracing sporting culture.[6]

The historiographical debate becomes more heated, however, when assessing the durability of the nation's sporting culture in the face of industrialised trench warfare. As early as October 1914, William Ralph Inge, the dean of St Paul's Cathedral, warned the congregation of Temple Church, London, that such had been the ferocity of operations in France and Flanders that he could not foresee a time when 'we shall feel the same zest for field sports and games again. They will remain a delightful form of recreation, but as a serious business I think their day is now over'.[7] Anthony Bateman, in his detailed study of the cultural significance of cricket in nineteenth- and early–twentieth-century Britain, made much the same point. The 'carnage' of the first few months of the war had, he maintained, exposed as a 'bitter fiction' the notion that sport had ever served as an ideal training ground for military service.[8] Other historians have differed only in the timing of this moment of national epiphany. Michael Paris viewed 1915 as the critical year when 'the squalor of the trenches and the anonymity of death by poison gas . . . did much to undermine the rhetoric of the "game of war"'.[9] For Paul Fussell, it was, as ever, the battle of the Somme in 1916 that proved to be the watershed. Citing the letters of Rupert Brooke as evidence, he posited that Britain's 'universal commitment to the sporting spirit' may have prevailed well into 1915, but it could not survive the slaughter of 1 July 1916.[10] Agreeing in principle but with less specificity, W. J. Reader contended that the public school cult of athleticism, a belief system that, he claimed, lay at the root of the volunteer movement of 1914, was rendered obsolete by the horrors of attrition in 1916 and 1917.[11] This was certainly the view of one anonymous correspondent to the editor of the *Spectator* in June 1917. Writing shortly after the Battle of Messines, 'Z' was absolutely convinced that any early idealism had been supplanted by a mood of stoic endurance: 'Joy and anxiety, we know none. Spirituality does not come into the scope of our thoughts. Idleness we enjoy thoroughly when we get it. Sport we have forgotten all about; even the sport of war is now finished!'[12] Yet, as James Roberts has shown, the army's commitment to sport in fact deepened as the conflict progressed. The 'proletarianization' of military culture in the wake of mass conscription in 1916 forced the authorities to adopt working-class pastimes, in particular football, as a ready means to assimilate and control new recruits.[13] As late as 1918, the practical benefits of army sport were being given official articulation in the revised version of the BEF's training manual:

> Too much attention cannot be paid to the part played by games in fostering the fighting spirit . . . If [the platoon commander] induces his platoon to be determined to produce the best football team in the battalion, he will have done a great deal to make it the best platoon in every way.[14]

A deepening devotion to team games and sporting culture in the later years of the war has also been recognised in J. G. Fuller's examination of the morale of the British and Dominion forces between 1914 and 1918 and in Tony Mason's and Eliza Riedi's longitudinal study of army sport. Although both works do make note of the military authorities' unshakable belief in the transferrable skills inherent in team games, more critically they both also lay stress on the enduring role of sport as a reassuring frame of reference for combatants and non-combatants alike. For Fuller, sporting values gave 'some pattern to a war which, as idealism and enmity both faded, was hard to comprehend in any other terms'.[15] Mason and Riedi developed this theme by focusing on the importance of amateurism in military sporting activity. Remarking on the undiminished war-time appeal of the games ethic, they noted that the assumed intrinsic worth of physical endeavour, which ensured that the realities of mass warfare did not 'curb the Edwardian tendency to see sport and war as versions of each other', was thought by contemporaries to be found only in competitions unsullied by 'the distribution of prize money'.[16]

The growing significance of the amateur ideal and the centrality of amateurism to the Victorian cult of athleticism firmly placed the sporting revolution of the late nineteenth and early twentieth centuries within the milieu of affluent polite society. The emerging middle classes, keen to differentiate themselves from the increasingly vocal masses, rejected the professionalism and commercialism of working-class sports, like football and rugby league.[17] Unsurprisingly, given the public-school dominance of the officers' mess in the decades leading up to the outbreak of the First World War, a similar sporting apartheid held sway in the ranks of the armed forces. As Colin Veitch has noted, prior to 1914 team games were largely the preserve of officers, while physical exercise for other ranks was delivered through gymnastics and drill.[18] This is not to say, however, that the rank–and-file recruit of the pre-1914 army was unreceptive to his superiors' belief in the ideology of amateurism. Gary Sheffield, Eliza Riedi and Tony Mason have all commented on the public schools' cultural hegemony of the military sporting world. Sheffield has argued that the fascination with games was so universal within the army that the public-school-educated sporting subaltern earned not only the respect of his peers by his athletic endeavours but also the loyalty of his subordinates, while Mason and Riedi have observed that 'the amateur model of sport' provided a 'common language and frame of reference which all men could be expected to understand'.[19] Thus, far from losing its appeal, the language and culture of sport assumed even greater meaning as the fighting on the Western Front degenerated into an attritional slog. Brandon Luedtke, for example, has commented on the frequency with which, in the later stages of the war, frontline soldiers reimagined and refashioned the battlefield as a games field. This served, Luedtke has maintained, 'to lend a sense of normalcy to the foreign experience of war'.[20] A similar conclusion has been arrived at by Iain Adams in his examination of the 'football charges' on the Western Front.[21] The fixation with playing sport, especially football, in the combat zone was, according to Adams, a 'displacement activity', which served the dual function of distracting soldiers from the task they were about to undertake while simultaneously demonstrating that their civilian identities had not been compromised by military life. Indeed, Adams has even suggested that, for some, sporting activity acted as an antidote to the fear of brutalisation; 'playing football was not an escape from the immediacy of one's own death but an escape from killing others'.[22] Simon John, in a wide-ranging examination of the role played by cricket in shaping Britain's wartime experiences, has elaborated on this line of reasoning. The language and culture of cricket not only helped civilians and soldiers cope with the brutal day-to-day realities of modern warfare, even during the seemingly endless months of dispiriting stalemate on the Western Front, but also furnished the war effort with a sense of nobility and legitimacy. An important cultural signifier that supposedly embodied the nation's commitment to fair play, John has shown that the game was repeatedly employed as a frame of reference to justify both the army's conduct and the country's war aims.[23]

The nexus between sport and war was, then, a topic that was firmly established as part of the national conversation by the onset of hostilities in 1914 and was one that continued to be addressed and debated until the signing of the Armistice in 1918. The British soldier's love of sport and the frequency with which, despite adverse circumstances, he continued to engage in athletic endeavour of some sort was given prominence in a range of war-time publications. Throughout the course of the war, the press regularly showed illustrations of, and commented on, soldiers playing football not only in home camps but also at the Front. *The Times*, for example, in a lengthy report on the 'Military Football Season' of 1914, highlighted the army's indomitable sporting spirit by noting that matches were even being played 'in the Tropics with a startling contempt for climate'.[24] The armed services' penchant for games was also quickly recognised by the *Daily Mail*, *Sporting Life* and the *Daily Express*, all three of which established within a few weeks of the outbreak of war public appeals to fund the delivery of sports equipment to the fighting front.[25] A similar story of military sporting devotion can be gleaned from the pages of school magazines. In the space of just four weeks in the summer of 1918, the 1st XI of Simon Langton Boys' School in Canterbury played five cricket matches against teams from the Army Service Corps, the Buffs and 'HQ Staff'.[26] More tellingly, perhaps, in the section of the magazine reserved for news from old boys serving in the forces, references were invariably made to impromptu kickabouts or inter-regimental tournaments. Typical was a report, in April 1917, from Private A. S. Nash, for whom sport seems to have been the defining feature of camp life on the Western Front:

> The billet is very pleasant, as there is plenty of sport. I have entered for wrestling, and I find it very interesting indeed. Most of the fellows are keen on

football, and whenever there is a match the touch lines are crowded. This Depot is split up into five camps, and every month sports are held, and camps compete one against another. The camp which score most points flies the flag and assumes the honour of 'cock camp'. I entered for football, and when the captain asked me where I played I said 'Anywhere'. He was after a back, and he had the cheek to tell me I was rather small. I was greatly disappointed.[27]

Indeed, so commonplace was sport in the combat zone that it even featured in some of the war art of the Western Front. Thus, impromptu football matches were incorporated into Samuel Begg's sweeping panorama of life behind the lines, *In the Wings of the Theatre of War*, which appeared in the *Illustrated London News* in December 1914, and into John Singer Sergeant's monumental canvass, *Gassed*, which depicts the scene at a casualty clearing station in the aftermath of a mustard gas attack.[28]

The inclusion of such scenes, it has been argued by Iain Adams and John Hughson, is a clear indication of just how ubiquitous football on the Western

Figure 3.1 Samuel Begg, 'In the Wings of the Theatre of War: Behind the Centre of the Fighting Line, Belgium', *Illustrated London News*, 5 December 1914

Front was.[29] Yet, images of sporting Tommies also served another purpose. They promoted, Adams has shown, a 'feeling of everydayness' and so served to reassure viewers on the home front that the fighting men had not shed their civilian sporting guises despite the brutal conditions of frontline life.[30] In fact, sport could also act as a reminder of pre-war identities for the soldiers themselves. Eighteen-year-old Private J. Gilham fused regimental pride with a nostalgia for his childhood when writing to the editor of his old school magazine in April 1917:

> I played in a cricket match today for 'A' Coy, the best coy, against the Signallers. They made 115 and we made 123 of which I made 52; so you see we still keep our eye in a little. It seems only a few months ago that I was playing football and cricket at Langton.[31]

The following year, the same editor once again received a letter in which past and present were connected through sport. Having been struck down by first dysentery and then appendicitis, Lieutenant E. Ireland was certain that his convalescence had been given a boost by being selected to keep wicket for the battalion cricket team. Life, he wrote, 'suddenly seemed just like the old days', and this had enabled him to 'feel like myself again'.[32] For some, so close were these associations between sport and civilian peacetime that the presence of any sporting activity near the frontline could, at least initially, seem, at best, incongruous and, at worst, inappropriate. Ernest Townley of the *Daily Express*, one of only four war correspondents invited by GHQ to witness the Battle of Neuve Chapelle in March 1915, was, on arriving at the Front, shocked to find an inter-company football match in progress.[33] He rather self-importantly dismissed the offer of a touchline seat, the paper's readers were told, because he 'preferred to see what could be seen of the other battle . . . [t]he life and death struggle four or five miles away'. Yet, as the day wore on and the men resolutely persisted with the match, Townley became increasingly appreciative of the role and importance of sport in such a hostile environment.

> Soldiers die every day when they are in the trenches but they can only play football when they come back from the trenches for a rest, and they don't have an inter-company match every day. You may think it sounded odd to hear a referee's whistle in between the thud of the guns. But if anyone earns his right to play football, it is these brave men at the front who for months have borne the wretchedness of trench warfare in such a winter as they have passed through. It is partly because they play football that they are bound to beat the Germans, and some day it may be said that Great Britain won the war on the playing-fields of Flanders.[34]

Gary Sheffield has noted that it was 'widely accepted' in early-twentieth-century Britain that sport was a useful training ground for war.[35] One of the earliest and most egregious manifestations of this belief was the raising of the First Sportsman's Battalion in September 1914.[36] Aimed at men over the official recruitment age, notices in *The Times* urged 'All Varsity Men, old Public School Boys,

The First World War 71

men who are hardened to the soldier's life by the strenuous pursuit of sport [to] enlist at once' and 'Show the King's Enemies what British Sportsmen are'.[37] So great was the response that a second battalion was formed in March the following year. Indeed, throughout the war, the perceived martial benefits of a range of sporting activities were publicly promoted. The advocates of hunting,

Figure 3.2 The Times, 8 December 1914

who faced increasing pressure from farmers and government officials lobbying for the greater protection of arable land, were especially keen to advance the indispensability of their sport in wartime. In December 1916, R. C. Drummond, the hunting correspondent for the *Manchester Guardian*, reacted to the news that the Game Laws were to be amended so that the requirements of agriculture should take precedence over those of the sporting community by presenting his readers with a detailed explanation of exactly why 'training in field-sports was a splendid preparation for the stern tests of battle':

> These men were accustomed to long hours and hard work in the open air. They were fit and healthy, and from habit, were quick to form a decision, prompt to act in an emergency. From the Chief downwards – General Sir Douglas Haig is a fine horseman and a first-rate polo player – they have proved time and again the usefulness of their peace training.[38]

The author and literary editor of the *Morning Post*, E. B. Osborn, was also quick to cite the commander-in-chief as proof of hunting's martial attributes. In a tribute to Colwyn Philipps, a captain in the Royal Horse Guards and keen point-to-point rider who had been killed in the Second Battle of Ypres in 1915, he asserted, 'You only had to look into the personal history of Sir Douglas Haig and other famous commanders past and present, to admit the truth of Sir Evelyn Wood's contention that the hunting-field is a fine school of military leadership.'[39] A willingness to carry out rather than give orders was the key quality that one correspondent to the *Daily Mail* felt marked out the boxer as being particularly suited to army life. Arguing that he had 'yet to discover a finer sport for producing men who will "go over" the parapet and rush a Hun trench', "An Officer" was keen to dismantle any preconceived notions that readers might have of the boxer as little more than 'a bruiser'. 'Take it from me', he informed the paper's editor, 'the best boxer in the battalion is one of the least likely men to give trouble; he is always brave, he is never a bully, and he accepts the discipline of the referee or his company commander without a murmur.'[40] Courage was also seen to be the hallmark of the rugby player. In a section entitled 'Records of Regiments in the War', the hugely popular part-work *War Illustrated* drew a parallel between the Leicesters and the city's renowned rugby team:

> Every lover of that manly game, Rugby Football, has heard of the 'Tigers', and most of them have, at one time or another, seen them play. To those who have played against them they were very sturdy opponents, and he was a plucky back who threw himself in their way when they came tearing down the field. The Leicesters, for such is the other name for the 'Tigers', carry the same dashing spirit into the greater game of war.[41]

It was the practical skill as well as the pluck of the cricket-playing soldier that frequently drew the approval of commentators. When that great master of the game, W. G. Grace, died in October 1915, the *Spectator* was certain that his influence had stretched beyond the cricket square to 'the battlefields of Flanders'.

'A generation', Grace's obituary read, 'reared on his exploits and trained to bowl and "throw in" hard and accurately are the best bombers the world can produce, and beat the Germans easily in length and precision.'[42] The following year a campaign was launched in the magazine's letters' column to have a statue erected at Lord's to honour the heroics of those players who had signed up. Inspired by James Norman Hall's stirring poem *The Cricketers of Flanders*, the former first-class batsman J. Gordon Crowdy led the way. In a poetic flurry, he insisted that satisfying Hall's injunction, 'Let splendid bronze commemorate/These men', would remind 'those/In less believing days, perchance/How Britain's fighting cricketers/Helped bomb the Germans out of France'.[43]

Throughout the war, then, sporting endeavour continued to be seen by many as one of the best ways, if not the best way, to prepare young men for combat. Sport, asserted E. B. Osborn in the introduction to his best-selling 1917 anthology of war poetry, *A Muse in Arms*, endowed 'the nation and its civilian soldiers with heroic virtues'.[44] The servicemen whose work featured in the collection all wrote, Osborn continued,

> in honour of the games and field-sports in which [they had] acquired the basal elements of all true discipline – confidence in [their] companions and readiness to sacrifice the desire of personal distinction to the common interest of [their] team, which is, of course, a mimic army in being.[45]

The army also remained convinced, right up to the cessation of hostilities, of the value of sport to military efficiency. Old Langtonian and keen rugby player G. E. Smith informed the current pupils of Simon Langton Boys School that the 'most pleasing feature' of the artillery course he had been sent on in 1917 was 'the importance attached to sport'.[46] Even as late as 1918, a *Times*' report on new army training schools in France, 'at which . . . the immediate and ostensible objects were instruction in the use of bayonet and musketry', could comment favourably on the amount of time devoted to physical recreation. 'The great thing', the paper's special correspondent enthused, 'is the games. What games? All games which teach combination and self-reliance and quickness of hand, foot, and eye – football, handball, basket-ball, boxing, wrestling, fencing of every kind, tug-of-war, medicine-bag-tennis, and a dozen other strange sports invented on the premises.'[47] Indeed, so all-embracing had this lionisation of sporting culture become by the second half of the war that one of the *Manchester Guardian*'s military contributors, who had previously 'held sport in contempt', underwent a remarkable *volte-face*. In a lengthy piece entitled 'Soldiering and Games', 'A Soldier' argued that football benefited not just the participant but also the spectator. Concluding with a rhetorical flourish that no doubt struck a chord with football fans in the Northwest, the article linked the emotional challenges of an FA Cup run with the mental trials of attritional warfare:

> And it is not claiming too much, is it, to say that the same cheery spirit which carried an Oldham crowd through the great discomforts of a Cup-tie trip to London is now carrying our men through the grave discomforts

of the trenches? The kindly tolerance of the gamely man, his forbearance and good humour, his instinctive desire to make the best of things and to maintain a cheerful demeanour in the worst circumstances, all these qualities which have reached their highest development in France and Flanders – qualities of incalculable value, begun on the playing-field and continued on the battlefield.[48]

It was, though, almost without exception, the active player rather than the passive observer who was thought to have profited from the games culture; and, more precisely, it was those who had gone through the public-school sports system who were believed to have benefited the most. The experience of captaining the House XI or the School 1st XV was, as Gary Sheffield has noted, considered by many to be an ideal apprenticeship for commanding a platoon of men.[49] Public school sport, it was believed, furnished young men with the moral as well as physical wherewithal to excel on the battlefield. Unsurprisingly, given his reputation as the unofficial poet laureate of the late Victorian cult of athleticism, Henry Newbolt was a leading proponent of this view.[50] His fanciful children's history of the chivalric roots of contemporary English society, *The Book of the Happy Warrior*, published in 1917, drew parallels between the training of squires in medieval times and the education of the public school boy in the early twentieth century. Central to both, it was claimed, was a 'love of games' and a 'sporting or amateur' view of them.[51] Bound by a 'natural fellowship of sport', the products of these regimens were fully grounded in 'the moral qualities, such as leadership and endurance and fair play, which are indispensable for war'.[52] The fusion of war and sport had, in fact, already been explored by Newbolt in semi-fictional form the previous year. *The Adventures of a Subaltern*, which appeared as one of a collection of short pieces in *Tales of the Great War*, followed the daring exploits of an unnamed young officer on the Western Front. In the very first paragraph, the story established the protagonist's credentials as a worthy hero by underlining his sporting pedigree. Having gone up to Oxford, the juvenile readership was informed, the anonymous subaltern had 'continued to play football, captained his College team and won the Cup Ties'. To reassure those sceptical about the significance of this sporting detail, Newbolt was quick to make abundantly clear why, in wartime, endeavour on the games-field mattered:

> Some writers think that this kind of thing has little to do with soldiering, but I have heard commanding officers say that the useful new subalterns in this war have mostly come from the Public Schools and Universities, and many of the best of them have been those who were accustomed to leading in games.[53]

The conviction that sporty public schoolboys possessed innate leadership qualities was by no means confined to the world of children's literature. General Horace Smith-Dorrien, the commander of the Second Army Corps during the early stages of the war, revealed he was of the same view when addressing his old school's war memorial committee at Harrow in 1917. Preaching, one can't help thinking, to the converted, Smith-Dorrien was quick, *The Times*' report on the meeting noted, to praise 'the magnificent public school spirit, and the fact that the best material for leading troops came from those who had public school training, of which such an important part consists of games and sport'.[54] Frank Hilllier, the foreign affairs editor of the *Daily Mail*, was equally certain that the natural authority of the nation's officer corps had been forged on the playing-fields of the public schools. In a lengthy article entitled 'The Public-School Boy in the War', published on 3 November 1914 at the height of the First Battle of Ypres, Hillier drew parallels between the battlefield and the rugby pitch:

> The man who coolly goes down to the ball under the feet of a rushing crowd of forwards, who tackles a galumphing giant twice his size, has learned, till it has become second nature, the calm courage he will require when it comes to facing hailstorms of bullets. The power of instant decision – 'Shall I pass or go on?' 'Blind side or open?' – he will have learned that too; it is all in football, and he will never hesitate what to do in a tight place. And then what man worth his salt ever stopped doing all he knew till the whistle went, no matter what the score against him? The only difference is that in this game there will be no whistle till the game is won![55]

Critically, Hillier concluded, on the cricket squares and rugby pitches, the public-school boy 'learned how to lead men, and also how not to lead them; he learned firmness, authority, justice, courage. . . . He learned to sacrifice personal glory to the glory of that wonderful whole of which he had the honour of being a humble part'.[56]

Hillier's belief in the sportsman's commitment to self-sacrifice and honour was widely shared and was, for many, central to the public-school games ethic. In his glowing eulogy for Old Rugbeian Ronald Poulton, the English Rugby Union captain who was killed at Ploegsteert in May 1915, E. B. Osborn singled out the player's 'chivalrous' approach to the game for special mention. 'The most important element in war', Osborn argued, 'and the most difficult to make sure of, is the moral element, and for that there is nothing like the old English School tradition which makes so much use of the hard, exhilarating discipline of team-games.'[57] The popular authoress Beatrice Heron-Maxwell also cited the playing-fields of the English public school as the birthplace of a 'chivalrous law that was unbreakable by any man, or boy, of honour'. This law, she informed readers of the *Daily Mail* in September 1916, 'became a creed, wherein though there might be thirty-nine articles and hundreds of minute variations, there was only one dogma – that of Fair Play'.[58] Adherence to this sporting code, even by those who had never had the advantage of a public school education, was often considered enough to be thought of as the equal, or very nearly the equal, of a British officer. Thus, in an article commending the French for the part they had played in stabilising the fighting on the Western Front over the winter of 1914/15, the *Daily Mail* judged the war to have been the making of the ordinary *poilu*:

> The majority of them have never heard of cricket; they have never rowed in a boat nor run a race in their lives. They are not physical sportsmen. They are something better. They are playing the greatest game of all, the game of life and death, and they are playing it like men, like gentlemen. The sense of honour, the spirit of sacrifice have become for them not an outward gesture but an inward instinct of the soul itself. They are moral sportsmen.[59]

The same thinking prompted the editor of the best-selling part-work *The Great War: The Standard History of the All-Europe Conflict* to conclude a section dedicated to 'Sportsmen who fell' with the observation: 'To mention all the sportsmen killed during the year would be to write down the names of nearly all the 190,000 [British dead].'[60]

The belief that an innate sporting instinct and concomitant devotion to fair play were peculiarly British characteristics had already become firmly established in the national consciousness by the turn of the twentieth century and, as John Horne has observed, was accentuated by the onset of war.[61] Stories of German atrocities were widely reported in Britain and acted as neat counterpoints to the assumed probity of the BEF's prosecution of the war and the rectitude of the British soldier.[62] Thus, in an advert for the leading country sports magazine, *The Field*, which appeared in the *Manchester Guardian* in February 1915, great play was made of the recent inclusion of a supplement that had provided 'authentic records of German atrocities'. The antidote to the horrors contained in 'this document of international importance', the copy concluded, could be found by reading *The Field*'s coverage of the war:

> To be known as a nation of sportsmen is Britain's just pride, for upon the sportsman's code of fair play the British Empire has been built. Today it is the sportsman's spirit that inspires the strong arm of the Empire, fighting for fair play, and nowhere is this spirit – a cherished tradition of our race – given more vigorous and effective expression than in the war section of *The Field*.[63]

Early criticisms in German newspapers that the reconfiguration of the war as a sport smacked of frivolity were quickly turned on their head by the British press. In October 1914, both *The Times* and *Punch* seized on the *Cologne Gazette*'s claim that the use of 'sporting expressions' revealed a misunderstanding of the 'high seriousness of war and . . . its moral importance' to make unfavourable comparisons between the German and British approaches to warfare. For the editor of *The Times*, a nation's affection for sporting metaphors was a telling indicator of moral fibre:

> An English commander might, in his vulgar sporting jargon, say that it was not cricket to make war on women and children, but he would not make it . . .

but for the German war is too sacred a thing to be compared with cricket and so he will make war on anyone who comes in his way.[64]

It was not only a commitment to fair play that Sir Owen Seaman, the editor of *Punch*, saw in the British soldier's obsession with sport but also a natural aptitude for combat. He concluded a poetic celebration of the rank and file of the BEF, which appeared in the magazine in October 1914 and which referenced the item in the *Cologne Gazette* by way of introduction, by outlining the martial qualities of his eponymous hero, *Thomas of the Light Heart*:

> He takes to fighting as a game;
> He does no talking, through his hat,
> Of Holy missions; all the same
> He has his faith – be sure of that;
> He'll not disgrace his sporting breed
> Nor play what isn't cricket. There's his creed.[65]

The *Daily Mail*, under the ownership of the virulently anti-German Lord Northcliffe, took particular delight in contrasting the barbarous nature of the Hun with the sporting inclinations of the British Tommy.[66] The tone was set early on in the paper's response to the German raids on Scarborough, Whitby and Hartlepool in December 1914. 'The cowardice and brutality achieved by the German raiders', a scathing editorial insisted, had 'proved conclusively that blood-stirring games do not brutalise and that the philosophical figure-spinning of spectacled [German] students is not guarantee against excess and violence when the helpless are encountered'.[67] Throughout the war any opportunity to highlight the German soldier's inability to comprehend Anglo-Saxon sporting culture was seized on with relish by *Daily Mail* reporters. Typical was a sardonic item from the paper's correspondent in New York. Under the headline 'The Sporting English: Quality that Perplexes the Hun', German bemusement in the face of nonchalant games-playing POWs was given full rein:

> German officers have been commenting to the correspondent of the *Chicago Tribune* on what they term British ideas of sport in relation to the war. They state that British prisoners who have been captured in enterprises which seem to the Germans to be mad invariably observe, 'Well, it was a sporting thing to do.' 'War,' severely observed one officer, 'is not sport, it is science.' The officers asked a captive English airman: 'What did you learn?' 'As it happened, I did not learn much,' the airman replied with a smile, 'but it was a good sporting proposition.' The correspondent says the Germans regard such a man as *verruckt* (cracked).[68]

Even on the rare occasion when a grudging acknowledgement of the existence of a physical culture in Germany was given, it was invariably depicted as a poor imitation of the English cult of athleticism. Lord Northcliffe, in his rather idiosyncratic ruminations on the progress of the fighting up to 1917, published under the unassuming title *Lord Northcliffe's War Book*, characterised the German soldier as courageous but lacking initiative. The reason for this, he asserted, was because

> his whole training from childhood upwards has been to obey, and obey in numbers. He has not played individual games. Football, which develops individuality, has only been introduced into Germany in comparatively recent times. . . . [German soldiers] are brave, but in a way very different from our kind of bravery. They do not take war in the British spirit, which they consider frivolous and too much akin to sport.[69]

Unsurprisingly, the *Daily Mail*'s 'eye-witness in Germany', D. Thomas Curtin, was in agreement. German sport, he opined in an article on life in Germany, was not the spontaneous sport of Anglo-Saxon countries, and consequently, 'German boys [were] bad-tempered losers and boastful winners'.[70] One interesting exception to the general rule that Germans couldn't be true sportsmen arose in the first few months of the war. Between August and November 1914, the German light cruiser SMS *Emden* carried out a series of successful raids on Allied merchant vessels in the Indian and Pacific Oceans.[71] For British commentators, the most notable feature of these operations was not the tonnage of shipping destroyed but the strict adherence to the rules of war by the *Emden*'s captain, Karl von Muller. Arthur Conan Doyle, in his early reflections on hostilities, *The German War*, published at the end of 1914, felt that Muller had earned the commendation of the British public 'because almost alone among Germans he played the game as it should be played'. By living up to '[Britain's] ideal to fight in a sporting spirit', Conan Doyle concluded, Muller ought to be differentiated from the 'murderers and brigands in Belgium'.[72] The same distinction was drawn by Fred T. Jane in volume 2 of *War Illustrated*. With his reputation 'untarnished by an act of barbarity such as his countrymen have perpetrated in their battles on land', Muller had earned the right to be regarded, Jane suggested, as 'a sportsman and a gentleman'.[73]

Jane's association of sportsman with gentleman is a telling one, for the British sporting ideal alluded to by Conan Doyle was very much the one rooted in the middle-class amateur tradition. As John H. Osborne has argued, in the decades leading up to the First World War the expanding middle classes, keen to assert their new-found respectability, quickly turned participation in amateur games into an important cultural signifier.[74] Pivotal to this new sporting ideology was the notion of self-sacrifice. Thus, Paul Jones, a lieutenant in the Tank Corps and former captain of Dulwich College 1st XI football team, could confidently assert, in a posthumously published collection of his letters from the Front, that it was 'only on our amateur playing-fields that we become really unselfish'. It was this 'spirit of unselfishness', Jones reasoned, that explained why 'the amateur has done so enormously better [in the war] than the professional'.[75] Jones' belief that the professional sportsman lacked the moral fibre of the amateur had widespread currency during the war years and most obviously manifested itself in the condemnation the professional football authorities received for refusing to abandon the 1914/15 league programme.[76] Within a few weeks of the declaration of war, the *Spectator* published a letter from H. B. Tristram, a former international Rugby Union player, in which the amateur's jaundiced view of the professional was given full voice. Noting that 'as soon as ever a game is perverted into a business[,] its followers seem to lose all sense of proportion', Tristram concluded with a stark warning:

> It is just about ten years ago that a man of understanding said to me: 'I am afraid that even if the first battle of Waterloo was won on the playing-fields of Eton, there is a terrible danger that the next may be lost on the football ground of Crystal Palace.'[77]

The magazine's editor gave the letter his full backing. In an editorial outlining the 'contribution of games to the war', he extolled the qualities engendered by cricket and football but lamented the 'fact that not all young and unmarried cricketers and footballers have signed up and that the county cricket season and football fixtures are still going ahead'.[78] The pressure on the FA was maintained with the continued publication of critical letters in subsequent issues of the magazine.[79] The anti-football lobby also found support in the Northcliffe press. Both *The Times* and the *Daily Mail* not only published a series of letters lambasting the FA for its unpatriotic stance but, probably to greater effect, employed the services of popular poets to urge, through the medium of patriotic doggerel, the nation's footballers to join 'the greater game'.[80]

To an even greater extent than the professional player, it was the football spectator who was on the receiving end of particularly vitriolic attacks. In a letter to the editor of *The Times*, A. F. Pollard, professor of constitutional history at University College London, conceded that football was a 'healthy recreation for combatants' but nonetheless insisted that 'there is no excuse for diverting from the front thousands of athletes in order to feast the eyes of inactive spectators who are either unfit to fight or unfit to be fought for'.[81] References to the complacency and moral deficiency of football fans also featured in the pages of *Punch* and the *Spectator*. A cartoon depicting two men avidly reading football results, which appeared in *Punch* in January 1915, branded such reporting 'The Shirker's War News'. To drive home the point, the accompanying text read: 'Football news has not receded into its true perspective; shirkers are more preoccupied with the defeat or victory of "Lambs" or "Wolves" in Lancashire than with the stubborn defence, the infinite discomfort and the heavy losses of their brothers in Flanders.'[82] The editor of the *Spectator* chose to publish an anonymous letter from the frontline that denounced as 'extremely stupid' the belief of the 'beer-swilling, football-match-watching mob' that the war would be won without sacrifices being made by the nation as a whole.[83] That such criticisms appeared in publications targeting the affluent elite reveals much about the inherent class bias in British sporting life at this time. For public-school-educated sportsmen, the emergence of football as a mass spectacle for the urban working class threatened to undermine all the physical and moral values that lay at the heart of the nation's sporting heritage.

The FA did attempt to defend its position by publicly celebrating the patriotic record of its members. In an announcement issued in late August 1914, it reminded critics:

> Thousands and thousands of the flower of British youth and manhood who, on the playing fields of this country have acquired and developed the splendid characteristics of the fearless and undaunted warrior are now, at the peril of their lives, fighting the battle of honour, honesty and uprightness against military despotism.[84]

The popular weekly sports paper *Athletic News* also lent its support to the footballing fraternity. The game, it was pointed out in an editorial of 10 August 1914, was not only of value at the fighting front but also important in the domestic war effort by helping non-combatants 'keep the body fit and the mind calm'.[85] But such arguments did little to assuage the growing clamour against the continuation of the league programme, and professional football formally ended for the duration of the war with the Khaki Cup Final between Sheffield United and Chelsea on 24 April 1915.

For some, however, the onset of hostilities had rendered abhorrent any suggestion that not just football but sporting culture as a whole retained any real significance. In his treatise, *The Public School in War Time*, published in 1916, S. P. D. Mais, a teacher at Sherbourne School, insisted, 'One of the greatest benefits that war has conferred upon us is the depreciation of the value of athletics.' 'We were', he continued, 'in grave danger of falling into the snare of making success in games one of the first standards by which we judged our fellow-men.'[86] Mais' view was echoed the following year by William Temple, a former headmaster of Repton School and future Archbishop of Canterbury, who argued in his work of popular philosophy, *Mens Creatrix*, that the struggle against Germany had laid bare the vacuity of the public-school cult of athleticism:

> The great danger of an education which proceeds largely by means of games . . . is that it gives the impression that the rules of the game may be treated as the rules of life. In England we speak of 'a good sportsman' and 'playing the game' as if these phrases embodied all morality; but in fact they are most misleading. In one case there is, or should be, nothing at stake . . . in the other there may be at stake the right to live with honesty.[87]

It was this new sense of sport's relative inconsequentiality that clearly prompted the father of Francis Henry Browning, the Irish rugby union and cricket international, to take the unusual step of correcting an obituary of his son that had appeared in the *Spectator* in June 1916. Noting that Francis had been described as 'the well-known football player and sportsman of Trinity', Browning pointed out that he had also formed the Irish Football Association Volunteers, 200 of whom were at that time serving in Gallipoli. 'Surely a record such as this', he admonished the journal's editor, 'far surpasses, and merits acknowledgement more than, his achievements in the cricket and football field, good as they were.'[88]

On the whole, though, these dissenting voices remained on the margins, and the widespread belief that playing sport cultivated valuable martial qualities continued to go unchallenged. However, there was an increasing tendency as hostilities progressed to question the extent to which sport fully prepared young men for the serious business of modern war. A letter to the editor of *The Times* in May 1916, in which W. G. Knox, a retired lieutenant-general who had served in the Second Boer War, proposed that riding to the hounds served as the best apprenticeship for a commission in the army, received only lukewarm support.[89] David Hannay, the eminent naval historian, in a response published the following day, agreed that sport may help build character. However, he was equally certain that 'the surest way to beat the Boche or any other enemy' was not by 'scampering across fields after a miserable fox' but by giving 'the best of your thought and energy to your work as a soldier'.[90] Hannay received the full backing of an anonymous correspondent three days later. Sport may be 'an excellent preparatory school' for the army, but the mismanagement of the fighting against the Boers should, 'W. T.' argued, have taught the nation that 'war must be taken in earnest and seriously'.[91] Even Henry Newbolt acknowledged that the war in South Africa had been something of a watershed. The final chapter of *The Book of the Happy Warrior* clearly outlined the impact the protracted struggle against the Transvaal and the Orange Free State had had on the sporting ethos that underpinned the nation's amateur-military tradition:

> Then came the Boer War; the army was outwitted in a new and peculiar kind of fighting, and a cry arose that we had wasted our time on mere games and sports, which were no preparation for war. The nation resented this cry, especially when uttered in verse, but it had truth in it: you may get from the playing-fields the moral qualities such as leadership and endurance and fair-play, which are indispensable for war, but you cannot get the scientific training which is also indispensable.[92]

Similarly convinced that a military training based almost exclusively on sporting prowess was deficient were the best-selling romantic novelist Marie Corelli and the master of Haileybury College F. B. Malim. In a collection of her wartime writings, published under the self-effacing title *My 'Little Bit'*, Corelli argued that although games helped with 'physical development', it was only through 'study' that true military efficiency could be guaranteed.[93] Malin, having outlined at some length the 'virtues' developed by sport, nonetheless warned, in a wartime essay on 'Athletics', which was published in A. C. Benson's edited volume *Cambridge Essays on Education*, that 'it may be desirable to reduce the time spent on games [for army recruits]'. This, he concluded, would allow greater attention to be paid to 'handicraft or military drill'.[94] A reference to A. C. Benson's work featured in what was one of the most damning indictments of the nation's anti-intellectual sporting culture to appear during the war. To a mixture of controversy and acclaim,

Alec Waugh's thinly disguised autobiographical account of his schooldays at Sherborne, *The Loom of Youth*, was published in 1917. In it, his cricket-playing hero, Gordon Carruthers, 'a blood – one of the best all-round athletes', rounded off a debate on whether the 'worship of games is harmful' with a withering dismissal of sport's relevance in wartime:

> I love cricket; but that does not make me worship it. I like eating; but I don't make a god of a chocolate éclair. We can like a thing without bowing down to it, and that's how we have got to treat games. Some fool said, 'the battle of Waterloo was won on the playing fields of Eton'; and a fool he was, too. Games don't win battles, but brains do, and brains aren't trained on the footer field. It is time we realised that.[95]

Unsurprisingly, the motion was carried with 'an enormous majority'.[96] Even readers of the *Daily Mail* had any romantic illusions that a sporting pedigree was all that an officer required to overcome the trials of the Western Front occasionally challenged. Having witnessed the BEF's retreat after the Battle of Mons in late August 1914, one of the paper's most experienced war correspondents, H. Hamilton Fyfe, was reluctantly forced to concede that 'war is not a sport any longer. It is a science. . . . Successful generals are no longer dashing soldiers. They are . . . spectacled, professional bookish persons'.[97]

Although the brutal realities of life and death on the battlefield may have led to a greater realisation about the serious nature of modern conflict, the reconfiguring of the war as a sporting contest, nonetheless, persisted. Both combatants and non-combatants used sporting analogies and metaphors to 'normalise' the fighting and impose a familiar frame of reference onto what was an emotionally dislocating experience.[98] For those who had to endure frontline conditions, employing the language and imagery of the games field to refashion the combat zone was an effective mechanism for coping with an alien world. The proletarian soldier frequently fell back on the familiarity of football to make sense of the landscape of war. Indeed, Iain Adams has gone so far as to claim that the language of the non-commissioned soldier was 'infiltrated by football'.[99] Thus, Private T. Connolly of the Royal Irish Rifles described for *War Illustrated* the role of his company at Givenchy in 1916 as 'playing inside left [in] the centre line of a football team', while *The Times* noted that, to one sergeant in the Highland Light Infantry, the German advance at Mons in 1914 was 'like a football crowd leaving Hampden Park'.[100] Those from privileged backgrounds often turned, perhaps unsurprisingly, to the rugby pitch and the cricket square to shape their understanding of the fighting. To one officer, quoted in the *Daily Mail*, German shells looked 'for all the world like a cricket ball coming through the air', although to Max Pemberton, war correspondent and alumnus of Merchant Taylors' School, their irregular trajectory reminded him more of a 'badly-kicked rugby football'.[101]

However, it was on the home front that it was more common for the battlefield to be transformed into a playing-field. In the early stages of hostilities, calls to the colours were occasionally forged using the imagery of football. R. G. Vernede's poem *The Call*, which appeared in *The Times* on 19 August 1914, presented the war as the greatest sporting contest of all:

> Here is the game of games to play.
> Never a goal – the captains say –
> Matches the one that's needed now:
> Put the old blazer and cap away –
> England's colours await your brow.[102]

In a similar vein, the following March an advertisement in the *Sporting Times* urged readers to sign up for 'the grand International Tours of the British Empire Football Club . . . the preliminary rounds to be played in France and Belgium'.[103] This refashioning of the fighting front as a sports field was not confined, though, to crude exhortations to enlist but rather permeated all aspects of war writing. By employing the conceit of portraying the war as a game, journalists and authors could represent the alien world of mechanised warfare within the parameters of a reassuringly familiar construct. Tony Collins has argued that, rather than football, it was, in fact, rugby union that lent itself most readily to this practice, the violent nature of the game providing obvious parallels with armed struggle.[104] Certainly, the rugby scrum was seized on by the *Spectator*, twice, *War Illustrated* and, in verse, Claude Burton of the *Daily Mail*, as the perfect analogy for the attritional fighting on the Western Front.[105] A more complex use of rugby terminology was used by Ernest Swinton in his short story 'The Full Back'. Published in 1915 as part of a collection of military adventure tales for boys, the story, echoing Newbolt's *Vitaï Lampada*, traced a young pilot's self-sacrificing strike against a German spotter plane back to a critical moment in a school rugby match: 'It is his old game. Subconsciously he sees before him a foggy field, and feels the hush that comes over it. Though the touch line – the final touchline – is some thousands of feet away this time.'[106] With our eponymous hero along with the German pilot and observer all killed, Swinton's concluding sentence left the young reader in no doubt about the sporting nobility of war: 'Three more of the salt of their respective nations are out of play. And though for the rest of the armies "No side" does not yet sound, and the great game goes on, full back has saved again.'[107]

Despite rugby union's physicality seeming to offer the perfect vehicle through which the war could be repackaged for a domestic audience, it was, once again, the gentler game of cricket that many writers felt fulfilled this function more readily. Cricket was thought to symbolise all that was good about British or, more specifically, English culture and identity. The game, it was assumed, fostered all the qualities that made the amateur sportsman the perfect role model.[108] Typifying this vision of the nation's summer sport was Jesse Pope's poem *Cricket 1915*, which graced the pages of the *Daily Mail* on 18 May 1915. With the FA succumbing to the pressure to discontinue its league programme for the duration of the war,

Pope, a regular contributor of patriotic verse to the *Mail*, was moved to remind the paper's readers of the decency and gallantry of the nation's cricketers:

> Where are those hefty sporting lads
> Who donned the flannels, gloves, and pads?
> They play a new and deadly game,
> Where thunder bursts in crash and flame.
> Our cricketers have gone 'on tour';
> To make their country's triumph sure.
> They'll take the Kaiser's middle wicket
> And smash it by clean British Cricket.[109]

In February 1915, a similar line had been adopted by W. Snow for subscribers to the *Spectator*. His poem, *Oxford in War Time*, in the preface of which it was pointedly observed that 'The whole of last year's Oxford Eight and the great majority of the cricket and football teams are serving the King', again reflected on the implications of abandoned cricket squares:

> Where are her sons who waged at Cricket
> Warfare against the foeman-friend?
> Far from the Parks, on a harder wicket,
> Still they attack and still defend;
> Playing the greater game, they'll stick it,
> Fearless until the end![110]

The nobility of the cricketer-warrior was a theme that was revisited by Ernest Raymond in his hugely successful post-war novel *Tell England*. Published in 1922, the story charts the progress of a group of boys from their days at Kensingstowe, a fictional public school, to their service as junior officers during the doomed Gallipoli campaign. In one of the final dramatic scenes, the book's narrator, Rupert Ray, witnesses his friend, Edgar Doe, a former stalwart of the Kensingstowe cricket First XI, pinned down in No-Man's land by an enemy machine-gun he has been tasked to disable. Ray has no doubt that Doe's sporting pedigree will come to the fore: 'from all I knew of Doe and his passion for the heroic, I felt assured that he would never stay in the crater like a diffident batsman in his block. He would reach the opposite crater, or be run out.' Inevitably Doe doesn't make it, and, as he falls fatally wounded, he is seemingly transported back to his natural environment: 'His cap fell off, and the wind blew his hair about, as it used to do on the cricket-field at school.'[111] Reports in the *Spectator* and *The Times* also figuratively relocated the last moments of serving cricketers from the battlefield to the sports-field. Coverage, in the *Spectator*, of a charity match between England and the Dominions at Lord's in July 1918 concluded by reflecting on those former players who, 'in the greater and ghastly game in France and Flanders . . . have played their last ball and closed a noble innings'.[112] The following year, *The Times* adopted a similarly contemplative tone. The resumption of first-class fixtures in the 1919 season would, the paper's cricketing correspondent noted, be tinged with sadness for those county players who had 'in the greater field played the game to the last ball'.[113] The use of such sporting metaphors helped those on the home front cope with the dislocation caused by the war and provided some mitigation of the overwhelming sense of loss felt by the bereaved. As Stuart Sillars has stated, there was consolation in being told that the fallen's ordeal should be regarded as no more than 'a glorified cricket match' and their deaths as 'something as painless as a fall on the cricket pitch'.[114]

Cricket as a conduit for consolation and pride was also a feature of the post-war boom in memorial construction. With, as Jack Williams has pointed out, the game's associations with sportsmanship and 'Englishness' being reinforced by the First World War, it became an attractive proposition for the war dead to be recalled as former players.[115] A sizeable number of public schools, including Haberdashers' Aske's, Bradfield College, Merchant Taylors' and the City of London School, chose to commemorate old boys who had died in the war through the dedication of cricket pavilions.[116] The significance of this choice of memory site was clearly spelt out in the inscription above the door of the pavilion at King's School, Worcester: 'This Pavilion was erected in memory of those who, having learnt in this place to play the game for their School, played it also for their Country during the years 1914–1919.'[117] It was, future generations were being informed, in their schoolboy sporting roots that the essential spirits of these institutions' Rolls of Honour resided. By sanitising the loss of life through the reclamation of the fallen as schoolboy cricketers, such memorials served the dual function of providing solace for those left behind while reinforcing the value of institutional ethos. This belief that traditional manly virtues fostered by the cult of athleticism had been validated by the war could be seen not only in the erection of cricket pavilions but also in the public-school predilection for the purchase of playing-fields as commemorative sites. Bury Grammar School, Tettenhall College, Bradfield College, Llandovery College, the City of London School, Monmouth Grammar School, Loretto School, Edinburgh, and the Perse School, Cambridge, all extended their sports grounds as part of their memorialisation schemes.[118] What was implicit in this utilisation of sporting facilities as loci for remembrance was made explicit by HRH Prince Henry at the unveiling of Lancing College's war memorial in June 1927. He told those assembled in the school cloisters that:

> [t]he spirit of unselfishness is that which we understand by the Public School tradition, and it is taught from the very beginning of our school days on the playing fields. To play for your side and not for yourself, this is the spirit so drilled into you that when you leave school to go out into the world it has become part of your very self. Keep before you that Lancing tradition of team play, which spells unselfishness. Keep that tradition before you. It will enable you to conquer manhood, as in your schooldays, when you excel in the sports field. . . . In doing this, you will honour not only the School, but also the memory of those whose services we commemorate today.[119]

Further evidence that the war years had buttressed the public-school games ethic can be discerned in the confidence with which the authorities of that other mainstay of the private pupil's sporting curriculum, rugby union, entered the interwar period. Proud of the hundreds of players who had died serving their country, including 27 England internationals, the RFU quickly reaffirmed its commitment to what was a central plank of the cult of athleticism: amateurism.[120] In a series of council meetings in 1919, the wartime practice of allowing professionals and amateurs to play in the same team was quickly abandoned, and the draconian prewar regulations prohibiting Northern Union players from having any association with rugby union clubs were reinstated.[121] This combination of confidence and pride was evident in an article published in *The Times* on 4 March 1919. Having 'lost more famous players than any of the other national games', the paper's rugby correspondent boasted, the sport would 'take over from football as the game for public schools and universities'. Indeed, such had been the sport's wartime record, the article concluded, that 'Rugby cannot help but become a great part of military training for which it is so curiously adapted'.[122] The interwar publishing boom in rugby union coaching manuals would appear to confirm the truth of this prediction. These manuals, the target markets for which were educational institutions and the military, made frequent references to the lessons of war and reflected, in the words of Tony Collins, 'the triumphalism that Rugby Union felt about its role in the British victory'.[123] In stark contrast, those controlling the two key professional winter sports, football and rugby league, were anxious to put the war years behind them and made little, if any, effort to commemorate fallen players. In part, as Tony Collins has pointed out, this was indicative of the different socioeconomic make-up of the two sports' members and supporters. The working-class communities, which provided most of the professional players and the bulk of the fan-bases for football and rugby league clubs, were less enamoured of the patriotic militarism and popular conservatism that underpinned many of the postwar rituals of remembrance.[124] However, the reluctance of the FA and the RFL to engage in the sort of self-congratulatory commemorative activities favoured by the cricket and rugby union authorities was, to a greater extent, a reflection of the public opprobrium that had been heaped on professional sport during the war. Indeed, the FA's awareness that the reputation of football had suffered a severe blow as a result of its war record can, as A. J. Arnold has pointed out, be seen in the fate that befell Leeds City in October 1919.[125] Having uncovered irregularities in the club's accounts, which suggested that the July 1915 regulation prohibiting the payment of players in wartime had been contravened, an FA disciplinary board chose to adopt the high moral ground, which they had so conspicuously failed to occupy in the first year of the war. Members of the syndicate that controlled Leeds City were barred for life from any future involvement with the sport, and the club itself was disbanded, its ground and place in the league pyramid being given to the amateurs of Leeds United.[126]

The Great War, therefore, saw the role of sport in British military and civil society closely dissected and widely discussed by the nation's journalists and authors. As the nature and costs of total warfare became ever more apparent, the questioning of the cult of athleticism as an ideal, or even adequate, preparation for the vicissitudes of war grew ever more intense. The need for a more scientific approach to the training of army recruits, which had been mooted during the South African War at the turn of the century, became generally accepted even by those for whom the games ethic continued to hold some of its pre-war allure. Yet, although the belief that playing games was directly correlated with military prowess may have been diminished by the British army's experiences on the Western Front, sport, nonetheless, retained in the popular consciousness its importance as a cultural signifier. In his recent survey of physical culture in Britain between 1914 and 1918, Tim Tate remarked that 'sport was a lightening conductor for wider anxieties about war'.[127] Certainly, the opprobrium heaped on professional footballers and, to a lesser extent, spectators at sporting events revealed widespread concerns in the first few months of the war about national degeneration. However, even the football league's most ardent critics were keen to differentiate between professional and amateur sport. John Astley Cooper, the founder of the Commonwealth Games, spoke for many when he told an audience at the Colonial Institute in May 1916 that amateur sport helped to counter 'the decadent influences at work within the British Empire'.[128] Of even greater significance, however, was the reassuring frame of reference for the home and fighting fronts that the idealisation of the nation's amateur sporting culture provided. Sporting imagery and language imposed some meaning and nobility on the chaos and horror of combat. Thus, notwithstanding the new-found appreciation of armed conflict as a professional rather than sporting undertaking, the amateur games ethos that underpinned so much of the war as sport rhetoric not only survived the industrialised fighting of the Western Front but was buttressed by it. Whether it would able to withstand the test of another total war, however, was by no means certain.

Notes

1. Tony Mason and Eliza Riedi, *Sport and the Military: The British Armed Forces, 1880–1960* (Cambridge: Cambridge University Press, 2010), pp. 60–65.
2. Dean Allen, '"Bats and Bayonets": Cricket and the Anglo-Boer War, 1899–1902', *Sport in History*, 25/1 (2005), pp. 31–32. See also J. D. Campbell, '"Training for Sport Is Training for War": Sport and the Transformation of the British Army, 1860–1914', *International Journal of the History of Sport*, 17/4 (2000), pp. 21–22, and Nic Clarke, '"The Greater and Grimmer Game": Sport as an Arbiter of Military Fitness in the British Empire – The Case of "One-Eyed" Frank McGee', *International Journal of the History of Sport*, 28/3 (2011), pp. 604–605.
3. *Minutes of Evidence Taken Before the Royal Commission on the War in South Africa (Volume II)* (London: Eyre and Spottiswoode, 1903), p. 108. *Bittereinders* was the name given to those Boers who fought on until peace was signed at Vereeniging in May 1902.
4. Campbell, '"Training for Sport Is Training for War"', pp. 24–25.
5. Peter Parker, *The Old Lie: The Great War and the Public-School Ethos* (London: Hambledon Continuum, 1987), p. 80.
6. Robert Hands, 'They Also Served – Re-evaluating and Reconsidering the Neglected', in Thierry Terret and J. A. Mangan (eds.), *Sport, Militarism and the Great War: Martial Manliness and Armageddon* (London: Routledge, 2012), pp. 107–110; Wray Vamplew,

'Exploding the Myths of Sport and the Great War: A First Salvo', *International Journal of the History of Sport*, 31/8 (2014), pp. 2306–2307.
7 *Daily Mail*, 5 October 1914.
8 Anthony Bateman, *Cricket, Literature and Culture: Symbolising the Nation, Destabilising the Empire* (Farnham: Ashgate, 2009), p. 42.
9 Michael Paris, *Warrior Nation: Images of War in British Popular Culture, 1850–2000* (London: Reaktion Books, 2000), p. 134.
10 Paul Fussell, *Great War and Modern Memory* (Oxford: Oxford University Press, 1975), pp. 25–29.
11 W. J. Reader, *At Duty's Call: A Study in Obsolete Patriotism* (Manchester: Manchester University Press, 1988), pp. 94–98.
12 *The Spectator*, 16 June 1917, p. 669.
13 James Roberts, '"The Best Football Team, The Best Platoon": The Role of Football in the Proletarianization of the BEF, 1914–1918', *Sport in History*, 26/1 (2006), pp. 36–37.
14 S. S. 143 *Instructions for the Training of Platoons for Offensive Action, 1918*, quoted in Roberts, '"The Best Football Team, The Best Platoon"', p. 37.
15 J. G. Fuller, *Troop Morale and Popular Culture in British and Dominion Armies, 1914–1918* (Oxford: Oxford University Press, 1991), p. 141.
16 Mason and Riedi, *Sport and the Military*, pp. 89, 105.
17 See Tony Collins, *Rugby's Great Split: Class, Culture and the Origins of Rugby League Football* (London Routledge, 1998), pp. 87–120. The Northern Rugby Football Union, or Northern Union, was the governing body of the professional game. In 1922 it changed its name to the Rugby Football League.
18 Colin Veitch, 'Sport and War in the British Literature of the First World War' (unpublished MA diss., University of Alberta, Edmonton, 1983), p. 37.
19 Gary Sheffield, *Leadership in the Trenches: Officer-man Relations, Morale and Discipline in the British Army in the era of the First World War* (Basingstoke: Macmillan Press Ltd., 2000), p. 45; Eliza Riedi and Tony Mason, '"Leather" and the Fighting Spirit: Sport in the British Army in World War One', *Canadian Journal of History*, 41/3 (2006), p. 498.
20 Brandon Luedtke, 'Playing Fields and Battlefields: The Football Pitch, England and the First World War', *Britain and the World*, 5/1 (2012), p. 99.
21 Iain Adams, 'Over the Top: "A Foul; a Blurry Foul!"', *International Journal of the History of Sport*, 29/6 (2012), pp. 813–831. Adams notes that the 'football charge' was limited to just a ten-month period, from the attack by the London Irish Rifles at Loos on 25 September 1915 to the East Surreys' ill-fated assault on the first day of the Somme, 1 July 1916. However, he also makes the point that the phenomenon petered out after the battle of the Somme not because of any diminution in the military's obsession with sport or use of sporting imagery but simply because the introduction of more sophisticated infantry tactics precluded the playing of football during an attack.
22 Adams, 'Over the Top', p. 823.
23 Simon John, '"A Different Kind of Test Match": Cricket, English Society and the First World War', *Sport in History*, 33/1 (2013), pp. 19–23.
24 *The Times*, 27 November 1914.
25 By December 1914, the *Daily Mail* and *Sporting Life* had supplied over 650 footballs to serving soldiers. Iain Adams, 'Football: A Counterpoint to the Procession of Pain on the Western Front', *Soccer and Society*, 16/2 (2015), p. 221; the *Daily Express*' Cheery Fund was even more successful, distributing, by July 1915, 18,000 footballs and 520 cricket bats. Peter Grant, *Philanthropy and Voluntary Action in the First World War: Mobilizing Charity* (Abingdon: Routledge, 2014), p. 20.
26 *Langtonian*, 10/2 (July 1918), pp. 345–349.
27 *Langtonian*, 9/4 (April 1917), pp. 162.
28 Samuel Begg, 'In the Wings of the Theatre of War: Behind the Centre of the Fighting Line in Belgium', *Illustrated London News*, 5 December 1914; *Gassed* was

commissioned by the British War Memorials Committee in 1918 and displayed in the Royal Academy of Arts in 1919. Iain Adams and John Hughson, 'The First Ever *Anti*-Football Painting? A Consideration of the Soccer Match in John Singer Sargent's *Gassed*', *Soccer and Society,* 14/4 (2013), pp. 503–504.

29 Iain Adams and John Hughson have argued that, as an artist who viewed his work as no more than 'visual reportage', Sergeant simply 'painted what he saw'. However, Anthony King has been inclined to regard Sergeant's work in general, and *Gassed* in particular, as possessing greater symbolic complexity. For King, the football match signified an army entranced by nationalism and blinded by their passion for war. Adams and Hughson, 'The First Ever *Anti*-Football Painting?', pp. 509–511; Anthony King, 'Sport, War and Commemoration: Football and Remembrance in the Twentieth and Twenty-First Centuries', *European Journal of Sport and Society*, 13/3 (2016), pp. 216–220.

30 Adams and Hughson, 'The First Ever *Anti*-Football Painting?', p. 509; Iain Adams, 'Football: A Counterpoint to the Procession of Pain', p. 220.

31 *Langtonian*, 9/4 (April 1917), p. 162.

32 *Langtonian*, 10/3 (December 1918), p. 404.

33 The other three correspondents were Philip Gibbs for the *Daily Telegraph* and *Daily Chronicle*, Valentine Williams for the *Daily Mail* and *Daily Mirror*, and Henry Nevinson for *The Times* and the *Daily News and Leader*. Martin C. Kerby, *Sir Philip Gibbs and English Journalism in War and Peace* (London: Palgrave Macmillan, 2016), p. 92.

34 *Daily Express*, 15 March 1915.

35 Sheffield, *Leadership in the Trenches*, p. 44.

36 The idea originated with Emma Cunliffe-Owen, who petitioned Lord Kitchener for the right to raise a battalion of over-age sportsmen; officially the 23rd (Service) Battalion, Royal Fusiliers. For more on the formation and service record of the Sportsman's Battalion, see Fred W. Ward, *The 23rd (Service) Battalion Royal Fusiliers (First Sportsman's): A Record of Its Services in the Great War, 1914–1919* (London: Sidgwick and Jackson Ltd., 1920).

37 *The Times*, 25 September 1914; 8 December 1914.

38 *Manchester Guardian*, 13 December 1916.

39 E. B. Osborn, *The New Elizabethans: A First Selection of the Lives of Young Men Who Have Fallen in the Great War* (New York: John Lane Co., 1919), p. 100. According to one of his fellow officers, Philipps died 'giving view-halloos as we advanced and shouting "Come on, boys", and waving his cap'. Josh Levithan, 'A View-Halloo from Colwyn Phillips' (14 March 2015), A Century Back: Writing the Great War Day by Day blog, <www.acenturyback.com/tag/colwyn-philipps/> [accessed 4 October 2017].

40 *Daily Mail*, 30 March 1917.

41 *War Illustrated Volume 8* (London: London Amalgamated Press Ltd., 1917), p. 2855.

42 *The Spectator*, 30 October 1915, p. 569.

43 *The Spectator*, 9 June 1916, p. 286. Crowdy was particularly taken by the second stanza of Hall's poem:

> Full sixty yards I've seen them throw/With all the nicety of aim./They learned on British cricket fields./Ah, bombing is a Briton's game!/Shell-hole to shell-hole, trench to trench,/"Lobbing them over" with an eye/As true as though it were a game,/And friends were having tea nearby.
>
> *The Spectator*, 2 June 1916, p. 264.

Despite Crowdy's poetic efforts, no statue was ever erected.

44 E. B. Osborn (ed.), *The Muse in Arms: A Collection of War Poems, for the Most Part Written in the Field of Action, by Seamen, Soldiers, and Flying Men Who Are Serving, or Have Served, in the Great War* (London: John Murray, 1917), p. ix. The anthology, which was republished in 1918, was, according to Stuart Sillars, 'the most celebrated collection of the war years'. Stuart Sillars, *Fields of Agony: British Poetry of the First World War* (Penrith: Humanities-ebook, 2007), p. 34.

45 Osborn, *Muse in Arms*, p. ix.
46 *Langtonian*, 9/3 (April 1918), p. 296.
47 *The Times*, 26 February 1918.
48 *Manchester Guardian*, 24 February 1917. In January 1915, on their way to the quarter finals of the FA Cup, Oldham Athletic had travelled to, and beaten, Croydon Common.
49 Sheffield, *Leadership in the Trenches*, p. 47. It is instructive that in R. C. Sherriff's enormously well-received play of 1928 (and film of 1930), *Journey's End*, the three officers who best embody leadership, Stanhope, Osborne and Raleigh, all excelled at sport in their public schools. R. C. Sherriff, *Journey's End* (London: Victor Gollancz Ltd., 1929).
50 *Vitaï Lampada*, to Newbolt's great surprise, became one of the 'most frequently quoted poems in the English-speaking world'. Cecil D. Eby, *The Road to Armageddon: The Martial Spirit in English popular literature, 1870–1914* (Durham: Duke University Press, 1988), p. 105. Indeed, Newbolt's reputation as a spokesperson for the imperial cause was such by the outbreak of the First World War that he was invited to attend the first meeting of the War Propaganda Bureau at Wellington House in September 1914. Gary S. Messinger, *British Propaganda and the State in the First World War* (Manchester: Manchester University Press, 1992), p. 92.
51 Henry Newbolt, *The Book of the Happy Warrior* (London: Longman's, Green and Co., 1917), p. vii.
52 Newbolt, *Happy Warrior*, pp. 263, 274. It should be noted that Newbolt does go on to say that the instruction received on the playing-fields of the public schools will need to be supplemented by some scientific training. Newbolt, *Happy Warrior*, p. 275.
53 Henry Newbolt, 'The Adventures of a Subaltern', *Tales of the Great War* (London: Longman's, Green and Co., 1916), p. 1.
54 *The Times*, 19 May 1917. David Monger has shown that General Henry Horne, commander of the First Army corps between 1916 and 1918, shared Smith-Dorrien's outlook. Monger has argued that Horne's devotion to the cult of athleticism and certainty that games were central to 'the formation of a soldier's character' was a legacy of his time at Harrow. David Monger, '"No Mere Silent Commander?" Sir Henry Horne and the mentality of command during the First World War', *Historical Research*, 82/216 (May 2009), p. 350.
55 *Daily Mail*, 3 November 1914. To public school men like Hillier, 'football' meant rugby union.
56 *Daily Mail*, 3 November 1914. The belief that sportsmen made the best leaders appears to have been an enduring one. As late as October 1918, Robert Graves recollected, in his autobiographical work *Goodbye to All That*, the final selection for officer cadets being made 'by watching the candidates play games, principally rugger and soccer'. Robert Graves, *Goodbye to All That* (London: Jonathan Cape, 1929), p. 203.
57 Osborn, *The New Elizabethans*, pp. 239–240.
58 *Daily Mail*, 15 September 1916.
59 *Daily Mail*, 3 February 1915.
60 H. W. Wilson (ed.), *The Great War, the Standard History of the All-Europe Conflict, Volume 8* (London: Amalgamated Press, 1917), p. 560.
61 John Horne, 'Introduction: Mobilizing for Total War, 1914–1918', in John Horne (ed.), *State, Society and Moblization in Europe During the First World War* (Cambridge: Cambridge University Press, 1997), p. 6.
62 Randal Marlin, 'Media and Propaganda: The Northcliffe Press and the Corpse Factory Story of World War One', *Global Media Journal: Canadian Edition*, 3/2 (2010), pp. 67–82.
63 *Manchester Guardian*, 26 February 1915.
64 *The Times*, 8 October 1914.
65 *Punch*, 14 October 1914.
66 For more on the extent of the *Daily Mail's* Germanophobia, see Adrian Gregory, *The Last Great War: British Society and the First World War* (Cambridge: Cambridge University Press, 2008), pp. 47–55.

67 *Daily Mail*, 21 December 1914.
68 *Daily Mail*, 11 January 1916.
69 Alfred Harmsworth, *Lord Northcliffe's War Book: With Chapters on America at War* (New York: George H. Doran Company, 1917), p. 86.
70 *Daily Mail*, 11 November 1916.
71 For more on the *Emden's* raids, see Dan van der Vat, *Gentlemen of War: The amazing story of Commander Karl von Muller and the SMS Emden* (New York: Book Sales, 1984).
72 Arthur Conan Doyle, *The German War: Some Sidelights and Reflections* (London: Hodder & Stoughton, 1914), pp. 92–93.
73 *War Illustrated Volume 2* (London: London Amalgamated Press Ltd., 1915), p. 570.
74 John Osbourne, '"To Keep the Life of the Nation on the Old Line": *The Athletic News* and the First World War', *Journal of Sport History*, 14/2 (Summer 1987), pp. 139–140.
75 Paul Jones, *War Letters of a Public-School Boy* (London: Cassell and Co. Ltd., 1918), p. 51. Jones was killed on the opening day of the Battle of Passchendaele, 31 July 1917. Tristram singled out Crystal Palace for special mention because it had been the venue for the FA Cup Final since 1895. Tristram's own sport of rugby union received far less criticism than football despite the season initially carrying own. Tony Collins has argued that the high enlistment rate of rugby union players, which forced the RFU to formally abandon fixtures on 4 September 1914, was the reason the rugby authorities got off so lightly. Tony Collins, 'English Rugby Union and the First World War', *Historical Journal* 45/4 (2002), pp. 802–804.
76 Colin Veitch, '"Play Up! Play Up! And Win the War!" Football, the Nation and the First World War', *Journal of Contemporary History*, 20/3 (July 1985), pp. 363–378.
77 *The Spectator*, 22 August 1914, pp. 260–261.
78 *The Spectator*, 22 August 1914, p. 292. In fact, with the cricket season more than half over by August 1914, and with a number of counties deciding to cancel their remaining fixtures, the cricketing authorities managed to avoid the level of vitriol directed towards the FA. Jack Williams, *Cricket and England: A Cultural and Social History of the Inter-war Years* (Abingdon: Frank Cass, 1999), p. 6.
79 See, for example, *The Spectator*, 29 August 1914 and 5 September 1914, p. 324.
80 See, for example, *Daily Mail*, 3 December 1914, and *The Times*, 24 November 1914. Jessie Pope's 'Play the Game' was published in the *Daily Mail* on 3 December 1914 and A. Lochhead's 'The Game' appeared in *The Times* on 24 November 1914. Lochhead encouraged footballers: 'Come, leave the lure of the football field/With its fame so lightly won,/And take your place in a greater game/Where worthier deeds are done.'
81 *The Times*, 7 November 1914.
82 Frank Reynolds, 'The Shirkers' War News', *Mr Punch's History of the Great War* (London: Cassell and Co., 1919), p. 22.
83 *The Spectator*, 16 February 1915.
84 Quoted in Simon Inglis, *League Football and the Men Who Made It: The Official Centenary of the Football League, 1888–1988* (London: HarperCollins, 1989), pp. 91–92. Although accurate figures are hard to come by, it has been suggested that, by November 1914, 2,000 out of the 5,000 professional players had signed up and a further 100,000 men had volunteered through footballing associations. James Walvin, *The People's Game: The History of Football Revisited* (London: Allen Lane, 1975), p. 93.
85 Quoted in Tony Collins, *Rugby League in Twentieth Century Britain: A Social and Cultural History* (Abingdon: Routledge, 2006), p. 10. It is hardly surprising that *Athletic News* lent its support to the football authorities. As John H. Osbourne has pointed out, its editorial board largely consisted of those who represented the interests of the professional football league. Osbourne, '"To Keep the Life of the Nation on the Old Line"', p. 138.
86 S. P. D. Mais, *The Public School in War Time* (London: John Murray, 1916), p. 105. As early as 1915, Edward Lyttelton, headmaster of Eton, had claimed in *The Spectator* that the war had caused the pupils to 'turn their backs on football' in favour of the OTC. *The Spectator*, 2 January 1915, p. 9.

92 The First World War

87 William Temple, *Mens Creatrix: An Essay* (London: Macmillan and co., 1917), pp. 231–232.
88 *The Spectator*, 10 June 1916, p. 716.
89 *The Times*, 29 May 1916.
90 *The Times*, 30 May 1916.
91 *The Times*, 2 June 1916.
92 Newbolt, *Happy Warrior*, p. 274. Newbolt's mention of 'verse' was a reference to Rudyard Kipling's poem *The Islanders*, which was published in *The Times* on 4 January 1902.
93 Marie Corelli, *My "Little Bit"* (New York: George H. Doran Company, 1919), p. 130.
94 F. B. Malim, 'Athletics', in A. C. Benson (ed.), *Cambridge Essays in Education* (Cambridge: Cambridge University Press, 1917), p. 167.
95 Alec Waugh, *The Loom of Youth* (London: Methuen Ltd., 1917), p. 263. Such was the book's popularity, no doubt fuelled by the furore caused by Waugh's allusion to the existence of homosexual relationships within the public-school community, that it was reprinted eight times before the end of the war. Waugh, much to his dismay, was dismissed from the Old Shirburnian Society as a result of the book's notoriety. See Harold Orel, *Popular Fiction in England, 1914–1918* (Lexington: University of Kentucky Press, 1992), pp. 135–146.
96 Waugh, *Loom of Youth*, p. 263.
97 *Daily Mail*, 9 October 1914.
98 George Mosse, *Fallen Soldiers: Reshaping the Memory of the World War* (Oxford: Oxford University Press, 1990), pp. 190–191.
99 Iain Adams, 'A Game for Christmas? The Argylls, Saxons and Football on the Western Front, December 1914', *International Journal of the History of Sport*, 32/11–12 (2015), p. 1410.
100 *War Illustrated Volume 7* (London: London Amalgamated Press Ltd., 1917), p. 2212; *The Times*, 11 September 1914.
101 *Daily Mail*, 25 January 1915; *War Illustrated Volume 8*, p. 2564.
102 *The Times*, 19 August 1914. It was, undoubtedly, no coincidence that Vernede's call to enlist, directed as it was at the amateur sportsman as the reference to cap and blazer makes clear, came at the same time as *The Times* was leading the campaign against the continuation of professional football.
103 *Sporting Times*, 6 March 1915, quoted in Luedtke, 'Playing Fields and Battlefields', p. 112.
104 Collins, 'English Rugby Union', p. 809.
105 *The Spectator*, 10 October 1914, p. 484; 9 January 2015, p. 33; *War Illustrated Volume 2* (London: London Amalgamated Press, 2015), p. 383; Ward, *The 23rd (Service) Battalion Royal Fusiliers*, p. 4. Claude Burton wrote patriotic verse for the *Daily Mail* under the pseudonym Touchstone.
106 Ole Luk-Oie, *The Great Tab Dope and Other Stories* (London: William Blackwood and Sons, 1915), p. 366. Swinton's pseudonym Ole Luk-Oie, sometimes translated as the Sandman, came from a fairy tale by Hans Christian Andersen.
107 Luk-Oie, *Great Tab Dope*, p. 368.
108 For most commentators, cricket was viewed as an amateur sport, although, of course, it had a long tradition of employing professionals. For more on the importance of cricket in shaping English national identity, see Brian Stoddart, 'Sport, Cultural Imperialism, and Colonial Response in the British Empire', *Comparative Studies in Society and History*, 30/4 (October 1988), pp. 658–659; and Dean Allen, 'England's "golden age": Imperial Cricket and Late Victorian Society', *Sport in Society: Cultures, Commerce, Media, Politics*, 15/2 (March 2012), pp. 209–226.
109 *Daily Mail*, 18 May 1915.
110 *The Spectator*, 18 February 1915, p. 82.

The First World War 93

111 Ernest Raymond, *Tell England: A Study in a Generation* (New York: George H. Doran, 1922), pp. 287, 312. *Tell England* remained in print until the 1940s and sold 300,000 copies by 1939. Dan Todman, *The Great War: Myth and Memory* (London: Hambledon Continuum, 2005), p. 133.
112 *The Spectator*, 6 July 1918, p. 9.
113 *The Times*, 19 February 1919.
114 Stuart Sillars, *Art and Survival in First World War Britain* (Basingstoke: Macmillan Press Ltd., 1987), p. 137.
115 Williams, *Cricket and England*, p. 6.
116 C. F. Kernot, *British Public School War Memorials* (London: Roberts and Newton Ltd., 1927), pp. 124, 213, 232 and 236.
117 Kernot, *War Memorials*, p. 206.
118 Kernot, *War Memorials*, pp. 7, 124, 130, 208, 213, 240, 257 and 144.
119 Quoted in Kernot, *War Memorials*, p. 206.
120 Although professionals did play cricket, the game was, nonetheless, popularly viewed as an amateur one. See Stephen Wagg, '"Time Gentlemen Please": The Decline of Amateur Captaincy in English County Cricket', in Adrian Smith and Dilwyn Porter (eds.), *Amateurs and Professionals in Post-war British Sport* (London: Frank Cass, 2000), pp. 31–59.
121 Collins, *Rugby League in Twentieth Century Britain*, pp. 18–21.
122 *The Times*, 4 March 1919. Certainly, rugby union suffered a high death toll; 27 England internationals were killed in the war. However, other sports were less assiduous in keeping records, so no clear comparisons can be made. See Collins, *Rugby League in Twentieth Century Britain*, p. 19.
123 Tony Collins, 'Amateurism and the Rise of Managerialism: The Case of Rugby Union, 1871–1995', *Sport in History*, 30/1 (2010), p. 110.
124 Collins, *Rugby League in Twentieth Century Britain*, pp. 20–22.
125 A. J. Arnold, '"Not Playing the Game?" Leeds City in the Great War', *International Journal of the History of Sport*, 7/1 (1990), pp. 111–119.
126 *The Times*, 14 October 1919; 20 October 1919.
127 Tim Tate, *For Team and Country: Sport on the Frontlines of the Great War* (London: John Blake Publishing Ltd., 2014), p. vii.
128 *Daily Mail*, 25 May 1916.

4 The Second World War
Winning in the 'ashes of civilisation'

In April 1939, the directors of Brentford F. C. placed a notice in the *Evening Standard* announcing the enrolment in the War Reserve Police of the club's entire squad.[1] Other teams quickly followed suit, with West Ham United, Bolton Wanderers and Liverpool all taking steps to ensure that the volunteerism of their professionals did not go unnoticed by the wider public.[2] The alacrity with which these teams responded, and, critically, were being seen to respond, to the call of patriotic duty on the eve of war is revealing of the football industry's new-found confidence in its role in British society. After the public condemnation of 1914–1918, the game had been rehabilitated in the interwar years, with widespread coverage in the popular media broadening its appeal to the suburban middle classes.[3] In-depth features and behind-the-scenes reporting by the tabloid press and newsreel companies turned professional players into national celebrities.[4] Such was the elevated status of football by the onset of war that a Mass Observation survey, published in 1940, could confidently claim that 'the sport . . . [is] as important to the masses as politics or religion'.[5] Although, perhaps, the most egregious example, football's dramatic rise in popularity in the 1920s and 1930s was by no means exceptional. Sport as a whole enjoyed a boom in the interwar years. As Jeffrey Hill has observed, by the mid-1930s a range of sporting activities, from traditional games like cricket to recent imports like speedway, had developed efficient commercial set-ups and, consequently, attracted new consumers.[6] With, then, sport assuming an ever more important place in popular culture, it was inevitable that there would be, to use James Walvin's phrase, a 'sea change' in the attitude of the ruling elite to sport and the role it could play in times of national crisis.[7]

Although most of the literature on sport and the British experience of total warfare has explored the First rather than the Second World War, where the focus has fallen on 1939–1945, it has been, unsurprisingly, this shift in government attitude that has received the most attention. For Neil Wigglesworth, Tony Mason and Eliza Riedi, the authorities' move towards a more favourable stance was underpinned by a belief that sport had become increasingly important in sustaining morale on the home front.[8] In support of this view, Mason and Riedi have pointed out that there were enormous numbers of troops, both non-combat and, between Dunkirk and D-Day, combat, stationed in Britain during the Second World War, and these men required some form of healthy diversion during their off-duty hours.[9] However, Matthew Taylor has presented a more nuanced interpretation. While accepting that the maintenance of morale played a part in shaping official policy towards sport, he has contended that there was, nonetheless, 'a matrix of shifting considerations and interests', not least of which were concerns over public safety and wartime waste.[10] The ambivalence of the government's position has also been noted by Robert Mackay. Ministers might well have tolerated sport as a distraction from the vicissitudes of war when Britain was in no immediate danger, but, he has argued, 'in times of national emergency it was not considered a priority'.[11]

The attitude of the armed forces towards sport has proven to be a less divisive issue. There is general agreement that the military valued team games and physical endeavour as an aid to fitness and esprit de corps and that it remained wedded to a comprehensive sporting agenda for these purposes. However, cracks in this consensus do begin to appear when the focus falls on the long-held belief that sporting prowess served as a useful measure of officer qualities. Jonathan Fennell, in his exhaustive study of British and Commonwealth Armies in the Second World War, has stressed the shift towards a more scientific approach to officer recruitment based on 'rigorous psychological and military situational tests'.[12] By contrast, Mason and Riedi have suggested that a significant number of senior commanders retained an unerring faith in good old-fashioned instinct and continued to lay great store by the Victorian model of the sporting warrior.[13] And, certainly, the Corinthian ideals of an earlier age were still evident in the Army Sport Control Board's war years' handbook. 'A sportsman', it was asserted in the preface, 'is one who: 1. Plays the game for the game's sake; 2. Plays for his side and not for himself; 3. Is a good winner and a good loser; 4. Accepts all decisions in a proper spirit; 5. Is chivalrous to a defeated opponent; 6. Is unselfish and always ready to help others to become proficient.'[14]

Michael Paris has claimed that this idealisation of the amateur sporting spirit stretched beyond the ranks of the military and was so deeply embedded in British popular culture generally that journalists and authors still felt able, despite the experience of 1914–1918, to portray the war using the romanticised imagery of earlier conflicts.[15] Although the evidence here is less than clear-cut, what does seem more certain is that many, if not the majority of, Britons continued to regard themselves as a sporting people. For all classes, sportsmanship and fair play were considered to be defining national characteristics. As Mike Huggins has shown, in the interwar years even professional sports like football were packaged for their largely working-class audiences in the language and values of amateurism.[16] The continuing hold of this Victorian cult of athleticism was, as one might expect, particularly strong in the public schools. Norman Longmate, a 14-year-old schoolboy at Christ's Hospital in leafy West Sussex when war broke out, recalled with bemusement his classmates' reaction when he opted to substitute the traditional games afternoon with voluntary war work: 'Curiously enough to work on a farm instead of playing games was regarded as rather unpatriotic. What contribution boys idling their afternoons away on the cricket or rugger pitch were making to the war effort I never discovered.'[17] What, of course, Longmate failed to appreciate was that sport for the British, even as late as 1939, was as much about moral qualities as it was physical proficiency. As such, British sporting culture could serve as shorthand for the values and principles for which the war was being fought.

From the very outset of war, the ordinary Briton's passion for sport was used as evidence of the nation's ability to weather crises with stoicism and resolve. An editorial in the *Daily Mail* greeted the news of the Russian offensive against Poland on 17 September 1939 with a carefully drawn vignette of working-class unflappability:

> There's a war on, but ... men met at street corners and talked not of the Russian invasion of Poland of which the special newspaper bills were talking but of the previous day's sport. 'I would have got ten home draws yesterday', I heard one man declaring, 'if only the Pools had been running!'[18]

Although, in the immediate aftermath of the declaration of war, fears over public safety persuaded the government to prohibit all events that involved mass gatherings, this proved to be only a temporary measure, and very quickly a full sporting programme resumed, with football, in particular, flourishing.[19] In stark contrast to 1914–1918, this resumption was greeted with almost universal acclaim. The *Daily Mail* was keen to acknowledge sport's critical role in the maintenance of morale. 'Sport and recreation', the editor informed the paper's readers, 'are necessary to a nation enduring the strain of war. We are all soldiers of a sort in this war. And every wise commander in history has known that troops must be kept in good temper.'[20] Organising and attending sporting fixtures could also be refashioned as acts of defiance in the face of German aggression. *No Black-Out for Football*, a feature for *British Movietone News* that appeared in cinemas on 21 September 1939, accompanied scenes of football fans entering grounds carrying their gas masks with the jaunty commentary, 'Football in Britain absolutely refuses to be blacked out. And even if wartime soccer is a bit different, it is soccer just the same.'[21] Even *The Times*, the scourge of the FA during the Great War, was prepared to concede that the return of professional football 'might be no bad thing', although this somewhat guarded welcome was tempered further by the observation that most matches 'will, in their essence, be friendlies'. This, the paper's editor hoped, would mean that 'without the pressure of league points, football may return in spirit to an earlier, more delectable, and less strenuous age'.[22]

In the first few months of the war, sport's governing bodies went to great lengths to ensure that there was no repetition of the public opprobrium they had received in the last war. Both the Rugby Football Union and the Rugby Football League were quick to associate their respective codes with the war effort by encouraging clubs to support war charities and offering grounds up for military use.[23] The MCC immediately cancelled Test and county cricket while letting it be known that a series of fund-raising games would be held at Lord's.[24] But it was the football authorities, desperate to avoid the condemnation of the 1914–1915 season, which took the greatest care to accede to, and to be seen to be acceding to, official directives. Over the course of September 1939, *The Times* regularly reported on the progress and results of the Football Association's and the Football League's collaboration with various government departments. Safety was prioritised by limiting spectators, waste minimised by establishing regional competitions, and the war effort protected by restricting matches to Saturdays and public holidays.[25] Yet, even these efforts were not enough to deflect fully public criticism. Although the imposition of conscription on the day war was declared precluded any possibility that professional footballers would again be condemned for not enlisting, there was, nonetheless, a residual belief that they were still not fully meeting their patriotic duties. In particular, it was felt that footballers were frequently being offered cushy numbers within the ranks of the Army Physical Training Corps. Typical of this view was a piece in the *Manchester Guardian* that asserted, 'there was considerable [public] dissatisfaction . . . that well-known footballers were, at once, made sergeant-instructors and given week-end leave regularly to maintain their practice'.[26] The fact that it was the FA that had come up with this scheme provided enough substance for accusations about the favourable treatment of sportsmen to be raised in Parliament in January 1940, and for the inspector of Physical Training, Colonel T. H. Wand-Tetley, to issue a public rebuttal. In a statement, printed in full by the *Manchester Guardian* on 18 January 1940, Wand-Tetley insisted,

> These men are doing a real job of work in the Army, and are serving the nation admirably. Far from having an easy time, physical and recreational instructors are some of the hardest-worked men in the Army. They are kept busy from eight in the morning until five o'clock tea, and after supper they open the gymnasia again and are responsible for providing the troops with all kinds of recreation, from darts to dances. By their experience gained from sport these instructors know the best P. T. methods to adopt. Irreparable damage can be done to recruits if the training is too severe. In the last war there were many cases of heart trouble caused by inspectors who did not know their business.[27]

This, at least temporarily, seems to have stemmed the worst of the criticism, although low-level grumbling about the preferential service conditions of elite sportsmen continued to rumble on for much of the rest of the war.[28]

Wartime sport may have enjoyed greater public acceptance in the early stages of the Second World War than it had in the Great War, but that does not mean that episodes of intense scrutiny and disapproval were avoided entirely. In moments of national crisis, attitudes towards sport hardened. The threat of invasion in the summer of 1940, the German Offensive against Russia in June 1941 and the fall of Singapore in February 1942 all led to upsurges in public condemnation, and government restriction, of sporting events.[29] Thus, as Allied troops fought for their lives on the beaches of Northern France in May 1940, an editorial in *The Times*, entitled 'Are We at War?', pressed for the cessation of all 'inappropriate pursuits'. 'Horse and greyhound racing', the paper's readers were lectured, 'employ people who might be doing useful productive work, and waste paper and petrol without helping the national war effort.'[30] Cinema-goers were treated to a similarly censorious message the day after Germany launched Operation Barbarossa in June 1941. Covering the wartime Derby at Newmarket, *Pathé Gazette* matched scenes of crowded stands and packed carparks with a voice-over dripping with disapproval:

> We agree with the authorities that war workers should have occasional relaxation, but we find it difficult to believe that these tens-of-thousands are war-workers who can be spared in mid-week; or that the use of petrol to bring thousands of cars to Newmarket for the substitute Derby is helpful to the war effort. Our already heavily taxed railways had to run trains in several sections. Somehow those sorts of things don't sound right in wartime. What do you think?[31]

For one *Times*' correspondent, even reading about racing when the nation was fighting for survival was unpatriotic. In a letter published during the 1941 Cheltenham Festival, Mr A. Ford of Brighton expressed his astonishment 'that 75 per. cent. of [a London evening paper's] total reading contents was devoted to horse or greyhound racing'. 'Apart', he reasoned, 'from the irksomeness of this, one cannot help thinking that this encouragement to gambling is not a contribution to the war effort, and that the paper used in the publication of these so-called "Sporting Editions" might have been employed in preventing the reduction in size of ordinary newspapers.'[32] Indeed, so febrile was the atmosphere in the summer of 1941 that institutions and sports, which rarely attracted censure, nonetheless took steps to advertise their adherence to the new mood of asceticism. The editor of the *Langtonian*, the school magazine of Simon Langton Boys' Grammar in Canterbury, felt obliged to follow a lengthy summary of the year's sporting fixtures and awards with a carefully worded postscript distancing the boys from charges of profligacy. 'Let not our readers suppose', he cautioned, 'that we are wasting our substance in riotous living. On the contrary, the School has possessed for some time a flourishing Savings Group, and we are informed that the very substantial sum of £30 has been paid in to date.'[33] In a similar vein, the governing bodies of football and rugby league both made it known that, for the first time, savings certificates rather than medals would be awarded to the finalists of the 1941 Challenge and FA Cups respectively.[34]

Public questioning of wartime sport reached a peak in February 1942 following the disastrous news of the Japanese occupation of Singapore. In a much-publicised speech, Sir Stafford Cripps, the Leader of the House of Commons, pronounced dog-racing and boxing displays to be 'completely out of accord with the true spirit of determination of the people in this crisis of their history' and vowed to bring to an end the culture of 'pleasure as usual'.[35] This call for public self-denial received almost universal acclaim in the press.[36] Typical was the response from the editor of the *Manchester Guardian*, who welcomed the promise of a 'new spirit', which would, he hoped, 'in a matter of days, not of weeks and months', introduce 'restrictions on frivolous sports and on personal waste and extravagance'.[37]

Sport, during these periods of national emergency, was not only charged with squandering vital resources but also faced moral outrage. In May 1940, Sir Percy Harris, the Labour MP for Bethnal Green, supported a call for greyhound racing to be banned until the end of the war, arguing that the public found it 'irritating to have this great extravaganza at a time when such appalling sacrifices of men were being made overseas'.[38] The following month, as the situation in France grew ever grimmer, the matter was raised in the Commons once again. MPs from across the party divide insisted that it 'offend[ed] decency' for people to attend or bet on race meetings when Paris was 'fighting for its life'.[39] This sentiment received the backing of the editor of the *Manchester Guardian*, who likened attending a greyhound race in such 'tragic circumstances' to 'playing a noisy game of pitch-and-toss at the graveside before the mourners had turned away'.[40] Robin Arden Hayes, director of Studies for Engineering at Trinity Hall, Cambridge, was concerned about how the betting public's 'craving for excitement' would affect Britain's image abroad. As news reached London that Brussels and Antwerp had fallen to the Germans, he wrote to *The Times* to express his 'sense of shame' that

> at a time when the whole of the world must be listening in to British broadcasts, when the life of France, of our own Army in France, and of all nations who love liberty seems to hang by the slenderest thread, our news bulletins should be associated with racing results. It is easy to imagine the feelings of our French, Norwegian, Dutch, or Belgium allies who should happen to be listening in, and I am certain that those feelings must be shared by millions of our own countrymen.

Clearly doubtful that the government would proscribe racing, Hayes finished with the exasperated plea that 'if anyone still needs racing results . . . then at least let us keep the deplorable fact out of the limelight instead of following broadcast news from France with news from the Turf'.[41] Although the moral assault on the racing fraternity died down as the threat of invasion eased, it was quick to resurface when the country faced another moment of self-doubt during the crisis of February 1942. A letter from Reverend Henry Carter, secretary of the temperance and social welfare department of the Methodist Church, which appeared in the *Manchester Guardian* on 3 March under the heading 'Moral Values', typified this new onslaught against the sporting world. 'It is time', Carter harangued the paper's readers,

> for citizens who really care about moral values in national life to speak up. . . . Vested interests, after their fashion, are striving to hold out as much as they can against the demand for the suppression of frivolous 'sports' and the elimination of personal extravagance. Those who believe that the national character will ultimately determine the future of Britain and its place of service in the world should be insistent that neither self-gratification nor money power should bar the way to drastic moral action. . . . All this is not primarily a question of a saving of petrol, paper, labour, and money, though that is

involved. It is that mankind is on its trial . . . that on the present quality of our personal and public life depends the future of the world in which our children, and our children's children, will dwell.[42]

Similar ethical concerns had, in fact, been raised briefly in Parliament the year before as fuel shortages had begun to bite. During a Commons' debate in July 1941, Manny Shinwell, the firebrand Labour MP for Seaham Harbour, had, in typically blunt fashion, challenged the government stance on sport by confronting Herbert Morrison, the home secretary, with the moral case for discontinuing wartime horseracing: 'We had no right', Shinwell had thundered, 'to allow seamen to sacrifice their lives to allow a lot of lazy scroungers to enjoy themselves.' Although Morrison had stood his ground, his response had, nonetheless, hinted at a shared sense of outraged decency:

> If [the government] appeared to be taking the view that they were making it difficult for the public to enjoy themselves in recreations which some might think were a little over the line of moral rectitude he was not sure that they would get more out of the people.[43]

This exchange is particularly revealing. Not only does it illustrate the importance of morality in the debates surrounding sport on the home front but it also points to another critical factor: namely class.[44] For both Shinwell and Morrison, products of the respectable working classes, horseracing was the preserve of the idle rich.[45] Thus, their distaste for those who persisted in placing the pleasures of race-going above the self-denial of wartime living had as much to do with an abhorrence of privilege as an unease over ethics.

That press and government hostility towards race-goers sprang from a deep-seated class-bias was certainly the view of A. B. Clements, the editor of the *Sporting Life*. Although, for Clements, it was the poor not the rich who were the subjects of this prejudice. In a strident letter to the editor of *The Times*, published in May 1940, he took issue with the sanctimonious sermonising of some of the paper's readers:

> The virtuous wrath of your correspondents against the continuation of some forms of sport in war-time is misplaced. They write from Olympus, with little thought for the conditions under which the masses of workers live. There is an enormous number of people in our industrial areas . . . who are unfitted, by temperament and learning, for spending their leisure in the comfortable role of armchair philosophers; and for whom 'talking it over at the pub' may not be all-sufficing. They may work 12 hours a day, seven days a week, but they still need some relaxation besides sleep. Watching horse-racing, greyhound racing, or football may not appeal to most of your correspondents, and it is conceivable that most working men could appreciate more refined enjoyment, but they must get their entertainment where they can. . . . We must

beware that the war is not used merely as an excuse by the *unco' guid* for prohibiting those things of which they do not approve.[46]

Tom Harrisson, the social anthropologist who, along with Charles Madge, had set up Mass Observation in 1937, was equally sure that the campaign against dog-racing specifically was a case of the powerful disregarding the social practices of the powerless.[47] In an unofficial Mass Observation paper exploring the impact on national unity of Sir Stafford Cripps' February 1942 speech, he drew attention to what he saw as a divisive cultural clash:

> MPs and others in high income levels are much more likely to be ready to favour the restriction of things like greyhound racing which have a working-class appeal, an appeal especially to male physical workers with limited leisure opportunities.[48]

Certainly, the frequency with which the press and those in power singled out dog tracks as a blight on the country's war effort would appear to confirm the significance class played in the debates surrounding the suitability of wartime sport. Although there had been a shift towards middle-class tolerance of, even support for, greyhound racing and associated betting in the interwar years, the sport had still found it difficult to shake off entirely its reputation for profligacy, criminality and gangland violence.[49] With the nation embracing calls for austerity after 1939, it was hardly surprising, therefore, that the racing industry became an easy target, around which long-standing middle-class prejudices against working-class leisure could coalesce. Cripps' speech in 1942, of course, hardly helped to ease this class discord. Indeed, for the *Manchester Guardian*, the leader of the Houses' intervention was a step too far, and it felt obliged to draw its readers' attention to the prejudice inherent in the government's position. Noting that 'only two illustrations of the general principle – boxing displays, and dog races' had been given, the paper's editor insisted, 'If the poor man loses his dog-racing the rich man must lose his horse-racing.'[50] This form of, what Huggins has called, 'upwards ... class resentment' was also evident in the 1943 docudrama *San Demetrio London*.[51] Produced by the Ealing Studios' boss Michael Balcon, the film was based on the true story of a British oil tanker, which, despite being extensively damaged by the German cruiser *Admiral Scheer* in October 1940, still managed to make its way back to Britain with its cargo intact. For Balcon, the youngest son of impoverished Jewish immigrants, the story served a political agenda. With the action centring on the ordinary seaman of the Merchant Navy rather than the commissioned ranks of the more fashionable and socially prestigious Royal Navy, the *San Demetrio*'s heroics presented, for once, the opportunity to extol the courage and sacrifices of the working man, revealing him to be every bit as important to the war effort as the privileged elite. This core message of working-class moral rectitude was hammered home in one of the film's concluding scenes through a pointed allusion to a key sporting controversy of the summer of 1940. As barrel after barrel of the *San Demetrio*'s vital cargo is unloaded, the captain leaves the bridge with the bitter observation: 'That ought to be enough to take quite a few racegoers to Newmarket.'[52]

These periodic eruptions of public antagonism towards sporting activities, whether on the grounds of waste or morality, placed the government in a difficult position. The consensus in Parliament was that sport helped to boost morale, and, consequently, most cabinet members favoured a light touch when it came to any state intervention. As Sir John Anderson, the home secretary, explained during a Common's debate in May 1940, 'if workers were to maintain their efficiency for more than a limited period some measure of relaxation was necessary. [The government is], therefore, anxious to avoid interfering unduly with facilities for sport and recreation.'[53] Further impetus to this hands-off approach was given by the government's desire to avoid, at all costs, becoming embroiled in the class resentments that any undue interference with horse and greyhound racing was bound to generate. Thus, when a limited horse-racing programme was resumed in September 1940, the prohibitions on less socially exclusive entertainments like dog-tracks and the football pools were, despite intense opposition, also lifted. Yet, it was also vital that Westminster should be seen to be taking the war seriously. This led, as has already been shown, to outright bans on some sporting activities being introduced during the dark days of the Battle of Britain. However, these were short-lived, and even at the height of the crisis in 1942, a moderate line was still maintained, with the government resisting the more extreme demands for permanent bans that appeared in the press.[54]

Indeed, just how committed the government was to wartime sport can be gauged by this refusal to bow to outside pressure, particularly during the poisonous press campaign in the aftermath of the fall of Singapore. Led by two of the *Daily Express*'s most influential reporters, Frank Butler and Trevor Evans, coverage of greyhound races and boxing matches in early 1942 repeatedly played on pre-war prejudices of corruption and immorality.[55] Typical was a first-hand account by Evans of a greyhound meeting at Stamford Bridge, which appeared in the *Express* on 27 February 1942. Under the sensationalist tag 'Refugees Bet with Rolls of Fivers', the piece was quick to place the event outside the bounds of respectable working-class leisure by noting that 'war workers formed only a tiny proportion of the crowd'. There then followed a pen-portrait of a sport mired in the black-market, in which wartime suspicion of gamblers and outsiders formed a toxic admixture:

> Two old hands at greyhound racing, who claimed they knew the crowds 'inside out', assured me that a crowd of at least two hundred follow the London meeting day after day, week in, week out. They told me the most conspicuous of these migrants are foreign refugees, mainly from France and Central Europe. I can confirm this was true of yesterday's meeting at Stamford Bridge. The accents of the voices in the tote queues, on the 6s 6d stand, and in the club room were over-whelming evidence. They play with big money. I watched rolls of five-pound notes being peeled off at the tote grilles.[56]

Although Evans' and Butler's reports represented the high (or maybe that should be low) point of the newspapers' campaign against racing, from the very outset of hostilities, sport in general had been marginalised by the press and treated as, at best, incidental, and, at worst, detrimental to the war effort. This shift in attitude was most obviously manifested in the reduction in column inches set aside for sports reporting. A Mass Observation report into the impact of paper rationing on newspaper content, published in May 1940, noted that, while the space devoted to general news remained largely the same, sports sections suffered the greatest cuts, with *The Times* reducing its coverage by 96 per cent and the *Daily Express* by 75 per cent.[57] Yet, how far this fall in press attention mirrored a genuine popular disenchantment with sporting culture is unclear. Certainly, both the *Observer* and Mass Observation agreed that sport had, for many, lost its appeal by the summer of 1940. However, they had widely divergent theories on why this was so. For the editor of the *Observer*, it was a new mood of defensive patriotism generated by the imminent threat of invasion that was responsible. 'Normal interests', he claimed, 'had gone, sport is being cancelled, and the people are asking to be armed.'[58] In stark contrast, Mass Observation felt able to offer a much more prosaic explanation. People had lost interest, not because sport had ceased to matter to them but simply because it was no longer what it used to be. 'Three of the most common objections to war-time sport', a file report on the press noted, 'were: "It hasn't the same atmosphere..." "I don't think they give their best on the field..." "Too tame; no competition."'[59]

Mass Observation was also doubtful that the press crusade against racing in 1942 truly reflected public attitudes. 'Sensationalist reporting', it was argued in a scathing file report published in March 1942, simply encouraged a vocal minority to 'react violently... and make itself much more conspicuous than the rest by *writing letters and showing strong feelings* [emphasis in original]'. By way of illustration, it was noted that Trevor Evans' targeting of refugees in his Stamford Bridge exposé had immediately prompted a supporting letter in *The Times* from Sir Waldron Smithers, 'a principal internment fan in the country'.[60] It was, therefore, almost certainly the case, the file report concluded, that 'dog racing would not offend even an appreciable minority of people if [it] had not been so greatly *emphasised* [emphasis in original] in the press'.[61] The use of the conditional here is, of course, particularly revealing. It may well have been the case that the wider populace had no innate antipathy towards dog racing, but it was what was believed to be true that was important, and public discourse was shaped, at least in part, by what appeared in the newspapers.[62]

Another important media outlet that not only reflected but also helped to mould popular attitudes was the newsreel. Established in the years immediately preceding the First World War, by the late 1930s newsreels had, in the words of the media historian Nicholas Pronay, 'joined the newspapers as suppliers of the sum of information and the range of interpretation upon which public opinion formed itself'.[63] Lengthier production processes and greater sensitivity to audience sympathies undoubtedly limited the scope of news the major broadcasting companies could, or would, cover, but producers and editors were, nevertheless, keen to address what were considered to be hot topics.[64] Thus, the continuation of major sporting events, and in particular of the horse-racing season, was an issue the newsreels repeatedly turned to between 1939 and 1945. The tone of this coverage, perhaps unsurprisingly given the close connection between newsreel owners and Fleet Street, followed a similar trajectory to that of the printed press.[65] Early criticism peaked in the first few months of 1942, albeit without ever assuming the vicious character of some of the *Daily Express* reporting, before quickly giving way to a lighter, more supportive style. Indeed, the speed with which the newsreels rehabilitated racing would appear to support Mass Observation's suggestion that the animus against racing was largely manufactured. As the crisis of 1942 receded and the popular mood in Britain lifted, the newsreel companies felt able to abandon forthwith the patriotic chest-thumping that had underpinned the moralising over waste in favour of a more sympathetic and empathetic approach. So, in *British Movietone*'s coverage of the St Ledger Stakes at Doncaster in September 1942, the commentary's gentle insistence, as the camera panned along endless rows of bicycles, that nobody could 'possibly be accused of wasting petrol' was a world away from the puritanical hectoring of just six months earlier.[66]

In striking contrast to the challenges the racing community faced during the crises of 1940–1942, professional football managed, for the most part, to avoid becoming the focus of parliamentary or popular censure. As we have already seen, collaboration and compliance were the hallmarks of FA policy from the outset of war.[67] Official requests to restrict or even, as was the case in Easter 1941, cancel fixtures were always respected.[68] Undoubtedly this willingness to subordinate the demands of soccer to the greater interests of the war effort helped to secure the government's stamp of approval. Yet, in many ways, administrators at Lancaster Gate were pushing at an open door. Such was football's popularity, especially in the industrial heartlands of Britain, that politicians were reluctant to criticise the sport for fear of alienating key war workers.[69] Indeed, wartime football, far from being denounced, was repeatedly endorsed by the attendance at matches of cabinet ministers and senior members of the royal family.[70] The media was equally supportive. As the Battle of Britain raged, the *Manchester Guardian* was quick to remind its readers that professional football was not an irresponsible self-indulgence but rather a much needed chance to relax: 'The game has', an article previewing the 1940–1941 season noted, 'a recreative value as much for the onlooker as the player that needs no special pleading; it will not interrupt the industrial effort and . . . will make only light claims on public transport services.'[71] The following year, the sport's benefits were once again extolled, this time for viewers of *British Gaumont News*. The voiceover for a short piece covering the FA Cup Final between Arsenal and Preston North End at Wembley in May laid stress on the game's role as a restorative:

> A good deal has been said against the holding of this Cup Final in wartime but a least it gave the opportunity for the services and other war workers to refresh their minds with complete change. It called for scores of police and others to be on duty but perhaps they found this duty not unpleasant. It's hard

to decide if we can afford this kind of festival today but we probably work better afterwards.[72]

In fact, so great had been professional football's rehabilitation since the dark days of 1914–1915 that its continuation during the hardships of Luftwaffe bombing raids could be considered as important for its symbolic significance as for its practical worth. Thus, the unveiling, in August 1940, of the upcoming league fixture list was greeted by the football correspondent of the *Observer* as a moment redolent with a potent combination of pride and defiance:

> When the time comes to write the history of the war, it may not pass unnoticed by the chronicler that as the Battle of Britain developed the Football League launched a season of competitive football. It is, at all events, no small act of faith and temerity on the part . . . of the League's flock.[73]

The following month Walter Farr of the *Daily Mail* presented in very similar terms an agreement between the FA and the Army Sport Control Board, which allowed professional footballers in the services to continue with their sporting careers. Having first noted, in an opinion piece published alongside the war news, that most of Europe had 'forgotten the very word "sport"', Farr concluded by conjuring up an image of a resolute Britain stubbornly and, to outside eyes, enigmatically maintaining its sporting heritage:

> The idea that men sit round a table working out schemes like this on the eve of blitzkrieg would certainly puzzle most of my Continental friends. But you only had to look at the faces of the crowd as they streamed out of the ground after the match (Millwall v Charlton) to realise that England is tackling the wartime sport question in the right way. You felt that each of them regarded the fact that he had managed to see a football match undisturbed as a kind of personal victory over Göring.[74]

The centrality of sport, and not just football, to a sense of Britishness was a conceit that was frequently returned to in the media. Typical was the 1941 British Council film *Island People, Lowland Village and Market Town*. Produced to provide both a domestic and an overseas audience with a timeless vision of Britain, the piece was an affectionate study of the nation's working week. Having covered a range of professions and roles, the final scenes focused on a people shrugging off their workday identities and resuming their true personas as all classes and ages relaxed by engaging in a wide variety of sporting activity, from skating to bowls, and tennis to cricket.[75] As had been the case in the last war, the latter, in particular, was thought of as having a heightened symbolic significance. Quintessentially English, the game was frequently, not least in the spring and summer of 1940 when the country's fate appeared to hang in the balance, deployed as shorthand for all that was good about the national character and spirit. Thus, in July 1940, *The Times* gave pride of place in its pictorial review of the war to an idyllic image of a local league match between the Hampshire villages of Hartley Wintney and Odiham. Accompanied by the caption 'Village cricket continues with as much keenness and local rivalry as ever', the picture's sub-text was clear: the soul of the nation had survived earlier crises and would survive the current one.[76] Local cricket as the purest embodiment of British (or, more precisely, English) resilience and temperament had also been a feature of the *Manchester Guardian*'s appeal for sporting equipment three months earlier. A defiant call for donations in April 1940 had opened with a loving description of the game that only a true Englishman would have been able to appreciate:

> To watch great players may be enthralling, but it can lack the zest of the local field and the enthusiasm of rival neighbours. It will take more than a war to stop the slow and sure innings, the forlorn and desperate batsmen, the steady and swerving bowlers, and the plodding fieldsmen.[77]

Similarly infused with notions of the game as emblematic of British stoicism was a report on Canterbury cricket week, which appeared in the regimental magazine of the Buffs in September 1940. Despite the curtailment of first-class cricket, meaning that 'no great players of the day' had been able to appear at the St Lawrence ground, the author was, nonetheless, keen to stress that this traditional sporting festival had been celebrated with the same dedication and intensity as years gone by: 'Regular pavilion habitués came wearing their Club colour on ties and hatbands. Not even Hitler could keep them from their yearly pilgrimage to the Mecca of Kent cricket.'[78] The idea that cricket in some way defined what it meant to be part of the wider imperial family was made explicit by the prime minister of Australia, John Curtin, the following year. In support of a proposal that five test matches between Australia and England should be played immediately after the war, he argued that such a series would be 'an effective way of demonstrating to the world the characteristics of the British race'.[79]

Cricket and football, as the leading summer and winter sports, may have lent themselves most readily to the idealisation of Britain's sporting heritage, but so deeply embedded in the popular consciousness was the belief that sport served as a vital cultural signifier that even horse racing, notwithstanding the wartime disquiet over its probity, could be used as a vehicle to celebrate the country's essential nature. The opening of the National Hunt season in January 1945, after an absence of over three years, was, in *British Paramount News*' coverage, presented as a moment of symbolic rather than sporting importance. As scenes of relaxed crowds checking meeting cards and placing bets signalled a return to normality, the buoyant commentary dwelt on the restoration of tradition. 'Much of the glory of pre-war Cheltenham, known as the Ascot of steeplechasing, was revived today', the narrator affirmed, by the return of 'this essentially English sport'.[80] Tradition was also the leitmotif of a *Times*' editorial on 'Derby Day' in June 1943. Although no longer held at Epsom on the first Wednesday in June, the 'ersatz' Derby at Newmarket, the paper's editor insisted, still retained 'its importance and prestige because, to paraphrase Tom Brown, "it is more than a race; it is an institution"'.[81] By way of support, he signed off by depicting the meeting as a unifying national festival that, at least in wartime, bore witness to the capacity of the British (and Britain's imperial subjects) to bear even the greatest misfortune with a calm good humour:

> Fiction and the distorting mirror of 'the write-up' occasionally offend by their blatant exploitation of the national weakness for understatement. The fictional hero after a raid will laugh off the holes in his fuselage and complain that what really worried him was the fact that the coffee in the flask was getting cold, but the editor of the *Times of Malta* was indulging in no flourish of self-conscious anti-heroics when she sent out an S.O.S. for the Derby runners at a time when the raids were at their worst. She was proving her loyalty to her public. Bombs could not be allowed to interfere with the harmless ritual of small sweepstake and smaller wager. For perhaps only five minutes in the year can news refer to any subject but one. That five minutes occurs tomorrow afternoon, when, in whatsoever far and fantastic places men find themselves, their thoughts will for a fleeting moment of time be set free from war, and the shout 'they're off' will be in no danger of being mistaken for a reference to the second front.[82]

The symbolic significance of Derby Day had, in fact, initially been raised by *The Times* two years earlier, although, with the anti-racing lobby in the ascendancy, the paper had chosen to focus not on the wartime substitute at Newmarket but rather on the suspended meeting at Epsom. An editorial, published on 11 June 1941, had viewed the traditional Derby as so pivotal to the nation's sporting culture and sense of identity that its restoration to the first Wednesday in June at Epsom had been employed as a reminder of why Nazism had to be defeated:

> We all have tougher jobs of work to do now, yet today remains Derby Day, and this day next year will be Derby Day. This assertion is more than an empty gesture. It is a declaration of our right to Derby Day. One, and perhaps not the least of the rights we are fighting for is that right to amuse ourselves in season, to be happy, to laugh, to put on holiday clothes, and live in the holiday spirit, unashamedly enjoying a spell of idleness, feeling no compunction at going all out for pleasure once in a way. Annually on Derby Day, England, with no small help from all the rest of the King's Dominions, has asserted this ancient claim. Derby Day, after all, is only a very obvious and superficial assertion of what one of the wisest of Englishmen, Sir Thomas More, knew to be the height of wisdom – the 'being merry together' which was possible on earth but would reach its perfection in Paradise.[83]

The Derby as a symbol of freedom was also evident in the 1939 propaganda feature *The Lion Has Wings*. Produced by Alexander Korda to promote the justness of the Allied cause, the fundamental distinction between liberal peace-loving Britain and militaristic expansionist Germany was firmly established in the opening shots by intercutting the harsh tramp of jackbooted Nazis with the happy chatter of Derby Day crowds.[84] Sporting culture and national identity were again interwoven in the film's final scene as Merle Oberon, Korda's wife, emotionally spelt out why Britain had to fight: 'We must keep our land. . . . [W]e must keep our freedom. We must fight for what we believe in – truth and beauty and fair play.'[85] The Boat Race was another iconic sporting event, which, although forced from its traditional setting by the exigencies of war, could still be deployed as a national institution worth fighting for.[86] So, in February 1945, the editor of The Buff's regimental magazine, *The Dragon*, recalled for his readers that the true importance of the race had been brought home to him when a squadron of bombers bound for the Ruhr had appeared in the skies above Henley-on-Thames just as the Oxford and Cambridge crews had been readying themselves for the start. This 'ironic contrast', he maintained, had served as a reminder of the reasons wartime sacrifices had to be made:

> But more than one of us down there on the quiet banks of Old Thames knew it was because of the young men in those throbbing giants up in the soft blue sky and of others like them in the waterlogged fields of Holland and elsewhere, that we should, all being well, see Boat-Races of peacetime quality again.[87]

Love of sport as a key British characteristic worth fighting for was frequently underlined by stressing German inability to grasp such a national obsession. The press reported with relish the more outlandish misconceptions of Nazi propaganda. In July 1940, 'Lucio', who produced a regular humorous feature entitled 'Miscellany' for the *Manchester Guardian*, took enormous delight in ridiculing a German claim that there had been 'a revolt [in London] against plutocratic cricketers'. 'The German wireless has just been putting out a story', he gleefully informed his column's readers, 'that people tried to destroy grounds at night. . . . This led to a sort of state of war between the population and the English sports clubs.' To ram home the sheer absurdity of this misinformation the item concluded on a farcical note: 'The next stage should be the news that in the absence of any Test matches this summer, Australia has decided to declare real war on England with body-line bowling by howitzer and siege artillery.'[88] The following week the same story was addressed in *British Gaumont News*' review of the annual Eton-versus-Harrow cricket match. Once again, the tone was mocking, although this time there was an added edge of steely determination:

> This year the Eton and Harrow match was played at Harrow instead of Lord's. At last we plutocratic freebooters are feeling the full weight of Hitler's anger. But there's another side to it; an old German gun which stood in the school was handed over for scrap on the same day. So, we shan't win the war exclusively on the playing-fields of the other place.[89]

The indomitability of Britain's golfers enabled *The Times* to launch an equally scathing attack on German propaganda in 1941. A set of light-hearted rules drawn up by the committee of Richmond Golf Club to cover 'every possible contingency' of playing during an air-raid had, a sarcastic editorial of 29 March noted, been treated by 'Dr Goebbels . . . with, if possible, more than his usual lightness of touch'. There then followed a damning critique of the lumpen nature of Nazi broadcasting, in which a lengthy golfing analogy was employed to illustrate both the hollowness of Goebbels' rhetoric and the ineffectiveness of Germany's bombing raids:

> Let us turn to Dr Goebbels and see how he deals with the matter [of Richmond's rules]. 'By means of these ridiculous reforms,' announced a German station, 'the English snobs try to impress the people with a kind of pretended heroism. They can do so without danger, because, as everyone knows the German Air Force devotes itself only to the destruction of military targets and objectives of importance to the war effort.' Curiously enough the German Air Force has lately given an illustration of this accuracy of aim on another golf course not very far from London. After some argument the committee decided to fill up a certain small bunker in the left-hand corner of a certain green. The work had just been finished when over came a German airman who presumably held strong views against making courses any easier. He might well have felt embarrassed by the riches of military objectives, for there were seventeen other greens; but with the perfect stroke he exactly reopened that particular bunker. The committee felt that it was useless to contend 'with the devil that was in his jerkin', and the bunker is now to be kept as a historical monument, a memorial of the most accurate approach shot ever played. Even German airmen cannot always live up to such a shot as that. . . . [He] cannot always take his time and his aim amid a perfect silence. His attention is distracted by the sudden barking of anti-aircraft guns and even night-fighters; and for just one fatal instant he fails to remember that rule of the game, so often dinned into him, 'keep your eye on the military objective'. If, then, he is a little inaccurate, if he misses the barracks and is bunkered in the hospital, the golfer at least will not blame him. The poor fellow is not allowed a second try, even with a penalty.[90]

Certainly, the determination with which Britain's citizen-soldiers pursued a full sporting calendar despite the war is revealing of the centrality of sport to the British way of life. Whether posted at home or abroad, on the fighting front or behind the lines, troops found themselves confronted by a dizzying array of sporting opportunities. As *The Times* noted in April 1940, 'wherever the Army goes, there goes sport.'[91] A glance though the pages of the regimental magazine of the Buffs is enough to confirm this point. Without fail, throughout the war years, each monthly edition devoted lengthy sections to reports detailing the regiment's extensive sporting exploits. Take, for example, December 1940. Over the course of ten days, members of the regiment based at its home depot in Canterbury played hockey against Maidstone under 20s, Dover Fixed Defences, the King's Shropshire Light Infantry and the Royal Artillery; rugby against the Royal Fusiliers,

110   *The Second World War*

Kensington Home Defence, the Royal Artillery and the Royal Engineers; football against the RAF and Simon Langton Boys' Grammar School, as well as finding time to squeeze in a squash match against the Royal Fusiliers.[92] And there was no let-up when England was left behind. In August 1944, a correspondent from the 5th Battalion, which had just arrived in Italy, was quick to reassure the magazine's editor that the men were 'making the most of it'. By way of proof, he noted, 'In no time at all two football pitches and a cricket pitch were going full blast.'[93] Even the more challenging conditions of the Middle East theatre failed to dampen the sporting enthusiasm of the men. Readers of the November 1939 volume of *The Dragon* were informed that within a week of arriving in Palestine, the 1st Battalion had not only uncovered 'an excellent squash court' but also 'organised swimming contests and established a sailing club'.[94] In this relentless pursuit of sport, the Buffs were by no means exceptional. *The Times* was full of admiration for the sporting facilities provided by the RAF in Iraq. An article published in February 1940 approvingly observed that the main station had

> a golf course, tennis courts, sailing club and bathing beach on a lake, and the kennels of the RAF pack of hounds, which hunt jackals and an occasional fox. These, together, with football, cricket and hockey grounds form some of the amenities which helped to sweeten life in a desert post some sixty miles from Baghdad.[95]

As one might expect, the military authorities gave their full backing to this perpetual round of sporting activities. The War Office, Brigadier-General John Charteris noted in an article for the *Manchester Guardian* in October 1940, regarded sport as not only 'the best way of meeting the threat of boredom' but also essential to 'the more important purpose of aiding the preparation of men for war'. To achieve this latter objective, Charteris continued, mass participation was considered to be crucial: 'The idea of gladiators, both in teams or individuals, performing for the delectation of the crowd has been discountenanced in every way.'[96] The Buffs were equally keen that men should play rather than watch. A note from the editor of *The Dragon* in November 1939 extolled the virtues of 'Stonyhurst football'. A throwback to the days before the sport's codification, it was pointed out that the key advantage of this version of the game was the fact that 'fifty or sixty a side can join in. This, therefore, ensures organised games being carried out by the maximum number of available men in a unit, instead of having the majority looking on at a few of the best players'.[97]

The practical benefits that were thought to ensue from mass participation were unquestionably at the heart of the army's drive to promote sporting activity. A War Office pamphlet on soldier's welfare published in 1941 defined sport as serving three main functions: 'to give healthy exercise, interest and amusement to as many as possible', 'to encourage unit esprit de corps and loyalty' and 'to teach men team spirit'.[98] The *Daily Mail*, reviewing the work of the Army Sport Control Board in August 1940, saw this inclusivity as evidence that the lessons of the previous war had been learnt. A lengthy and supportive piece outlining the military's plans to 'satisfy the sporting needs of the three million soldiers on guard in our island fortress' concluded with a quote from the Board's first president, General Sir C. H. Harington, on how important sport had been to the frontline troops of 1914–1918:

> How many times did one see a battalion which came out of the line battered to pieces and sad at heart at the loss of so many officers and men hold up its head again in a few hours by kicking a football or punching with a glove?[99]

Yet, the press was also keen to stress that another critical lesson had been taken on board since 1918: namely that sport was no longer regarded in army circles as the be all and end all. A special correspondent for *The Times*, who had spent a day on exercises with the Grenadier Guards in March 1941, advised the paper's readers that 'although the battalion still finds time for occasional football matches . . . athletic games do not occupy the place in training that might be expected'. The focus, he reassuringly continued, was now on 'weapons training'.[100] The same message had lain at the heart of an item covering the selection of pilots at the RAF's Initial Training Wing that had been published by the *Manchester Guardian* three months earlier. 'A Range of sports' may have been used to test the recruits' 'state of fitness', the anonymous author had insisted, but it was their knowledge of 'an intensive technical syllabus' that had really counted.[101]

However, some remained unconvinced by this apparent *volte-face*. Major H. A. Sisson, who had served as the deputy assistant director of Gas Services in the Great War, was concerned that there existed within the ranks of senior officers a reactionary rear-guard for whom brawn still took precedence over brains. In a letter to the editor of the *Manchester Guardian*, he urged moves to be taken to exclude from Army Selection Boards 'officers of the old school, more interested in sport than in science and engineering'; otherwise, he warned, there would be 'more stress on physical than on mental qualifications'.[102] And there was certainly evidence to suggest that Sisson's fear was not entirely without foundation. As British forces under General Archibald Wavell had swept the Italian 10th Army out of Sidi Barrani in early 1941, *The Times* had seen fit to give its seal of approval to Wavell's thoughts on 'the qualities essential in a high command' by revisiting the text of a speech he had delivered at Trinity College, Cambridge, on the eve of war. Clearly unfazed by his surroundings, Wavell had instructed his audience that '[n]o amount of study or learning will make a man a leader' unless he had 'character'. This quality, he had continued, could best be found on the sports ground: 'You all know and recognise it in sport, the man who plays his best when things are going badly, who has the power to come back at you when apparently beaten, and who refuses to acknowledge defeat.'[103] Admiral Sir William James, the chief of Naval Intelligence, and Sir Noel Curtis-Bennett, a board member of the British Olympic Committee and founder of the Civil Service Sports Association, were equally certain that sport did more than simply enhance physical fitness. The provision of sports facilities for every 'day school' would, James argued in a letter published in *The Times* in July 1943, 'pay colossal dividends' by not only building up the pupils' 'physical strength' but also 'raising . . . the moral standards of our race'.[104]

Curtis-Bennett was also looking to the future. His voluntary work as chairman of the National Playing Fields Association was, he declared in a speech to mark his retirement from public life, 'now of the utmost importance' as the country was in desperate need of 'sport to inculcate the ability for leadership among youth'.[105] That such beliefs were not entirely restricted to a few ageing establishment figures but rather had some wider purchase in the national consciousness can be discerned by the frequency with which the sporting achievements of servicemen who had been killed in action were given prominence in press obituaries. Typical was the notice in *The Times* announcing the death of Pilot Officer Rowland Mytton Hill. With just one sentence devoted to military matters, the short item read like a sporting roll of honour, in which Hill's receipt of 'every sports award' at Rottingdean School; his captaincy of Wellington College's rugby, football, hockey and racquet teams; and his subsequent victory in the South of England Lawn Tennis Boys' singles at Eastbourne were all covered.[106] In a similar vein, in Sub-Lieutenant Norman Parsons' obituary it was his schoolboy games career at Queen Elizabeth's School, Barnet, the award of colours for both rugby and football for four consecutive years, rather than his wartime service in the Fleet Air Arm that was singled out for special mention.[107] What both these notices implied about the conflation of the sporting and military worlds was made explicit in the obituary of Captain F. E. Allhusen. The qualities, it was noted, that had made Allhusen a 'superb soldier' were 'courage, fairness, and a love of sport'.[108] Indeed, so common was the practice of obituary writers regarding athleticism as evidence of greater worth that Ivor Brown, chief drama critic for the *Observer*, felt obliged to use his tribute to Prince Alexander Obolensky, the great England rugby union winger who had died in a training accident at Martlesham Heath Airfield in March 1940, as an opportunity to take a swipe at this 'middle-class moralising of games'. Obolensky had been a 'beauty on the field', Brown informed readers of the piece, which appeared in the *Manchester Guardian* in April 1940, and that alone was enough to make him exceptional without the need for 'misty talk about a thing called Leadership, which is apparently acquired only on green fields and in gymnasiums'.[109]

As in previous conflicts, the enduring hold that sport had on the British psyche was also evident in the regularity with which both combatants and non-combatants turned to sporting language and metaphors to make sense of the fighting. The war, a Mass Observation review of the public mood in late 1939 noted, was

> being treated by the press very much as if it was an enormous sporting event, in which one side brings down the other's aeroplanes, 15 love, then there is a retaliation, 15 all, and so on, to innumerable deuce games and sets stretching far beyond the horizon.[110]

And it was not just journalists, the review continued, but also the wider public who 'talked about [the war] in terms of the sport news'. By way of proof, a brief cameo of street life was provided: 'Two women and an old man are gossiping by a bus stop. "What about this 'ere war?" says woman, opening evening paper. "Well", says the old man and laughs. "Germans have the score 5–3"'.[111] This reversion to the cosy world of sport helped to not only simplify the complexities and chaos of war but also mitigate the misery and depredations of life on the home front. In his regular feature for the *Evening News* entitled 'Smiling Through', Joseph Lee, the paper's veteran cartoonist, frequently deployed chirpy sporting imagery to frame topical war stories.[112] Typical was his football-themed response to reports that Tripoli, the last remaining Italian-held city in Mussolini's African empire, had fallen to Montgomery's forces in January 1943. A middle-aged man, wielding a rattle and resplendent in scarf, hat and rosette, weaves his way down the road, as his wife confides to a neighbour, 'His team's had an away win. He's an Eighth Army supporter.'[113] Sport was also a useful way to convey the heroism of combat without having to dwell on the associated dangers. By equating the battlefield with the playing-field, the price that might be exacted for victory over the enemy could appear to be no higher than the risk of a sporting knock. Thus, for readers of the *Daily Express*, the sudden recall of Irish rugby union international Peter Doherty to active duty in November 1943 was presented in reassuringly familiar terminology. 'Lincoln [RUFC] would', a short item noted, 'have to do without Doherty because he is playing for the RAF in an international match against Germany.'[114]

The appeal of packaging the war in the language of sport reached to the highest echelons of power. At the height of the Blitz, Herbert Morrison, the home secretary, mobilised the nation's passion for football in an attempt to generate enthusiasm for a new governmental scheme to conscript firefighters. He was certain, he informed the country in a radio broadcast in January 1941, that

> the men to whom the call comes . . . will answer it with absolute readiness and determination to give of your best. . . . You will absorb and express the same spirit of aggressive sporting zeal that has made accounts of our defence against recent raids sound almost like reports of a football match – such thrusting keenness, such dashing courage have been shown![115]

Perhaps, though, the senior figure who was most inclined towards the sporting metaphor was Lieutenant-General, later Field Marshal, Bernard Montgomery, the hero of El Alamein. In a letter to Brigadier F. E. W. Simpson, the deputy director of Military Intelligence, Montgomery couched his first, successful encounter with Rommel in terms of a tennis match: 'I feel that I have won the first game, when it was his service. Next time it will be my service, the score being one love.'[116] Three years later the gentility of tennis had been replaced by the brutality of a much more vigorous athletic pursuit. In his personal message to the troops on the eve of 21st Army Group's thrust into Northern Germany, Montgomery used an extended boxing metaphor to present operations as the culmination of a protracted bout, albeit one that had emphatically not been conducted under Marquess of Queensbury rules:

> In 21st Army Group we stand ready for the last round. There are many of us who have fought through the previous rounds, we have won every round

on points. We now come to the last and final round, and we want, and we will go for, the knock-out blow. The rules of the last round will be that we continue fighting till the final count; there is no time limit. . . . We embark on the final round . . . with complete confidence in the successful outcome of the onslaught being delivered by our Russian allies on the other side of the ring. Somewhat curious rules you may say. But the whole match has been most curious. The Germans began this all-out contest and they must not complain when in the last round they are hit from several directions at the same time. Into the ring then, let us go. And do not let us relax till the knock-out blow has been delivered.[117]

Reprinted in full in *The Times*, the address received a ringing endorsement from Robert Barrington-Ward, the paper's editor. Taken by Montgomery's use of 'homely language', Barrington-Ward felt moved to conclude an effusive editorial on 23 February 1945 with a Shakespearean flourish:

We have always liked our battlefield metaphors to be taken from the more familiar fields of sport. 'I see you stand like greyhounds in the slips, Straining upon the start. The game's afoot.' That is today as appropriate as it is incomparable.[118]

But the sport that Montgomery most frequently returned to in an effort to conceptualise the war was cricket. Let two examples suffice. In the aftermath of victory at Alamein in November 1942, he warned war correspondents that although Rommel had been 'hit for six . . . we must not rest; we must hit him for six right out of Africa'.[119] The following year, in a letter to Lord Louis Mountbatten, he insisted that 'the 1st XI' would be required for Operation Husky, the Allied invasion of Sicily, as he had yet 'to get the thing on a good wicket'.[120]

Indeed, even before war had broken out, cricketing metaphors had been employed to explain the growing threat posed by fascist Europe. Britain's failure to stem German and Italian military aid to Nationalist Spain had been presented to readers of the *Evening Standard* as an egregious breach of cricketing conduct. A David Low cartoon, which had appeared in the paper in June 1938, had featured a combined bowling team of Mussolini, Hitler and Franco ready to deliver a grenade to a nervous-looking Neville Chamberlain.[121] The following year, as German troops had occupied Czechoslovakia, the Yorkshire and England opening batsman Herbert Sutcliffe had told the *Rotherham Advertiser* that Hitler's perfidy would have been avoided if only he had been 'educated in Yorkshire for . . . he would have learned the principles of sportsmanship and what it is to play a straight bat'.[122] Once hostilities commenced, cricket continued to be used as a frame of reference. Sir Home Gordon, the honorary secretary of Sussex County Cricket Club, who had served in the Air Ministry in 1918, perhaps unsurprisingly fell back on familiar ground as he faced the uncertainties of another war against Germany. 'England', he stated in the September 1939 issue of Sir Pelham

Warner's cricket magazine, *The Cricketer*, 'has now started the grim Test Match with Germany', the objective of which was to 'win the Ashes of civilisation'.[123] *The Times* was full of praise for this transmission of cricketing jargon to military affairs. An eye-witness account of the daring amphibious assault on St Nazaire in March 1942, in which the obsolete destroyer HMS *Campbeltown* was described as giving the dock gates 'a devil of a clout', was applauded for its use of 'the everyday vocabulary of sport'. 'That', the paper's editor insisted, 'is just what we landsmen and laymen wanted. No statistics would have availed. The hardness of the blow can only be described in general and picturesque terms.'[124] It was, however, the attritional aerial struggle over southern Britain in the summer of 1940 that lent itself most readily to the cricketing metaphor. As Michael Paris has noted, dogfights during the Battle of Britain, although clearly visible from the Home Counties, were remote enough not to dent the romantic image of air combat as a heroic sporting contest.[125] The press, particularly the tabloid press, seized on the cricket scoreboard as the easiest way of conveying the progress of Britain's fighter pilots during these tense weeks of attritional engagement. So, on 11 July 1940, the *Daily Mirror*, with the banner headline, 'RAF's battle score – 37', was able to celebrate another triumphant day over the Luftwaffe without having to resort to dense explanatory text.[126]

Yet, as the Battle of Britain raged, the incident that ultimately provoked a public debate on the appropriateness of using the language of sport to capture the drama in the skies had its roots in rather more vigorous physical pursuits than cricket. On Sunday 14 July, from a vantage point on the cliffs at Dover, the BBC's Charles Gardner recorded in tones of breathless excitement an aerial dogfight he could see taking place over the Channel. The commentary was broadcast a few hours later during the 9 O'clock News. Gardner's animated tone, far removed from the more sombre manner customarily adopted by BBC reporters, immediately caused a stir.[127] Both the *Daily Mail* and the *Manchester Guardian* likened the piece to the reporting of a boxing or football match.[128] For some, this shift in approach was too much. Reverend R. H. Hawkins from Carlisle found Gardner's manner so 'revolting' that he felt compelled to write in to editor of *The Times*. 'Where men's lives are concerned', he concluded in a damning rhetorical flourish,

> must we be treated to a running commentary on a level with an account of the Grand National or a cup-tie final? Does the BBC imagine that the spirit of the nation is to be fortified by gloating over the grimmer details of the fighting?[129]

Vera Brittain was equally appalled. Broadcasters such as Gardner, she argued in her autobiographical account of the war's opening stages,

> who treat war as though it were a blood-sport and describe it in terms of a cup-tie final, do not represent the spirit of ordinary men and women who offer cups of tea to crashed German pilots, or go out to rescue them in small boats when they fall into the Channel.[130]

For one correspondent to the *Daily Mail* it was the deleterious effect such reporting might have on the combatants' loved ones that was the greatest concern. 'The mothers of England are proud of their sons in the RAF', Donald Bibbs informed the paper's editor. '[D]oes the BBC imagine they care to hear a commentary similar to that on a heavyweight contest when their sons are fighting to the death?'[131] The gendering of criticism implicit in Bibbs' letter was made explicit in a Mass Observation report on Air Propaganda published in July 1940. Disapproval of Gardner's tone, it was noted in an appendix, 'was almost entirely confined to women (who also often dislike sport)'.[132]

Yet, such negative views, even among female respondents, were, the same report continued, the exception; 'the vast majority of people', it was observed, 'received [the broadcast] exceptionally well, and with actual active enthusiasm.'[133] Qualitative evidence in a subsequent Mass Observation file confirmed this conclusion. Two 'typical' respondents were quoted as regarding Gardner's commentary as 'exciting' and 'good for morale', although their likening of his tone to that more commonly employed in the reporting of such middle-class events as 'rugger' or 'boat race[s]' does cast some doubt on just how representative these views really were.[134] The attitudes of the working class were, however, addressed in a BBC Listener Research Report, commissioned as a direct result of 'the controversy aroused by [the] broadcast'. Having noted that Gardner's approach had garnered 'widespread appreciation' from 'large groups of manual workers', the report concluded on a cautiously optimistic note. Exceptional times, it was claimed, warranted exceptional methods:

> There is an appreciable amount of feeling that the 'football style' was only justified, if at all, by its complete spontaneity; i.e. a *policy* [emphasis in original] of treating war as sport would be asking for trouble. The replies of [industrial] welfare workers suggest that a large proportion of responsible and sensitive people do not like this sort of thing, contemplated in cold blood, but as their blood does not run cold in war, they appreciate broadcasts of this kind, however much they despise themselves for doing so.[135]

The Corporation's director-general, Frederick Ogilvie, was equally sure that 'people in all walks of life . . . found [the new approach] heartening and a tonic'. In a vigorous defence of Gardner's style, published in *The Times* on 22 July 1940, he argued,

> It would be a bad day for listeners – and that is the great mass of ordinary people of this country, faced at the moment with all the monotony and anxiety of waiting – if the BBC stood out of deference to the gravity of the situation, with bowed head and arms reversed.[136]

For once, Ogilvie even received backing from Basil Dean, the head of ENSA and long-time critic of the BBC. Writing in *The Sunday Times* a week after the broadcast, Dean was full of praise for Gardner's refusal to conform to the 'uninspired prose and flat microphone technique' of traditional BBC reporting. 'Last Sunday', he enthused,

> was one of those rare occasions when the BBC got up off its knees, and touched the deep pulse of the people's will to victory, an occasion for relief and not feeble criticism. This is an evil foe; and we must be allowed to exult in his destruction, especially when he is on his way to bomb our homes and families.[137]

Indeed, just how successful the new 'football style' was can be gauged from the fact that, although only meant to be 'an initial offering', it was quickly adopted as the accepted technique for the remainder of the war.[138]

As Britain found itself embroiled in another global conflict, the function of sport and its place in the life of the nation were once again brought into high relief. Although, within official circles, there was a new-found awareness and acceptance of the role sport could play in sustaining morale on the home front, this did not prevent some of the assaults on sporting culture, particularly working-class sporting culture, which had been all too apparent in the last war from resurfacing. In moments of national crisis, with the nation gripped by what Mass Observation neatly described as 'war puritanism', moral outrage was directed towards those sports, such as horse and greyhound racing, which seemed to be most distant from the amateur sporting ideals of an earlier and, in the popular imagination, more innocent age.[139] These moments were, though, relatively fleeting.[140] For most of the war, the public's vision of what constituted the national sporting culture was much more inclusive than it had been between 1914 and 1918. In June 1940, the *Manchester Guardian*, in an article eulogising sport as a 'unique part of England's heritage', was at pains to point out that the nation's sporting passion encompassed not just the playing of games but also 'the watching of sports and the learned, even pedantic study of sport'.[141] The backing the FA and the Football League received from the wartime authorities for the continuation of a professional programme certainly revealed a recognition that the boundaries of the national sporting life were not simply defined by the recreational player. This new-found appreciation of professionalism was not restricted to the sporting world. Although, in certain quarters, there was a residual belief in the sportsman's innate martial ability, the military, for the most part, regarded sport as an adjunct to, not a substitute for, professional training. However, that is not to say that sport did not, for many, continue to serve as an important frame of reference. Not only were sporting language and imagery used to make sense of a dislocated world but they were also mobilised to provide a beleaguered public with a sense of moral purpose and identity. In this, at least, threads of continuity with 1914–1918 can be seen.

Notes

1 *Evening Standard*, 15 April 1939.
2 Anton Rippon, *Gas Masks for Goal Posts: Football in Britain During the Second World War* (Stroud: Sutton Publishing, 2005), p. 10; Eamon Dunphy, *A Strange Kind*

of Glory: Sir Matt Busby and Manchester United (London: Heinemann, 1991), p. 80. In fact, the directors of West Ham had encouraged the club's players to enlist in the War Reserve Police as early as September 1938, in the aftermath of the Munich Crisis. Rippon, *Gas Masks*, p. 10.

3 Pierre Lanfranchi and Matthew Taylor, 'Professional Football in World War Two Britain', in Pat Kirkham and David Thoms (eds.), *War Culture: Social Change and Changing Experience in World War Two Britain* (London: Lawrence and Wishart Ltd., 1995), pp. 189–190.

4 See, for example, *Pathé Gazette's* 'Famous Football Teams at Home' series of 1936, which provided behind-the-scenes footage of, and brief items on, key players. The first club to feature in the series was (who else?) Brentford. *Pathé Gazette*, 39690, 'Famous football teams at home, No. 1 Brentford', 2 November 1936.

5 Tom Harrisson and Charles Madge, *War Begins at Home by Mass Observation* (London: Chatto & Windus, 1940), p. 275.

6 Jeffrey Hill, *Sport, Leisure and Culture in Twentieth Century Britain* (Basingstoke: Palgrave Macmillan, 2002), pp. 33–38.

7 James Walvin, *The People's Game: A Social History of British Football* (London: Allen Lane, 1975), p. 151.

8 Neil Wigglesworth, *The Evolution of English Sport* (Abingdon: Routledge, 1996), p. 111; Tony Mason and Eliza Riedi, *Sport and the Military: British Armed Forces, 1880–1960* (Cambridge: Cambridge University Press, 2010), p. 179.

9 Mason and Riedi, *Sport and the Military*, pp. 178–179.

10 Matthew Taylor, 'Sport and Civilian Morale in Second World War Britain', *Journal of Contemporary History*, 53/2 (2018), p. 318. A similar point has been made by Norman Baker, who noted that criticism of sport peaked with the war's low points. Norman Baker, '"A More Even Playing Field?"' Sport During and After the War', in Nick Hayes and Jeff Hill (eds.), *Millions Like Us? British Culture in the Second World War* (Liverpool: Liverpool University Press, 1999), p. 131.

11 Robert Mackay, *Half the Battle: Civilian Morale in Britain During the Second World War* (Manchester: Manchester University Press, 2002), p. 118.

12 Jonathan Fennell, *Fighting the People's War: The British and Commonwealth Armies in the Second World War* (Cambridge: Cambridge University Press, 2019), pp. 282–283.

13 Mason and Riedi, *Sport and the Military*, pp. 179–180.

14 Quoted in Tony McCarthy, *War Games: The Story of Sport in World War Two* (London: Queen Anne Press, 1989), p. 127. The Army Sport Control Board was established shortly after the signing of the Armistice in November 1918 with the nominal aim of overseeing and regulating all army sport. However, as Mason and Riedi have noted, it was also tasked with sustaining and promoting the ideals of amateurism. Mason and Riedi, *Sport and the Military*, pp. 113–114.

15 Michael Paris, *Warrior Nation: Images of War in British Popular Culture, 1850–2000* (London: Reaktion Books, 2000), p. 221.

16 Mike Huggins, 'Projecting the Visual: British Newsreels, Soccer and Popular Culture 1918–39', *International Journal of the History of Sport*, 24/1 (2007), p. 92.

17 Norman Longmate, *How We Lived Then: A History of Everyday Life During the Second World War* (London: Hutchinson & Co. Ltd., 1971), p. 196.

18 *Daily Mail*, 18 September 1939.

19 For more on the initial prohibition, subsequent resumption and scope of sport in 1939, see Matthew Taylor, 'The People's Game and the People's War: Football, Class and Nation in Wartime Britain, 1939–1945', *Historical Social Research*, 40 (2015), pp. 270–297; Tony Collins, *Rugby League in the Twentieth Century: A Social and Cultural History* (London: Routledge, 2006), pp. 74–75; Peter Davies and Robert Light, *Cricket and Community in England: 1800 to the Present Day* (Manchester: Manchester University Press, 2012), pp. 98–99.

20 *Daily Mail*, 16 September 1939.

21 *British Movietone News*, 537A, 'No Black-Out for Football', 21 September 1939.
22 *The Times*, 23 September 1939. Indeed, *The Times* was not alone in thinking that the war might, in fact, be beneficial to the professional game. Frank M. Carruthers, writing in the *Daily Mail*, felt that 'the most conspicuous feature of the new football [was that] the iron had gone out of the game, and there is nothing to be regretted about that'. *Daily Mail*, 23 October 1939.
23 Collins, *Rugby League*, p. 75; Baker, '"A More Even Playing Field"', p. 133.
24 Davies and Light, *Cricket and Community*, p. 98.
25 *The Times*, 19 September 1939; 22 September 1939; 26 September 1939.
26 *Manchester Guardian*, 24 January 1940.
27 For more on the FA scheme to enlist players as PT instructors, and the subsequent fall-out, see Mason and Riedi, *Sport and the Military*, pp. 183–185; *Hansard* HC Deb. vol. 356, col. 361, 23 January 1940 [Online]. www.parliament.uk/ [accessed 31 July 2019]; *Manchester Guardian*, 18 January 1940.
28 Mason and Riedi, *Sport and the Military*, p. 185. Indeed, as late as 1945, Tommy Lawton, the England centre forward, recalled being heckled by the crowd with jeers of 'Come on the D-Day dodgers' during an army exhibition match in Florence. Tommy Lawton, *My Twenty Years in Soccer* (Norwich: Heirloom, 1955), p. 113.
29 Taylor, 'Sport and Civilian Morale', pp. 324–328; Baker, ' "A More Even Playing Field?" ', pp. 131–132.
30 *The Times*, 28 May 1940. The same edition of *The Times* contained a spirited defence of horseracing by the paper's racing correspondent, Captain R. C. Lyle. His central argument, that the supply of war workers was not diminished as most of those working in racing were Great War veterans who were 'not fit physically, nor in some cases mentally, to be employed in any other capacity', was somewhat undermined the following day when, in a letter to the editor, he was sarcastically (and, it has to be said, rather insensitively) thanked for revealing that the industry was of little value as 'apparently, much of it can safely be left in the hands of the mentally deficient and physically unfit'. *The Times*, 28 May 1940; 29 May 1940.
31 *Pathé Gazette*, 38941, 'Wartime Derby at Newmarket 1941', 23 June 1941.
32 *The Times*, 20 March 1941.
33 *Langtonian*, 33/2 (July 1941), p. 177.
34 Collins, *Rugby League*, p. 75; *Derby Daily Telegraph*, 29 January 1941.
35 *Hansard* HC Deb. vol. 378 col. 314, 25 February 1942. [Online]. www.parliament.uk/ [accessed 31 July 2019].
36 See, for example, *Daily Mirror*, 26 February 1942 and *Daily Express*, 26 February 1942.
37 *Manchester Guardian*, 27 February 1942.
38 *Manchester Guardian*, 31 May 1940. For further details, see *Hansard* HC Deb. vol. 361 cols. 655–658, 30 May 1940. [Online]. www.parliament.uk/ [accessed 31 July 2019].
39 *Manchester Guardian* 14 June 1940. For further details, see *Hansard* HC Deb. vol. 361 cols. 1368–1369, 13 June 1940. [Online]. www.parliament.uk/ [accessed 31 July 2019].
40 *Manchester Guardian*, 20 June 1940.
41 *The Times*, 24 May 1940. Hayes was certainly not alone. In the same edition of *The Times*, there were two more letters making exactly the same point. In fact, Hayes' scepticism about the government's willingness to embroil itself in this issue proved to be unfounded, and all racing, both horse and dog, was suspended from mid-June to September. Mike Huggins, 'Sports Gambling During the Second World War: A British Entertainment for Critical Times or a National Evil?' *International Journal of the History of Sport*, 32/5 (2015), pp. 674–676.
42 *Manchester Guardian*, 3 March 1942.
43 *The Times*, 3 July 1941. For further details, see *Hansard* HC Deb. vol. 372 col. 1462, 2 July 1941. [Online]. www.parliament.uk/ [accessed 31 July 2019].
44 See Taylor, 'Sport and Civilian Morale', p. 331.

45 The *Manchester Guardian* had the same view about the socio-economic make-up of horseracing's clientele. An editorial of June 1940 considered it 'hard to think that many workers are able to get relaxation from a midweek afternoon's racing at Newmarket'. Instead, racegoers were portrayed as a car-driving elite who wasted petrol and failed to 'take the war seriously' or do 'something more useful'. *Manchester Guardian*, 14 June 1940. The paper returned to the same theme two months later after emergency restrictions on the racing season had been lifted. Implying that the decision was the result of 'wire-pulling in high places', the paper's editor concluded with the despairing question, 'must we really risk men's lives and squander our resources on imported petrol to indulge a rich man's sport . . .?' *Manchester Guardian*, 28 August 1940.

46 *The Times*, 29 May 1940. *Unco guid* is a Scottish term, which loosely translated means excessively religious or self-righteous. It's most famous usage is in the title of Robert Burns' poem *Address to the Unco Guid*, published in 1786.

47 During the war, Mass Observation was contracted by the Home Intelligence Department of the Ministry of Information to explore and analyse public attitudes on the Home Front. J. Hinton, *The Mass Observers: A History, 1937–1949* (Oxford: Oxford University Press, 2013), pp. 152–162.

48 Mass Observation, FR 1149 'Some thoughts on greyhounds and national unity', March 1942, p. 7. A similar point about the appeal of gambling and dog-racing had been made by Mass Observation in one of its first publications in 1938. In *First Year's Work*, it was noted that, for the industrial worker, the racing industry served as an 'outlet for personal frustrations, ambitions and faith'. Charles Madge and Tom Harrisson (eds.), *Mass Observation: First Year's Work 1937–1938* (London: L. Drummond, 1938), p. 32.

49 Mike Huggins, '" Everybody's Going to the Dogs?" The Middle Classes and Greyhound Racing in Britain Between the Wars', *Journal of Sport History*, 34/1 (2007), pp. 111–116; Donald Thomas, *An Underworld at War: Spivs, Deserters, Racketeers and Civilians in the Second World War* (London: John Murray, 2003), p. 275.

50 *Manchester Guardian*, 26 February 1942.

51 Huggins, 'Sports Gambling', p. 672.

52 *San Demetrio London*, dir. Charles Frend, 1943.

53 *Manchester Guardian*, 31 May 1940.

54 Huggins, 'Sports Gambling', pp. 677–678. As the war gradually turned in Britain's favour, the campaign against racing died down and no further restrictions were imposed. Huggins, 'Sport Gambling', p. 679.

55 Frank Butler was the *Daily Express*'s chief boxing writer and, in 1941 at the age of just 24, became the *Sunday Express*'s youngest ever sports editor. Trevor Evans, who joined the *Daily Express*'s editorial team in 1933, was better known as a champion of the industrial worker. He went on to be a director of Express Newspapers. Edward Pickering, 'Evans, Sir Trevor Maldwyn (1902–1981)', Oxford Dictionary of National Biography (Oxford: Oxford University Press, 2018)); online edition, Lawrence Goldman (ed.), May 2008, <www.oxorddnb.com/article/31088>.

56 *Daily Express*, 27 February 1942. Similar assaults on greyhound racing were made by the *Daily Express*'s sister paper, the *Sunday Express*. See for example, Frank Butler's articles '£80,000 a day still gambled' (*Sunday Express*, 18 January 1942) and 'A cleanup is needed, and now is the time to kick-out sport racketeers' (*Sunday Express*, 1 March 1942).

57 Mass Observation, FR113 'Space distribution in the press 1937, 1939, 1940', 16 May 1940, pp. 11–13. The report confirmed the findings of a Mass Observation study from the previous year, which noted reductions of 83 per cent and 65 per cent in the sports coverage of *The Sunday Times* and the *News of the World*, respectively. Harrisson and Madge, *War Begins at Home*, p. 263.

58 *Observer*, 23 June 1940.

59 Mass Observation, FR126 'Report on Press', May 1940, p. 69.

60 Smithers, Conservative MP for Chislehurst, had written to *The Times* on 28 February 1942 to insist that total war demanded 'total effort and total sacrifice'. *The Times*, 28 February 1942.
61 Mass Observation, FR1149, pp. 2–13. It should be noted that there has been some debate about how accurately Mass Observation represented public opinion. Matthew Taylor, for example, has made the point that most of the organisation's respondents came from the 'letter writing classes'. Taylor, 'Sport and Civilian Morale', p. 330.
62 For more on the role of newspapers in shaping reader perception, see Glenn R. Wilkinson, '"The Blessings of War": The Depiction of Military Force in Edwardian Newspapers', *Journal of Contemporary History*, 33/1 (January 1998), pp. 97–98.
63 Pronay, 'British Newsreels', p. 411. Indeed, Mike Huggins has argued that the influence of newsreels was so great that *Pathé Gazette*'s negative coverage of the 1941 Derby prompted questions to be raised in Parliament. Huggins, 'Sports Gambling', p. 677.
64 The five major companies involved in the production of newsreels were: *British Gaumont News*, *British Movietone News*, *British Paramount News*, *Pathé Gazette* and *Universal News*. For more on newsreels in wartime, see Scott L. Althaus, 'Global News Broadcasting in the Pre-Television Era: A Cross-National Comparative Analysis in World War Two Newsreel Coverage', *Journal of Broadcasting and Electronic Media*, 62/1 (March 2018), pp. 147–167.
65 Anthony Aldgate, 'British Newsreels and the Spanish Civil War', *Film and History*, 3/1 (2013), p. 3.
66 *British Movietone News*, 693A, 'The King's Fourth Classic', 17 September 1942. Indeed, by the summer of 1944, the directors of *Movietone* considered the war to have turned sufficiently in Britain's favour for even the ultimate scourge of the racing world, gambling, to be treated with an indulgent humour: 'Holidays in wartime', mused the voiceover for the news short 'Whitsun 1944', 'are rare events and not everybody got one at Whitsun; all the same, in the South, Ascot was a big draw. You might have thought that what with war savings and income tax no-one would have much left to put on a horse, but as a pleasant change from Pay as You Earn, thousands enjoyed a spot of Lose as You Watch'. *British Movietone News*, 782A, 'Whitsun 1944', 1 June 1944.
67 See pp. 96–97.
68 *The Times*, 3 April 1941.
69 Taylor, 'Sport and Civilian Morale', p. 318.
70 The King's first attendance at a football match since the outbreak of war was captured by *British Movietone News* in its coverage of the Inter-Services Cup Final at Samford Bridge in May 1942. *British Movietone News*, 676A, 'King and Queen see services cup final', 21 May 1942.
71 *Manchester Guardian*, 31 August 1940.
72 *British Gaumont News*, 1130, '1941 FA Cup Final at Wembley', 15 May 1941.
73 *Observer*, 31 August 1940. A Mass Observation file report of April 1942 certainly confirms football's positive image noting that, of all sports, it was the one that received the highest approval rating from the public. Mass Observation, FR1229 'Attitudes to the Continuance of Organised Sport in Wartime: April 1942', 26 April 1942.
74 *Daily Mail*, 2 September 1940.
75 Edward Corse, *A Battle for Neutral Europe: British Cultural Propaganda During the Second World War* (London: Bloomsbury, 2013), p. 121.
76 *The Times*, 1 July 1940.
77 *Manchester Guardian*, 20 April 1940. The *Guardian*'s sports gear appeal again deployed cricket as a symbol of defiance and resistance the following month. Under the heading 'The Drake Touch', the preamble to the request for subscriptions noted, 'The threat of war once did not stop a game of bowls, nor need its presence now prevent a game of cricket.' *Manchester Guardian*, 3 May 1940.

78 *The Dragon*, 490, September 1940, p. 199. Established in 1842, Canterbury cricket week is the oldest cricket festival in England. Keith Sandiford, 'English Cricket Crowds During the Victorian Age', *Journal of Sport History*, 9/3 (1982), p. 13.
79 *The Times*, 29 November 1941.
80 *British Paramount News*, 1447, 'Winter racing starts again after three years', 11 January 1945.
81 Regulations governing crowd safety, which had been introduced at the start of the war, had forced the Jockey Club to reschedule the Derby to the second Saturday in June and relocate it to Newmarket.
82 *The Times*, 18 June 1943.
83 *The Times*, 11 June 1941.
84 Paris, *Warrior Nation*, p. 189; Huggins, 'Sports Gambling', p. 681.
85 *The Lion has Wings*, dir. by Alexander Korda, Michael Powell, Brian Hurst and Adrian Brunel, 1939.
86 Only four races were organised during the war: two at Henley in 1940 and 1945, one at Sandford-on-Thames in 1943 and one at Ely in 1944. Richard Burrell, *One Hundred and Fifty Years of the Oxford and Cambridge Boat Race* (London: Precision Press, 1979), pp. 16–17.
87 *The Dragon*, 544, March 1945, p. 35.
88 *Manchester Guardian*, 12 July 1940. 'Lucio' was the pen-name of the *Manchester Guardian*'s assistant editor, Gordon Phillips.
89 *British Gaumont News*, 682, 'Roving Camera Reports: Eton v Harrow Cricket Match: Harrow Gun Presented for Scrap Iron', 18 July 1940.
90 *The Times*, 29 March 1941.
91 *The Times*, 2 April 1940.
92 *The Dragon*, 494, January 1941, pp. 14–15. The one sporting club from the regiment that curtailed its competitive fixtures for the duration of the war was the golfing society. Having participated in a tournament at Rye on 6 August 1939, it did not then enter another competitive event until a meeting at the Infantry Training Centre in Canterbury on 18 December 1945. Although the society's minute book provides no explanation for this hiatus, it is interesting to note that golf had, since the late nineteenth century, been regarded with disdain by many social commentators, who labelled its largely bourgeois devotees as obsessive and self-centred. This reputation would have hardly sat easily with the supposed character-building qualities of team sports like football and rugby. Canterbury, Templeman Library Special Collections, U327, The Buffs Golfing Society Record Album, volume 1, no date or page number; John Lowerson, 'Golf', in Tony Mason (ed.), *Sport in Britain: A Social History* (Cambridge: Cambridge University Press, 1989), p. 190.
93 *The Dragon*, 537, August 1944, p. 135.
94 *The Dragon*, 480, November 1939, p. 377.
95 *The Times*, 23 February 1940. Even at the height of the fighting in the western desert in 1942, sport, at least for some, still seems to have been a priority. Keith Douglas, the war poet and a captain in the Royal Armoured Corps, recalled, in a posthumously published memoir, his astonishment at being told that a delivery of new tanks would require work as the troops supplying them 'had not had time for maintenance because in their units sport took precedence over it'. Keith Douglas, *Alamein to Zem Zem* (London: Editions Poetry London, 1946), p. 109.
96 *Manchester Guardian*, 12 October 1940.
97 *The Dragon*, 480, November 1939, p. 381.
98 'The Soldier's Welfare: Notes for Officers, issued by the War Office' (1941), p. 13, quoted in Mason and Riedi, *Sport and the Military*, p. 196.
99 *Daily Mail*, 13 August 1940.
100 *The Times*, 19 March 1941.
101 *Manchester Guardian*, 7 December 1940.

102 *Manchester Guardian*, 31 July 1942. Geoffrey Wellum's reminiscences of his years as a Spitfire pilot would appear to confirm Sisson's fears. He recalled that the officers on his selection panel seemed much more interested in his prowess as a cricketer than his ineptitude as a mathematician. Geoffrey Wellum, *First Light* (London: Viking, 2002), pp. 4–7.
103 *The Times*, 17 February 1942. Wavell's enthusiasm for sporting prowess as an indicator of military proficiency received further support in the pages of *The Times* in the last year of the war. In a letter to the paper's editor in February 1945, Henry Garwood, a retired lieutenant-colonel in the Royal Artillery, approvingly recalled another of Wavell's pre-war speeches, this time delivered at the Royal United Services Institute in 1933, in which it had been claimed that the 'ideal infantryman should be athlete, sharpshooter, stalker'. Field sports, Garwood concluded, developed all 'the qualities we require in an officer'. *The Times*, 20 February 1945.
104 *The Times*, 20 July 1943.
105 *The Times*, 10 June 1942.
106 *The Times*, 5 August 1941.
107 *The Times*, 1 March 1941.
108 *The Times*, 2 September 1941.
109 *Manchester Guardian*, 6 April 1940.
110 Harrisson and Madge, *War Begins at Home*, p. 270.
111 Harrisson and Madge, *War Begins at Home*, p. 148.
112 The feature had originally been entitled 'London Laughs', but this was changed to 'Smiling Through' for the duration of the war. 'Joseph Lee' (21 March 2016), University of Kent British Cartoon Archive, <www.cartoons.ac.uk/cartooinst-biographies/k-l/JosephLee.html> [accessed 3 December 2018].
113 Joseph Lee, 'Smiling Through: Greater Game', *Evening News*, 21 January 1943.
114 *Daily Express*, 13 November 1943.
115 *The Times*, 20 January 1941.
116 Stephen Brooks (ed.), *Montgomery and the Eighth Army; A Selection from the Diaries, Correspondence and Other Papers of Field Marshal the Viscount Montgomery of Alamein, August 1942 to December 1943* (London: Bodley Head for the Army Records Society, 1991), p. 70. The engagement to which Montgomery was referring was the Battle of Alam el Halfa (30 August to 5 September 1942), at which an attempt by Rommel's German and Italian forces to engulf the British Eighth Army was repulsed. See Fennell, *Fighting the People's War*, pp. 62–66.
117 *The Times*, 19 February 1945.
118 *The Times*, 23 February 1945.
119 *The Times*, 7 November 1942. This quote was seized on by Sir Pelham Francis Warner, the former international cricketer and deputy secretary of MCC, to advance the cause of his sport. A letter to the editor of *The Times*, in which the cricketing pedigrees of both Montgomery's father and 'his great chief', General Alexander, were noted, concluded with the following observation: 'It is surely a remarkable tribute to a game that amidst the breathless business of waging war our greatest soldiers can give a thought to cricket.' *The Times*, 18 November 1942.
120 Brooks, *Montgomery and the Eighth Army*, p. 290.
121 David Low, 'Test Match', *Evening Standard*, 15 June 1938.
122 *Rotherham Advertiser*, 22 April 1939, quoted in Davies and Light, p. 97.
123 Quoted in Derek Birley, *A Social History of English Cricket* (London: Arum Press Ltd., 1999), p. 261.
124 *The Times*, 6 April 1942. Not everyone, however, was quite so enamoured of this linguistic crossover between the sporting and military worlds. C. M. Sterm, writing in the *Library Assistant*, was concerned about the effect it might have on impressionable minds. It might be 'funny', he argued, to suggest that the Allies were 'capable of beating the Italians with the aid of a cricket bat . . . but it won't help the young reader appreciate Crete or Norway or Dunkirk'. Quoted in Paris, *Warrior Nation*, p. 196.

125 Paris, *Warrior Nation*, p. 196.
126 *Daily Mirror*, 11 July 1940. Garry Campion has noted that as the raids shifted focus to London and other major cities, coverage moved away from the 'cricket score' approach. Garry Campion, *The Good Fight: Battle of Britain Propaganda and the Few* (Basingstoke: Palgrave Macmillan, 2009), p. 101.
127 For more on the context of Gardner's report, see Campion, *The Good Fight*, pp. 123–127 and Brian D. P. Hannan, 'Creating the War Correspondent: How the BBC Reached the Frontline in the Second World War', *Historical Journal of Film, Radio and Television*, 28/2 (2008), pp. 185–187.
128 *Daily Mail*, 15 July 1940; *Manchester Guardian* 15 July 1940.
129 *The Times*, 17 July 1940.
130 Vera Brittain, *England's Hour: An Autobiography 1939–41* (London: Palgrave Macmillan, 1941), p. 129.
131 *Daily Mail*, 18 July 1940.
132 Mass Observation, FR261 'Air Propaganda', 12 July 1940, p. 56. Although the report pre-dated Gardner's broadcast, the appendix was added after it had been aired. The issue of gender was also hinted at during a Parliamentary debate on the Gardner broadcast on 24 July 1940. Dismissing the suggestion that people might have found the tone offensive, Robert Bernays, the Liberal MP for Bristol North, insisted that 'we are not a nation of cissies [sic]'. *The Times*, 25 July 1940.
133 Mass Observation, FR261 'Air Propaganda', 12 July 1940, p. 56.
134 Mass Observation, FR279 'Charles Gardner Broadcast', 16 July 1940, p. 2.
135 'Listener Research Report: Air Battle Commentary by Charles Gardner' (1940), BBC online archives, <www.bbc.co.uk/archive/battleofbritain/11432.shtml?page=1> [accessed 19 April 2019].
136 *The Times*, 22 July 1940.
137 *The Sunday Times*, 21 July 1940.
138 Hannan, 'Creating the War Correspondent', p. 186. The BBC's decision to release, and the public's willingness to purchase, a gramophone record of Gardner's broadcast provides further evidence of the popularity of these 'football style' eyewitness reports. S. Nicholas, *The Echo of War: Home Front Propaganda and the Wartime BBC, 1939–45* (Manchester: Manchester University Press, 1996), p. 197.
139 Harrisson, *War Begins at Home*, p. 263.
140 Indeed, just how transitory such periods of criticism were can be seen in the rapidity with which not just racing but associated gambling was rehabilitated. As Mike Huggins has pointed out, by 1943 there was a general consensus in government that sports betting contributed positively to morale, and revenue from gambling increased annually between 1943 and 1945. Huggins, 'Sports Gambling', p. 679.
141 *Manchester Guardian*, 5 April 1940.

5 War in the nuclear age, 1945 to the present

'Top guns 1, mad dog 0'

At the beginning of April 2003, with Coalition forces poised on the outskirts of Baghdad for a final push against Saddam Hussein's fast-disintegrating Republican Guard, the *Guardian*'s Washington correspondent, Matthew Engel, used the opening of the new baseball season to explore the 'fraught' relationship between war and sport. Why, he wondered, 'when their contemporaries were playing a deadly game', were sportsmen and women not facing some of the restrictions and criticisms their predecessors had faced in the two total wars of the twentieth century? The reason, Engel determined, was due to an essential disconnect between home and fighting fronts:

> This war is far away, conscription has long gone and, though events in Iraq command universal attention, they don't command universal support. Thus, the rituals of American springtime are being observed. Baseball has begun; college basketball is reaching its climax; the Masters is imminent – and world events will probably do more harm to the feminist protests than to the actual golf.[1]

For many commentators, however, the implications the marginalisation of combat had for the sport/war paradigm were far more significant than this assessment appeared to suggest. Thus, both Michael Paris and Peter Gilroy have argued that the contentious nature of what Paris has called the 'inglorious little wars' that Britain has found herself embroiled in since 1945 not only has allowed the domestic sporting calendar to carry on unabated but, more critically, has blurred the boundaries between sport and conflict.[2] For Paris, this could be seen in the 'trivialisation of war as entertainment', while Gilroy has pointed to the fact that sport and war have acquired 'the same value . . . in the indices of a distinctive national axiology'.[3] Michael Mann, in an article exploring the evolution of popular militarism from the seventeenth century onwards, has also linked warfare's limited scope in the nuclear age with its refashioning as a sporting spectacle. 'Wars', he has argued, 'like the Falklands are not qualitatively different from the Olympic Games. Because life-and-death are involved, the emotions stirred up are deeper and stronger. But they are not backed-up by the commitment of personal resources. They do not involve real or potential sacrifice, except by professional troops.'[4] Colin McInnes has been equally keen to point out that the 'minimising of risk and exposure' inherent in the 'localization of war' has allowed people to 'become spectators – experiencing war through the media'. As a result, he has concluded, conflict, just like sport, is now experienced 'remotely through the screen' and is carefully packaged to present 'ideas about community, loyalty and national identity'.[5]

Sue Jansen and Don Sabo have identified the Gulf War of 1991 as the pivotal moment when this repackaging of war as sport assumed 'a historically unique social, rhetorical and ideological role'. The end of the Cold War and the collapse of 'world communism', Jansen and Sabo have maintained, had left the West needing to find new ways 'for making sense of – and thereby exercising some control over and within – the worldwide realignments of power relations'; the mobilisation of 'sport/war tropes', they have noted, was thought to provide a solution to this dilemma.[6] For others, it was the attack on the twin towers in September 2011 that served as a watershed. In his study of the work of Arabella Dorman, official war artist during the Iraq and Afghanistan campaigns, Anthony King has argued that the 'unjustifiable costs' and 'lack of clear strategic purpose' of the post-9/11 War on Terror have been compensated for by sport.[7] According to King, sporting rituals, imagery and language have been used to cloak military operations in the 'symbol[ism] of common humanity'.[8] Samantha King, although equally certain that 9/11 was the turning-point, has presented a more politicised interpretation of sport's function. Since 2001, she has posited, 'a variety of sporting events and celebrities have become key vehicles for reproducing and channelling militarist and national identifications'.[9] This line of reasoning has been developed by John Kelly in a series of essays exploring sport and militarism. Britain, he has claimed in a recent study on army rituals in British sporting culture, in order 'to encourage and facilitate public engagement with, and universal support for . . . the War on Terror', has followed America's lead by 'placing nation-state and stare-sponsored militarism at the centre of cultural and civic society'.[10] And sport has played a key part in this state-sponsored discourse. For, Kelly has insisted, as a 'floating signifier of national sentiment and an apolitical arena of untainted, virtuous commodified spectacle', sport has been used to 'neuter political opposition to western militaristic violence'.[11]

In the late 1940s and 1950s, however, Britons frequently chose to look to the past rather than the future, focusing not on the challenges of a new world order but instead on the glories of the recent struggle against Nazi Germany. John Ramsden, in a study of the charged post-war footballing relationship between England and Germany, has even gone so far as to suggest that British popular culture in these years remained in a '1940s time-warp, saturated in television programmes, jokes, situation comedies, old war films, tabloid newspapers, children's comics and thrillers, each of which highlighted the war'.[12] This obsessive craving to refight the Third Reich was most evident in the cinema. Production studios churned out a seemingly never-ending supply of action-adventures and thrillers in which plucky British troops outwitted, outfought and outlasted the massed ranks of the German army. Such films, although rarely well-received by the critics, proved to be hits with the British public.[13] Particularly popular was the prisoner-of-war (POW) genre.[14] Frequently based on the memoirs of former POWs, these offerings presented romanticised tales of gallant British officers heroically evading their brutal (and remarkably bumbling) German captors.[15] The effect, according to Jeffrey Richards, was to rewrite the People's War as a 'celebration of the officer class'.[16] In this refashioned celluloid war, the patently middle-class heroes differed very little from the sporting-warriors of pre-1914 imperial literature. As Michael Paris has observed, at the centre of the action was 'the same old stereotype, . . . [the] public school educated officer who looked on war as a game; a sporting adventure'.[17] Innate martial superiority was once again underlined by emphasising the protagonists' insouciant attitude to combat. Imprisoned British officers were portrayed as confronting the challenges of camp life as they would a particularly tricky fixture in inter-house rugby.[18] This all had the effect, film historian Ralph Donald has insisted, of 'blurring the distinction between war-making and sports participation, effectively melding these two contemporary constructions of masculinity'.[19]

Certainly, the spate of POW films in the two decades following the end of the Second World War invariably deployed sport as a central motif. As Dilys Powell, *The Sunday Times*' film critic, astutely observed in her review of the 1950 classic *The Wooden Horse*, the impression given of camp life in such films was that it bore a striking resemblance to that of a typical English boarding school:

> Someone or other – he was talking about poets – once said that the English were all schoolboys. I am aware that there is not much room for schoolboys in the modern battle and the welfare state, and I am aware that the English schoolboy spirit has contributed plenty to international exasperation. All the same I find its emergence in the incidents of war and its re-incarnation in this particular film against a backdrop of boredom and wretchedness pleasing and touching.[20]

And, of course, a central device that signalled this regression by camp inmates to their schooldays was sport. British prisoners in *The Wooden Horse* are seen playing endless games of football, and the escape itself is only made possible because of, in the camp commandant's words, 'the English craze for exercise'.[21] For the reviewer in the *Sunday Despatch*, so dominant was the sporting motif in the film that he felt the men 'might as well have been preparing a cricket pitch instead of a daring escape'.[22]

However, the film that did the most to embed in the public consciousness the public school yoking of sport and war was *The Colditz Story*. Directed by Guy Hamilton and released in 1955, the film was, according to S. P. MacKenzie, 'central in creating an enduring set of popular assumptions in which life behind the wire was interpreted, both figuratively and sometimes literally, in sporting terms'.[23] Prisoners in the castle are portrayed as engaging in a seemingly never-ending round of team games. Fiercely competitive football matches are constantly being played in the outer-field, while volleyball and a rather curious adaptation of rugby, called stoolball, which looks for all the world like the Eton wall-game, are pursued with single-minded intent in the castle's courtyard.[24] This sporting sub-text is firmly underlined in the film's concluding frame as a list of successful escapes by nationality is presented to the viewer in the form of an inter-school rounders competition:

Until the liberation of Colditz in April 1945, there were approximately 320 attempted escapes, resulting in:

5 Polish Home Runs
15 Dutch Home Runs
22 French Home Runs
14 British Home Runs.[25]

As MacKenzie perceptively noted, 'Escape was the name of the game, with the team from Oflag IVC topping the league table in terms of home runs.'[26]

The golden age of the British POW film essentially came to an end with the release of John Sturges' American blockbuster *The Great Escape*, in 1963.[27] Not only was British cinema unable to compete with the high production values of Hollywood but, as Nicholas Cull has pointed out, revelations about Nazi atrocities made during the Eichmann trial 18 months earlier had the effect of rendering the sporting escapades of a few imprisoned Allied officers rather feeble fare.[28] Indeed, any lingering suggestion that life in the camps specifically, or during wartime generally, could be equated with sport is shattered in *The Great Escape*'s final scene when Squadron Leader Roger 'Big X' Bartlett, the mastermind behind the escape plan, and 49 other recaptured British prisoners are summarily executed by the Gestapo.[29] However, this was not, in fact, to be the end of the traditional POW film, and the enduring hold the genre had on the British imagination was made apparent in 1981 by the popular, if not critical, acclaim garnered by John Huston's footballing potboiler *Escape to Victory*. In a fanciful tale, in which international football and resistance to Nazi tyranny are conflated, war is once again packaged as sport. Described by *The Financial Times* as 'match of the day crossed with *Stalag 17*', the film uses sporting ability as a barometer of decency and moral worth; it is surely no coincidence that the German who is depicted as treating the camp inmates with the most respect is supposed to have played soccer against England in 1938.[30] Although the old public school sporting ethos is gently challenged when Michael Caine's character, an avowedly working-class officer, unable to contain his exasperation with the resolutely middle-class escape committee, exclaims, 'Your escaping is just some bloody upper-crust game'; victory over the Germans is still ultimately defined in sporting terms.[31] It is the last-minute equalizer in the show-piece match in Paris between an Allied POW XI and a crack team from the Wehrmacht, rather than news of the prisoners' subsequent escape, that prompts the hitherto cowed crowd to break into a defiant rendition of *La Marseillaise* and is held to be truly symbolic of democracy's triumph over dictatorship. This reversion to the metaphorical approach of 20 years earlier proved to be immensely popular. The film was voted 'the greatest soccer film of all time' by Channel 4 viewers, and a special DVD edition was produced for the 2006 World Cup in

Germany.[32] David Castell, in a review for the *Sunday Telegraph*, attributed the film's high approval rating to the enduring appeal of sport/war tropes. 'The picture's image', he argued, 'of the soccer-field as a battleground is one that modern audiences will not have difficulty in recognising.'[33] John Ramsden, former professor of modern history at Queen Mary's University and author of a best-selling cultural study charting Anglo-German relations in the twentieth century, was equally sure the film provided a valuable insight into public attitudes to conflict. *Escape to Victory*, he concluded a scholarly critique for the *Historical Journal of Film, Radio and Television*, 'highlights the continuing interconnectivity between war and sport in British popular memory'.[34]

Just a year after *Escape to Victory* hit the cinemas, the connection between sport, or more precisely football, and war was again thrown into high relief. On 2nd April 1982, Argentinian forces invaded the British-held Falkland Islands and swiftly entered the capital, Port Stanley, forcing governor Rex Hunt to surrender. In an emergency Commons' debate to discuss Britain's response, held less than 48 hours later, the invasion was immediately coupled with the upcoming football World Cup Finals in Spain. Sir Nigel Fisher, Conservative MP for Surbiton, in calling for 'all available sanctions to be taken', demanded that, as a 'first step, . . . the very least we should do is to ensure [Argentina's] exclusion from the World Cup'.[35] Although the British government chose not to follow up Fisher's proposal, the expulsion of one or other of the belligerents from soccer's premier competition continued to be a very real prospect. By early May, with both sides having suffered devastating casualties at sea and with British troops poised to effect landings at San Carlos, FIFA, desperate to avoid becoming embroiled in the conflict, drew up plans to have the three qualified home nations of England, Scotland and Northern Ireland replaced.[36] Neil MacFarlane, the minister for sport, was quick to make clear that Britain would not voluntarily comply with any such ruling. 'The Government sees no objection', he informed the Commons on 19th May, 'to the three British teams taking part in the World Cup Finals next month. Many millions of people would find it odd if we as the non-aggressor nation were not taking part in the World Cup.'[37] The editor of *The Times* was equally certain that pulling the British sides would send out the wrong message:

> Argentine football does not have to be seen as representing the Argentina government. We have many times said that we have no quarrel with the Argentine people, and that we are limiting our actions against them to what is strictly necessary for the recovery of the Falkland Islands. It is inconceivable that the scratching of the three British teams from the World Cup would, in any way, facilitate that objective.[38]

This conflation of events in the South Atlantic with the conclusion of the football season was given a little extra piquancy by the presence in the Tottenham Hotspur squad of two Argentine internationals, Osvaldo Ardiles and Ricky Villa.[39] Villa, who had not been included in Argentina's line-up for the World Cup, was due to play in the FA Cup Final on 22 May. Unsurprisingly, there was some concern at both White Hart Lane and Lancaster Gate about how the Wembley crowd would receive him. Speculation that he would be dropped by Spurs' management or even prohibited from playing by the authorities featured regularly on the back pages in the days leading up to the match. This prompted John Samuel, the sports editor of the *Guardian*, to issue, on the morning of the final, an impassioned plea for the footballing community to take the moral lead and rise above the base-jingoism that appeared to have gripped the nation. In a lengthy piece entitled 'Uplifting Power', he expressed the hope that the sight of Villa paying his respects while *God Save the Queen* was played before kick-off would 'bring some moment of reflection to the 100,000 present and to the bulk of the nation watching on television'. Although prepared to admit that 'recent soccer history' hardly pointed towards an auspicious outcome, Samuel nonetheless concluded on a note of optimism: 'Football has the power to show an impulse to rise above the brute in the way it receives Villa this afternoon. . . . It will be tragic indeed if Keith Burkinshaw [the Tottenham manager] feels he cannot risk Villa.'[40] For Ardiles, it was not his possible omission from the Tottenham team but his actual absence from the country that drew the full glare of the media. The day after Argentina had seized the Falkland Islands, he turned out in the FA Cup semi-final against Leicester City before flying out to join the national squad for a pre-World Cup training camp. Although Burkinshaw insisted Ardiles' period of leave had been pre-planned, the press still chose to interpret it as a political statement. The *Mirror* accused Ardiles of 'turning his back on Britain', while the *Sun* painted him as a naïf who was being 'unwittingly' exploited by the Galtieri regime.[41] What was remarkable was that this footballing trivia appeared alongside genuine war stories on the newspapers' front not back pages. Indeed, the *Daily Express* chose to place its report, 'Final Whistle for Ardiles', not with the sports section but in a newly created Falklands feature, 'Battle Briefing'.[42]

The merging of the sporting action in Spain with the military struggle in the Falklands was further underlined by British television's decision not to broadcast live Argentina's three opening group matches against Belgium, El Salvador and Hungary.[43] Such a decision firmly cast the Argentine team as representatives of an enemy nation rather than a sporting rival.[44] Indeed, the press repeatedly conflated the fervour of the football fan and the bellicosity of the junta's supporters when reporting on the mood in Argentina. *The Times* noted that the seizure of the Falklands had been greeted in Buenos Aries by 'genuine enthusiasm among the people – who put the invasion on a par with winning a football match'.[45] Brian Glanville made the same point in *The Sunday Times*, seeing in the Argentine public's response to the invasion, 'that nasty, uncouth nationalism, that released hysteria, which seems at the bottom of [the country's] football passions'.[46] A similar parallel was drawn by Robert Cox, a former editor of the *Buenos Aries Herald* who had been forced by the military regime to flee Argentina in 1979, although he thought on balance, the battlefield was probably trumped by the playing-field:

> Twenty-eight million Argentines have realised a dream. At last, they have forced the world, and Britain particularly, to take them seriously. They

specifically wanted Britain's attention, and now they have got it. Most Argentines would have preferred an epic victory over England on the football field in a final of a World Cup that would have erased memories of that defeat at Wembley when Sir Alfred Ramsey called their team 'animals'. But they can celebrate the occupation of the Falkland Islands with almost as much jubilation.[47]

A month later, in the aftermath of the sinking of the *Belgrano*, Christopher Thomas informed *The Times*' readers that the mood in the Argentine capital had become even more impassioned and warlike. Thomas attributed this intensification to the constant flow of government communiqués that interrupted television programmes and were 'read by a breathless announcer in the manner of an overexcited football commentator'.[48] Even in defeat, according to the *Daily Express*' man in Buenos Aries, Ross Benson, the Argentine public found it hard to distinguish between football and war:

> Argentina was at war again on Sunday. Against Belgium. The streets of Buenos Aries were deserted, the inhabitants taking refuge in front of their TV sets. The war, the real one, being fought to its bloody conclusion on the Falkland Islands, was forgotten – Argentina was at the serious business of defending the World Cup. The reality in Spain, however, looks like being as indigestible as it is on the Falklands. Argentina's most famous radio commentator sobbed when Belgium scored the winner. The newspapers bore black-rimmed headlines like those used for death. Argentina could, of course, retain the World Cup. But people here are beginning to realise that their country, like their football, is all but bankrupt.[49]

Yet, for others, the practice of blurring the boundaries between football and combat was as much a characteristic of British popular culture as it was of Argentinian. Julian Cooper, who held citizenship for both countries, was appalled by the public reaction in Britain to the recapture of South Georgia on 25 April. In a letter to the editor of *The Times*, he warned of the dangers of treating the war as a sporting triumph:

> I believe it would be unwise to regard the re-taking of South Georgia with the enthusiasm of a football supporter whose side have just scored. In terms of Britain's long-term interests, let alone the far more vital question of simple humanity in one's behaviour to other human beings, every Argentine death inflicted by Britain and every injury to Argentine self-respect is equivalent to our scoring an 'own goal'.[50]

Writing in *Contemporary Review* two years after the war, Peter Beck, principal lecturer in international history at Kingston Polytechnic, was equally concerned about the impact the British fixation with sport would have on Anglo-Argentine relations. Disappointed that the English football team had, for the second time since the end of hostilities in 1982, withdrawn from a fixture with Argentina, he felt certain that any future contact between the two nations would be complicated by the fact that 'in England one is encouraged by the media and others to believe that sporting victory is perhaps the most important thing in present-day society'.[51]

A more sinister aspect of the bearing the Falklands conflict had on Britain's obsession with football also drew the attention of cultural observers in the years following the fighting. As British or, more precisely, English football became mired in crowd-trouble and hooliganism in the 1980s, many commentators began to make a connection between the fighting in the South Atlantic and the violence on the soccer terraces. Thus, the TV journalist Ed Vuillamy, in May 1985, traced the roots of the Heysel Stadium disaster to the tabloid-fuelled jingoism of three years earlier. 'I saw one English fan', he reported,

> with a t-shirt: 'Keep the Falklands British' as though he and his mates were the Task Force. . . . Indeed, there was little to differentiate the drunken hysteria in the bars of Brussels and one night in Tufnell Park in 1982, when gleeful patriots celebrated the sinking of the *Belgrano* in a wash of beer.[52]

In the same year, Nick Perry's Samuel Beckett Award-winning play, *Arrivederci Millwall*, located the vicious exploits of a group of hardcore England supporters during the 1982 World Cup in the wider context of a Falklands-induced culture of xenophobia.[53] This sense of a generation brutalised by the rabid bigotry of war fever also lay at the heart of Paul Greengrass' 1989 film *Resurrected*. Based on the true story of the summary justice meted out to a Falklands veteran who had returned to his regiment after being listed as missing in action, the film, D. George Boyce observed in his 1991 history of the conflict, depicted 'a harsh inconsiderate society, over-influenced by a scandal-mongering press and underpinned by a military culture whose behaviour is little different from the violent tribalism of football hooliganism'.[54] It was this equivalence between the experience of the combat soldier and the world of the football delinquent that really interested Greengrass. 'A line of sorts', he claimed in 1991, could be drawn 'between the Paras yomping their way across the Falklands to the lager louts of today, laying waste to European cities in the name of football'.[55]

The footballing sub-text of the war in the Falklands was so deeply entrenched in the public consciousness that the game could even be employed by the *Daily Express*' in-house cartoonist, Raymond Jackson ('JAK'), to satirise the moment of Argentine capitulation in June 1982. Referencing the need for the British negotiating team to use a local football pitch as a helipad when it flew in to discuss terms of surrender with the beleaguered Argentine forces in Port Stanley, Jackson depicted a forlorn marine in a telephone box informing the British secretary of state for defence, 'It's bad news, Mr Nott, the Argentines have beaten us 3–1!'[56] However, for some, the loss of young lives in the Falklands, both Argentine and British, had cast a shadow on the appropriateness of connecting sport and war and provided the nation with a golden opportunity to take stock and re-evaluate its all-consuming obsession with the beautiful game. This view was articulated by both David Lacey of the *Guardian* and Ian Wooldridge of the *Daily Mail*. Scenes of dead and dying aboard *HMS Sheffield* prompted Lacey to ask for a sense of proportion to be preserved in sports reporting:

> There is a tendency to describe football matches in the language of war. When war breaks out such language becomes immoderate to say the least. . . . Goalkeepers may commit fatal errors, but they live to tell the tale. . . . Worse things, as we have seen demonstrated all too graphically over the past few days, happen at sea.[57]

For Wooldridge, ensconced with the England squad in Spain, it was the conclusion of hostilities that had served to remind him and his fellow professionals of the superficiality of their work and the gravity of their responsibilities:

> There is not an England footballer or British sports writer here who is not aware that the World Cup, for many the zenith of their careers, is grimly overshadowed by death and sorrow and a vastly different kind of heroism. Suddenly the vivid rhetoric of the sports page, with its familiar battlefield allusions, must be muted.[58]

This issue of warfare imposing perspective was revisited almost a decade later during the first Gulf War. Three days after Operation Desert Storm had seen coalition forces launch a devastating aerial bombardment of Iraq in an attempt to liberate Kuwait, Peter Corrigan told readers of the *Observer* that 'the opportunity we now have to tone down the hysterical importance we grant our sports and sportsmen should not be ignored'. Appalled that the 'very phrases being used to describe the conflict in the Gulf would have been glibly colouring the reports of tennis, snooker or football a week ago', he somewhat derisively concluded that 'the time had come to redefine a hero as a young man who doesn't burst into tears when the going gets tough'.[59] Corrigan's sentiments were echoed by *The Times* the following week when an editorial appealed for a 'toned-down output' from 'the more purple sports writers and commentators'. However, the paper was anxious that any call for restraint should be kept in perspective. It ridiculed the BBC's decision to cancel the broadcast of the comedy film *Carry on up the Khyber*, pointing out that 'it has never been a rule of war that the British sense of humour has to be suspended for the duration.'[60] During the Second Gulf War in 2003, Mark Pougatch, who fronted BBC Radio 5 Live's sports coverage, was similarly keen that requests for moderation should not spill over into demands for prohibition. Aware that sport can appear to be 'rendered meaningless when people are dying', and although in agreement that 'it was more important than ever' that reporters 'watched [their] language', he was, nonetheless, insistent that that should not mean the wholesale abandonment of the nation's sporting programme. Quoting Glen Roeder, the manager of West Ham United, Pougatch maintained that it was the sports professional's role in wartime 'to play correctly and in the right manner and try and take people's minds off things'.[61]

Certainly, just as had happened in the two total wars of the twentieth century, Britain's involvement in armed conflict after 1945 initiated discussions about the role of sport in wartime. Three days after RAF Harrier and Tornado fighters, as part of a NATO force, had helped to open the bombing campaign against Yugoslavia in March 1999, Simon Barnes wrote a lengthy piece for *The Times* on whether it was fitting for England's Euro 2000 qualifier against Poland to be played that afternoon. Sport, he conceded, may pale into insignificance when compared to the deepening crisis in the Balkans, but that was a reason to go ahead with, not postpone, the match:

> Human beings need frivolity and distraction and pleasure in the face of the general over-seriousness of life. Caring about something that does not matter is perhaps, in these circumstances, the deepest pleasure that sport can offer.... This afternoon, we can turn away from war for a couple of hours of frolics and groin strains. Amid the terrible, we need the silly more than ever. Amid the inhumanity, we turn with relief to the all too foolishly human.[62]

In March 2003, on the eve of the second Gulf War, it was the turn of the sports journalist and author Simon Kuper to address 'the question that always reoccurs – "what can football mean at a time like this?"' A lengthy article in *The Game*, the soccer supplement of Saturday's *Times*, presented many of the same arguments Barnes had delivered four years earlier. 'In times of war', it was noted, 'football's insignificance is its charm.' Yet, Kuper also identified a subtle shift in the public's temperament since the war in Kosovo:

> With a new war about to start, the mood in the stadium is different. Fans and newspapers continue to talk about football as if it mattered – as if, in fact, it was a variety of war. Liverpool hold Celtic in the 'Battle of Britain', fans sing about being a 'blue and blue army', or abuse rival teams' followers with talk of plane crashes and Auschwitz.... Normally football provides a pleasant distraction from war. This time, however, the war seems incapable of distracting people from football. In British newspapers, David Beckham regularly trumps Saddam Hussein.

This increase in intensity of public sporting interest made Kuper uncomfortable. Instead of serving as a temporary escape, sport now, he concluded, acted as a 'lifelong holiday, and, at times like these that can feel childish'.[63] The *Guardian*'s Stephen Brierley also felt some disquiet at the importance attached to football as the death toll in Iraq mounted and cited the hateful coverage of Arsenal's French striker, Robert Pires, who had threatened to boycott matches to publicise his anti-war stance, as evidence of the tabloid press' failure to recognise that the game was no more than a diversion.[64] Despite these misgivings, however, Brierley felt the season should continue uninterrupted. 'Such is the power of sport in the middle of the most terrible and incomprehensible crises', he informed his readers in an opinion piece published on 25 March 2003, 'that there have already been tales of servicemen emailing home and urging that all sporting events go ahead so that the troops have something to take their minds off the terrible danger.'[65]

Press reporting, almost without fail, did indeed ensure that frontline troops' attitude towards, and engagement with, sport was presented in a positive light. It was generally assumed, as had been the case between 1939 and 1945, that sporting events helped to boost morale. In May 1982, *The Times* came out against the withdrawal of the home nations from the World Cup, arguing that, '[British servicemen's] morale would benefit from their being able to follow the fortunes of British teams on the radio'.[66] Peter Corrigan of the *Observer* was similarly convinced that those serving in war zones would be eagerly awaiting the results of key fixtures. 'You can well imagine', he wrote during the first Gulf War, 'a Tornado pilot jumping down from his cockpit last night and demanding to know the England-Wales result before reporting if he'd hit anything.'[67] During the second Gulf War, the *Sun* used an interview with Inverness Caledonian Thistle defender Bobby Mann to make the same point. With his team due to meet Dundee in a keenly awaited Scottish Cup semi-final clash, Mann explained why the match meant so much to him:

> I thought I didn't need any reminding of what Saturday's game means to Calley Thistle supporters until a few days ago when a letter arrived at the club from one of our troops in Iraq. It made me feel totally humble to think that one of the things that was keeping Kenny going throughout the brutal war was the success of our team. And I couldn't stop laughing after reading one of his greatest pleasures in the last few weeks has been winding up Celtic fans in his regiment.[68]

Yet, service personnel were, of course, not simply presented as passive consumers of sport. Conforming to a well-established practice that stretched back to the nineteenth century, British troops were also portrayed as enthusiastic participants in sporting activity. This media representation, again following precedents established in earlier conflicts, regularly imbued sport in combat zones with a wider meaning. This was particularly true of the two Gulf Wars when the British government's commitment to the coalition cause did not enjoy universal support. Thus, fears that there might be some friction between the US and British forces in 1991 was tackled by the *Daily Mirror* with a piece covering a good-humoured rivalry on the playing-field. American marines and British soldiers, the paper's readers were informed, had initiated their own form of cultural exchange by challenging each other to first a game of American football and then a rugby match.[69] More commonly, however, press depictions of frontline sport avoided any allusions to contentious political issues and focused instead on personal attributes. *The Times* couldn't resist resurrecting the image of the nineteenth-century gentlemen-warrior when, in December 2003, it reported on a rudimentary six-hole golf course constructed by the 101st Airborne Division at its base-camp outside Mosul in Northern Iraq. 'Not since the glory days of the British Raj', it was stated in a lengthy illustrated feature,

> have fighting men ridden into battle with a set of golf clubs in their baggage, but Lieutenant White, 36, who has a passion for the game, crossed the demarcation line dividing Iraq from Kuwait in the thick of the US-led invasion to topple Saddam Hussein with a seven-iron, a three-wood and, appropriately, a sand wedge.[70]

The re-taking of the British embassy in Baghdad by 1st Battalion, The Parachute Regiment in April 2003 received similar treatment. Leading with the breezy headline 'Innings resumed after war stops play', an article noted that having 'secured the ancient building on the Tigris', paratroopers then 'marked their return by playing a game of cricket on the embassy lawn'.[71] The message couldn't have been clearer. No matter what the rights and wrongs of the war itself, British troops were carrying out their mission with all the *sangfroid* of the imperial heyday.

Indeed, sport could be used to divorce the military from the controversial high politics of Western entanglement in the Middle East and instead forefront the basic humanity of the soldiers. During the second Gulf War, the *Daily Star* and the *Sun* ran stories about British units challenging local Iraqis to football matches. And both papers were keen to ensure that their readers realised the games were, in the true sense of the word, friendlies. The *Star* insisted that the Royal Marines' 9–3 defeat by 'eleven lads from Iraq's second city, Basra, . . . didn't matter'. Buttressed by photographs of smiling children in the crowd, the feature stressed that 'the only winner that Juliet Company, 42 Commando, wanted was peace'.[72] The *Sun*, reporting on a match at Umm Khayyal in southern Iraq, took a more direct approach. Leading with 'Marines lose match but win friends', the paper made abundantly clear from the outset what the purpose of the encounter had been and who the real winners were:

> Royal Marines challenged Iraqis on the football pitch in the battle for the nation's hearts and minds. And our boys emerged the winners – despite a 7–3 defeat. Thoughts of war were set aside as the men swapped weapons and helmets for T-shirts and trainers.[73]

Although, after 1945, the impact of conflict on the domestic sporting calendar may have been negligible, and the depiction of sporting activity on the frontline positive, this did not mean that the intersection between sport and war ceased to arouse passions. Fears continued to be voiced about the media's apparent insistence on treating the life-and-death struggles of the battlefield in the same manner they would the triumphs and disappointments of the playing-field. It was the tabloid press that seemed to be particularly prone to this practice. Special editions were frequently published in which the 'highlights' of wars were presented as if events in the Falklands or Iraq were comparable to an Olympic Games or a football World Cup.[74] Key 'players' were regularly featured with post-action interviews and in-depth studies, and even, on occasion, associated ephemera were made available, most infamously the *Sun*'s 'War Traitors' Dartboard' of 2003.[75] Indeed, this approach to war reporting had become so deeply embedded in the popular consciousness by the turn of the twenty-first century that the *Guardian* felt able to run a spoof item, 'The news for sports fans: Hans Blix v The Security Council', in the lead-up to the second Gulf War in March 2003.[76] However, for some, this packaging of war as a sport was no cause for levity. Stephen Baxter of the *New Statesman*, appalled by the 'barely restrained glee' with which the opening of hostilities against Libya in 2011 had been greeted, was concerned the tabloid's portrayal of 'war as a football match' would anaesthetise people to the real horror of what was taking place. 'I feel like I'm spoiling all the fun', he wrote in a damming article entitled 'War is sport, Sport is War',

> but I find it distasteful to reduce the Libya campaign to a football match ... an away win, a penalty kick. This, then, is the tabloid view of war. Our boys are attacking The Mad Dog and it's one-nil already. How can we not support it? How can we not be shocked and awed by the beautiful photos of explosions, the family-friendly pictures, without mangled corpses or that messy business that gets left behind when the clouds disappear? IT'S WAR [emphasis in original]. War is sport, sport is war. Look away now if you don't want to know the score.[77]

But, as the television age dawned, written journalism found itself increasingly challenged by broadcast news. As the former editor of the *Guardian* Peter Preston noted in 2003, newspapers, unable to compete with television's live coverage, were no longer able to break war stories but instead had to recognise that they were now 'just there for the pre-match yack and the post-match inquest, the latter-day Saints and Greavesies of high-tech conflict'.[78] However, any divergence in the function of the printed and broadcast news was not matched by a difference in approach. From the 1990s onward, television mirrored the tabloids' habit of packaging armed conflict as a sporting event. Battlezone coverage was filtered by the news studios, with content edited for specific purposes and viewers guided through the images by expert commentary.[79] Reviewing the BBC's coverage of the first Gulf War in 1991, Greg Philo, the research director of Glasgow University Media Unit, made just this point. 'Like two sports commentators', he noted, 'David Dimbleby and defence correspondent David Shukman were almost rapt with enthusiasm. They called for freeze-frames and replays and they highlighted 'the action' on screen with computer light-pens.'[80] And, as the *Guardian* pointed out in an item entitled 'Washington's Armchair Warriors', viewers, no matter how lofty their status, tended to take their lead from the tone set by the television companies: 'The first eleven days of the Persian Gulf War have had the feeling of a surreal spectator sport here, with the president constantly flicking the television channels and with other senior officials gathered in semi-circles with sandwiches around television sets.'[81] By the time of the second Gulf War, this televisual merging of war and sport had become so common that even the tabloid press felt able to lampoon it. Thus, on the eve of the opening of Operation Desert Storm, the *Daily Star*'s Dominik Diamond could wryly observe, 'So it's 99 per cent certain that war will begin this week. I'm not sure what time – I guess it depends who's got the TV rights. If it's the BBC, they really won't want it to clash with the Six Nations Rugby!'[82]

Unsurprisingly, not all viewers were impressed by this style of television news broadcasting. One *Guardian* reader, presumably with the jingoistic press journalism of earlier conflicts in mind, denounced the media reporting of the second Gulf War as a retrograde step. 'This constant, live TV coverage', he complained in a letter to the paper's editor,

> appears no more shocking than watching *Grandstand* with 'results' coming in and interviews with 'key players'. At a time when civilisation teaches us that war is abhorrent, this sport event-style coverage brings us back to square one in the portrayal of war.[83]

This viewpoint was endorsed by one of the paper's feature writers, Emma Brockes, the following day. Under the damning heading 'War Porn', Brockes condemned the TV channels for using sports-style 'jazz graphics, fact boxes and breathless statistics' in an attempt to 'pass something ugly off as something beautiful'.[84] The need for domestic audiences to be faced with the brutal ugliness of war was also picked up on by John Peacock, the director of Sharpham College for Buddhist Studies, in an article for the *Independent* towards the end of March 2003. Responding to the furore surrounding Al Jazeera's decision to broadcast images of two dead British soldiers, Peacock echoed Brockes in calling for the truth about the fighting in Iraq to be revealed:

> Television coverage of the Middle East has so far borne an uncanny resemblance to sports reporting with emphasis being placed on techniques, skills and a totting up of 'goals', or casualty figures, both for and against us.... It is of overwhelming importance to show the 'truth' of war – and confront those who support conflict with the 'unglamorous' reality of warfare.[85]

For some media professionals, the advent of smart technology and surgical strikes had made the burden of reporting war as it actually was all the more pressing. Bob Deans, who covered Operation Desert Storm for Fox News, was worried that 'television's around-the-clock "War in the Gulf" coverage . . . had bordered on war as entertainment – the ultimate contest, the ultimate football match'. This could, he feared, have grave repercussions:

> There is a frightening seduction . . . to the unfolding drama of war as television theatre. And therein lies a warning: people who speak with bland detachment of the random violence of war have taken a dangerous first step toward accepting that violence. For just as language mirrors our thoughts, so can it

help to shape them. Words, after all, represent ideas, and there's something chilling about war reports that ignore the concept of human suffering.[86]

David Cole of the *Guardian*, equally uneasy about the toxic effect on domestic sensibilities the popular media's treatment of coalition operations to oust Saddam Hussein in 2003 would have, felt compelled to air his grievances in the pro-war *Daily Mail*. 'If we treat war as a new Olympic sport', he argued in a letter to the editor published under the banner 'War is not a Game', 'we lose sight of the impact on our own society. Support the war if you will but understand that it brings with it horrors no-one should have to witness.'[87] For both Mathew Paris, writing in *The Times*, and Julian Barnes, for the *Guardian*, the threats posed by television's resolve to deliver war as a sporting entertainment extended beyond the domestic sphere. If, Paris insisted, 'war becomes riveting simply as a spectator-sport', then the public will be blind to its wider implications. In particular, he cautioned, people will fail to see that 'after the success of Shock and Awe will come despair. And despair may not mount much resistance to a daisycutter, but so long as there are jetliners and there are skyscrapers, despair will always be able to fly the one into the other'.[88] Barnes, although rather more facetious in tone, was no less stark when it came to warning about the consequences of the Iraq conflict's trivialisation as a televisual sporting encounter. 'War', he argued in a lengthy opinion piece published the day after the fall of Baghdad in April 2003,

> depends on public support. Public support depends, in part, on disguising the reality of war and on calculating the acceptability of death. So, what would be the best way of scoring the game? . . . Let's start with the basic unit: one dead Iraqi soldier, score one point. Two for a dead Republican Guard or fedayeen. And so on up to the top of the regime: 5,000 let's say for Chemical Ali; 7,500 for each of Saddam's sons; 10,000 for the tyrant himself. Now for the potentially demoralising downside. One Iraqi civilian killed; if male, lose five points, female 10, a child 20. One coalition soldier killed deduct 50 points. And then, worst of all (as it underlines the futility and hazard of war), one coalition soldier killed by friendly fire, deduct 100 points. On the other hand, gain 1,000 points for each incident which a couple of years down the line can give rise to a feel-good Hollywood movie: witness 'Saving Private Lynch'. By this count, the war is a success. And television has more or less reflected the weighting of the above scoresheet. . . . But I have two questions for you. Do you honestly believe that the staggering bombardment of Iraq, televised live throughout the Arab world, has made Britain, America, and the home town of Torrie Clarke, safer from the threat of terrorism? And if so, let me remind you of another statement by your war leader, Mr Blair. He told us, in full seriousness, that once Saddam was eliminated, it would be necessary to 'deal with' North Korea. Are you getting hot for the next one – the humanitarian attack on Pyongyang?[89]

140 *War in the nuclear age, 1945 to present*

It was not only in the way news from the battle zone was packaged but also, just as had been the case in earlier conflicts, in the manner language and imagery were deployed that war was conflated with sport for the British public after 1945. Both combatants and correspondents regularly couched accounts of fighting in sporting terms. Predictably perhaps, given the temporal proximity of the World Cup Finals, football was often used as a frame of reference during the Falklands campaign.[90] As the British task force began to gather in the South Atlantic, Major Mike Norman, who had been detained and then deported during the initial invasion, was reported to be keen to get back into the action for the 'return leg' against the Argentine forces. 'It's a straightforward case of nobody liking coming second', he told the *Daily Mirror*; 'nobody likes losing a football match.'[91] The *Daily Express* approached the story in the same fashion. Leading with the heading 'Team of thirty-seven Royal Marines to go back to battle', and accompanied by a photograph of some of the men in the pose of a victorious soccer squad, the item concluded by noting that 'this time the odds are a little more even'.[92] The following day, it was the *Daily Mail*'s turn to provide the footballing twist. A lengthy interview with Rear Admiral Sandy Woodward, the commander of the naval task force, closed by locating the forthcoming hostilities firmly in the sporting sphere. 'My battle group', Woodward was quoted as saying, 'is properly formed and ready to strike. This is the run-up to the big match which, in my view, should be a walkover. I'd give odds of 20–1 on, to win.'[93] Even once the actual fighting had begun and substantial losses had been borne by both sides, there was still a sense that what was occurring on the Falklands was no more than a re-run of England's World Cup encounter with Argentina in 1966. Reflecting on the success of his mission after a ceasefire had been called on 14 June, Major-General Jeremy Moore, the commander of the British land forces, couldn't resist the chance to single out his star 'player'. 'I would like to name', he disclosed to the *Daily Express*, 'my man of the match. There is no doubt that the success of the landing forces is due to the resolution, drive, professionalism and determination of Brigadier Julian Thompson.'[94] A Mahood cartoon, which had appeared in the *Daily Mail* at the end of May, had further buttressed the impression of the land war as a proxy football fixture. As two British paratroopers are shown fighting their way through a rainstorm to escort a bedraggled Argentine soldier into captivity, one says to the other: 'This is idiotic. In these conditions the whole damn thing should have been turned over to the Pools Panel.'[95] And reconfiguring the Falklands conflict as a soccer match was not exclusively the preserve of the tabloid press. Shortly after Port Stanley had been overrun by the Argentinians, *The Times*' defence correspondent, Henry Stanhope, exploited a detailed understanding of the professional game's tiering to apprise his readers of the challenges the country would face should the Conservative government choose to opt for a military solution. Under the apparently reassuring strapline, 'Third Division takes on Britain', images of tricky away cup ties against lower league opposition were invoked to caution against complacency:

> Argentina's armed forces are, on paper, smaller, less well-equipped and much less experienced than Britain's but in terms of football they belong to the

second or perhaps third division, not the Isthmian League, and pose problems which, for British forces far from home and a friendly port, could prove insoluble.[96]

The sports metaphor as a vehicle for sanitising and naturalising war was to assume even greater importance as Britain became embroiled in a series of increasingly contentious conflicts from the 1990s onwards. With the nation becoming more and more divided over coalition operations in the Gulf and the subsequent War on Terror, the language and imagery of sport served to rationalise warfare by infusing the act of war itself, regardless of root causes, with the structure and rules of a sporting event.[97] War correspondents and army representatives were able to detach military operations from their wider political contexts and, instead, portray hostilities as stand-alone sporting contests. And this they certainly did. Again and again battle strategies were referred to as game plans.[98] Complex manoeuvres were made more understandable for civilian audiences by framing them in sporting terms. The failure of the long-awaited clash between Iraqi and Coalition forces to materialise in 1991 was interpreted by General 'Stormin' Norman Schwarzkopf, the commander of the international forces, as a no-show at a key match. 'You know', he explained in one of his regular press briefings,

> a football game can be over very quickly if the other team decides not to play. And that's what you had in this case. When the kick-off came, okay, our team was there to play. Our team came to play ball. And they were not willing to fight.[99]

During the second Gulf War, America's national game was again used to shed light on the campaign's progress. With an assault on Republican Guard positions south of Baghdad expected to commence at any time, a spokesperson from US Central Command bullishly reminded assembled journalists in March 2003, 'We have many, many options now and the enemy don't know what we've got planned. It's like a game of American football. We have all the plays and if they come out to play, they're going to get waxed.'[100]

This refashioning of the battlefield as a playing-field was further underlined by the press, which regularly resorted to sporting language and imagery as conceptual tools to market war. The opening of the campaign to free Kuwait from Iraqi occupation was greeted by the *Daily Mirror* as if it was a pantomime boxing contest. Dividing its front page in two, photographs of Saddam Hussein and British service personnel were, respectively, labelled 'villain' and 'heroes', with an RAF pilot quoted as saying, 'It would be a hell of an end to my career to KO Saddam.'[101] Boxing metaphors were again used in 2003. As the Battle for Basra was reaching a critical stage, the *Sun* led its war coverage on 27 March with the headline 'Marines poised to KO Saddam troops on key Iraqi highway', while the *Daily Mirror*, by now firmly in the anti-war camp, maintained it was only because Americans 'felt sucker-punched' after 9/11 and were looking for a 'rematch to land that KO punch' that such appalling devastation was being tolerated.[102] The progress of coalition forces was also frequently couched in crude sporting terms. The *Daily Star* celebrated the destruction of an Iraqi armoured unit on the outskirts of Basra at the end of March 2003 with the front-page banner '14–0: Brits whack Iraq in huge tank battle'.[103] A rather more elaborate scoring metaphor was used by the *Daily Mirror* three days later to describe another one-sided engagement, this time in central Iraq near the city of Najaf. 'When you're playing soccer at home', Tom Newton Dunn told the paper's readers, '3–2 is a fair score, but here it's more like 119–0. And Alpha Company were on unfamiliar ground and playing by the rules. The enemy was in disguise and on home turf.'[104] Most infamously, the *Sun*, in March 2011, heralded the first strike of the air campaign against Muammar Gaddafi's regime in Libya with the triumphant front-page heading 'Top Guns 1, Mad Dog 0'.[105] This use of sporting terminology, Matthew Nadelhaft has noted, could have pernicious repercussions. Not only did it permit war news to be marketed as entertainment but it also helped to normalize armed conflict. The metaphorical linking of sports and war enabled domestic audiences to 'conceptualize war as an arena in which victory was decided by merit, as in sports as we know them . . . [and] triumph achieved against an equally-matched opponent through hard work, careful planning and execution'.[106] As if this wasn't enough, the conflation of sport and war, according to Riikka Kuusisto, had one further critical impact. By 'urg[ing] active engagement', it made it seem impossible 'to have the game called off or settled off the court'.[107] In the more direct language of Sue Jansen and Don Sabo, presenting war as a sport permitted nations to 'flex their muscles and . . . "kick some ass"'.[108]

The *Sun*'s branding of Colonel Gaddafi as 'Mad Dog' was a foretaste of a subtle shift in the use of sporting language and imagery, which was to gain momentum in the new millennium. As an American-led coalition embarked on what was dubbed the War on Terror in the aftermath of the attack on the World Trade Center on 11 September 2001, the press increasingly resorted to the use of hunting metaphors and similes in which military campaigns were portrayed as blood sports and enemy leaders as prey.[109] In a reversion to the custom of earlier times, Saddam Hussein, Muammar Gaddafi and Osama bin Laden were all branded as rats or beasts by the tabloids, with Hussein's and bin Laden's hideouts routinely described as lairs or pits. Even the broadsheets were not immune from representing military operations as hunt expeditions. Thus, as the search for Saddam Hussein intensified in the summer of 2003, the *Observer* used the strapline 'How American trackers picked up the scent of the missing Iraqi dictator', while the *Guardian* noted that 'Saddam's scalp' would represent the coalition forces' 'biggest catch'.[110] Although, in the immediate aftermath of Osama bin Laden's death, *The Times* did print a brief letter claiming the use of such language smacked of 'the law of the jungle', this did not prevent the paper from continuing to refer to the site of the killing as a lair.[111] This practice not only reinforced the normalisation of military operations but, as Deborah Wills and Erin Steuter noted in an article for the *Journal of War and Culture Studies* in 2009, could have more damaging long-term effects. 'When an enemy is depicted neither as worthy opponent nor as antagonistic human combatant but as animal quarry', Wills and Steuter contended, 'outcomes such as ceasefires, negotiations or treaties become less imaginable, subsumed in a hunt narrative whose successful end is the capture, the kill and the trophy.'[112] The parallels with war reporting in the high imperial age are, of course, all too apparent.

It was not only through a subtle shift in the use of sporting language and imagery that the escalation of the War on Terror had an impact on public perceptions of conflict but also through a delicate recalibration of sporting rituals and traditions. John Kelly, Roger Penn and Damon Berridge have all commented on the growing militarisation of sport and concomitant ' "hero"-fication' of militarism in Britain since the post-9/11 campaigns in Iraq and Afghanistan.[113] This manifested itself in a number of ways. Service personnel increasingly became viewed as central players in pre- and post-match ceremonies during major sporting fixtures. In 2011, Corporal Mark Ward, who had won the military cross in Afghanistan, presented the FA Cup to Manchester City, while in the 2014 and 2015 finals, the honour of bringing the trophy onto the pitch before kick-off was given to Medical Assistant Liam O'Grady and Sergeant Dipprasad Pun respectively, both of whom were also decorated veterans of the war against the Taliban.[114] A similar trend could be seen in Rugby Union. Injured servicemen and women were received as guests of honour before kick-off in the Six Nations match between England and Wales in 2010, while serving soldiers in new desert camouflage combat uniforms escorted the teams onto the pitch for the Autumn international between England and New Zealand at Twickenham in 2014.[115] Indeed, as Penn and Berridge have noted, the involvement of the military in these key sporting events had become so commonplace after 2010 that it rarely warranted a mention in the media coverage.[116] And it was not just on the playing-field that this militarisation of sport occurred. A number of sports-related military charities were set up from 2007 onwards, the two most high profile being Help for Heroes and the Invictus Games Foundation.[117] These initiatives, without exception, claimed to be entirely apolitical, with their primary functions being to provide financial support for past and present service personnel. Both Bryn Parry, the co-founder of Help for Heroes, and Prince Harry, the patron of the Invictus Games Foundation, went to great lengths to distance themselves from the politics of the War on Terror. Parry, reflecting on the phenomenal success of Help for Heroes in 2010, insisted that the charity was 'not about the rights and wrongs of the war, it's about a 22-year-old boy who's had his legs blown off', while Prince Harry echoed this sentiment at a press conference in 2014, maintaining that the Invictus Games Foundation was 'not about supporting the conflict in Afghanistan' but was rather there to remind people 'of the journey [wounded veterans] had been through'.[118] Yet, both charities, through official pronouncements and, indeed, through their very appellations, looked to generate respect not just for the service personnel themselves but also for the duties they carried out.[119] Perhaps the clearest example of this came in March 2010 when all 72 football league clubs agreed to hold a Help for Heroes week. In announcing the move, former Conservative minister Lord Mawhinney, the chairman of the

Football League, firmly connected sporting philanthropy and military realpolitik by asserting:

> The contribution being made by our armed forces around the world is truly humbling. As a nation we do not thank them enough for the sacrifices they make. The Football for Heroes week will provide an excellent opportunity for supporters to show their appreciation for the outstanding work being done.[120]

Such rhetoric, as John Kelly has noted, ensured that the public was in no doubt 'what their financial support represent[ed] ideologically'.[121]

Undoubtedly, the most overtly political initiative, and certainly the one that caused the most contention, was the football authorities' ruling that all Scottish and English Premiership clubs, as well as the national teams, should have a specially embroidered poppy displayed on their shirts for Remembrance weekend fixtures.[122] When viewed in conjunction with the increasing ceremonial presence of troops at grounds, the move appeared, to some at least, to be detaching the poppy from its traditional associations with the two world wars and instead realigning it with the more recent campaigns in Afghanistan and Iraq.[123] This belief was most clearly demonstrated in a series of protests carried out by supporters of Glasgow Celtic. In 2008 and 2009, some fans chose to vacate their seats as the minute's silence was being held, while in 2010, at half-time during the match with Aberdeen, a banner was unfurled which read, 'Your deeds would shame all the devils in Hell. Ireland, Iraq, Afghanistan. No bloodstained poppy on our Hoops.'[124] Although the demonstrators' insistence on accompanying their actions with the distribution of anti-war literature firmly placed them in the wider political context of the War on Terror, the press still branded them sectarian extremists.[125] Indeed, the ferocity of the tabloids' backlash against the oppositionist stance adopted by these Celtic fans highlighted just how far the series of sporting initiatives introduced since 2007 had resulted in the normalisation of conflict and, in John Kelly's words, had helped 'in foreclosing doubt around wars in Afghanistan and Iraq in the face of critical commentary of official accounts'.[126]

Yet, the sporting world could still, on occasion, be marshalled to challenge the dominant discourse during the War on Terror. One notable example of this was Arabella Dorman's 2013 artwork, *Wazha-pa-Wazha* (Shoulder to Shoulder). In the painting, Dorman, who had been appointed by the Ministry of Defence to record British operations in Iraq and Afghanistan, focused on the death of Captain Walter Barrie of 1st Battalion The Royal Regiment of Scotland during a football game at Forward Operation Base Shawqat in Helmand Province on Remembrance Day 2012. Barrie had been playing football with members of the Afghan National Army when an Afghan soldier, whom he had been mentoring, shot and killed him. Such "Green on Blue" attacks had been occurring with increasing regularity throughout 2012, and it was the mood of uncertainty and futility which they generated that Dorman chose to place at the heart of *Wazha-pa-Wazha*.[127] Although a football is visible in the painting, the two central figures appear to be caught up in a tussle for a separate ball. This, combined with goals partially obscured by swirling dust and players rendered indistinguishable from one another by military fatigues, creates an overwhelming impression of confusion and purposelessness.[128] For Dorman this sense of disorder was key. Her aim, she stated before the painting went on exhibition in London in November 2014, was to 'counter the dominant narrative' and encourage viewers 'to engage more deeply with the Afghan conflict – with the impact on those that fought and those caught up in it'.[129] The football match in *Wazha-pa-Wazha*, therefore, not only raised unsettling questions about the realities of the War on Terror but, more critically, also offered up a challenge to the mass media's dominant vision of combat as a sporting endeavour.

In the immediate aftermath of the Second World War, it was hardly surprising that the British public sought solace in the traditional heroic tropes of the sporting warrior when reimagining conflict. Yet, as the nuclear age progressed and fewer and fewer people had direct experience of combat, a significant adjustment in the portrayal of war took place. The media certainly continued to use sporting metaphors to make the confusion of battle more readily comprehensible to civilian audiences, but it also increasingly resorted to packaging warfare as a sporting entertainment. This was particularly evident in television coverage. The advent of the 24-hour news cycle brought added pressure to bear on television companies to attract and retain viewers. Paradoxically, therefore, just as warfare was becoming ever more remote as a part of civilian life, so was it being delivered to people's homes with ever-greater immediacy as a sporting spectacle. After 9/11, as Britain joined the American-led coalition in the War on Terror, the conflation of war and sport was extended to encompass a more general militarisation of sporting ceremonial acts and rituals. Although all this did lead to some concerns being raised about the appropriateness of deploying sporting language and imagery, and indeed of actually continuing to play sport, during times of war, these were, for the most part, relatively subdued. As had been the case during the age of imperial conquest in the nineteenth century, so, in the post-nuclear era, military operations carried out by small professional elites in theatres of war far from home could be easily divorced from their wider contexts and presented to domestic populations hungry for news as little more than alternative sporting events.

Notes

1 *Guardian*, 3 April 2004. The National Council of Women's Organisations staged a protest rally during the 2003 Masters as part of a campaign against Augusta National Golf Club's men-only membership policy. *Daily Telegraph*, 14 April 2003.
2 Michael Paris, *Warrior Nation: Images of War in British Popular Culture, 1850–2000* (London: Reaktion Books Ltd., 2000), p. 239.
3 Paris, *Warrior Nation*, p. 259; Peter Gilroy, 'Foreword', in B. Carrington and I. McDonald (eds.), *Race, Sport and British Society* (London: Routledge, 2001), p. xii.
4 Michael Mann, 'The Roots and Contradictions of Modern Militarism', *New Left Review*, 162 (March 1987), pp. 48–49.
5 Colin McInnes, *Spectator-Sport War: The West and Contemporary Conflict* (Boulder: Lynne Reimer Publishers, 2002), pp. 143–149.

6 Sue Jansen and Don Sabo, 'The Sport/War Metaphor: Hegemonic Masculinity, the Persian Gulf War, and the New World Order', *Sociology of Sport Journal*, 11 (1994), pp. 8, 13.
7 Anthony King, 'Sport, War and Commemoration: Football and Remembrance in the Twentieth and Twenty-First Centuries', *European Journal for Sport and Society*, 13/3 (2016), p. 210.
8 King, 'Sport, War and Commemoration', p. 226.
9 Samantha King, 'Offensive Lives: Sport-State Synergy in the Era of Perpetual War', *Cultural Studies – Critical Methodologies*, 8/4 (2008), p. 528.
10 John Kelly, 'The Paradox of Militaristic Remembrance in British Sport and Popular Culture', in Michael L. Butterworth (ed.), *Sport and Militarism: Contemporary Global Perspectives* (London: Routledge, 2017), p. 149.
11 John Kelly, 'Western Militarism and the Political Utility of Sport', in Alan Bairner, John Kelly and Jung Woo Lee (eds.), *The Routledge Handbook of Sport and Politics* (London: Routledge, 2017), p. 277.
12 John Ramsden, 'England Versus Germany, Soccer and War Memory: John Huston's *Escape to Victory* (1981)', *Historical Journal of Film, Radio and Television*, 26/4 (October 2006), p. 580.
13 Paris, *Warrior Nation*, p. 238.
14 Nicholas Cull has attributed, at least in part, the popularity of camp films to the public's desire to find an antidote to the Korean War, when not only were POWs not escaping but, even worse, were being forced to appear on screen admitting to war-crimes. Nicholas J. Cull, 'Great Escapes: "Englishness" and the Prisoner of War genre', *Film and History*, 14 (2002), p. 282.
15 Non-commissioned ranks, unlike officers, were not obliged to attempt to escape and so made less heroic subjects for film treatment.
16 Jeffrey Richards, *British Films and National Identity: From Dickens to Dad's Army* (Manchester: Manchester University Press, 1997), p. 144. The exception to this cinematic fixation with officer's camps was the 1962 film *The Password Is Courage*, directed by Andrew L. Stone.
17 Paris, *Warrior Nation*, p. 238.
18 See G. Geraghty, *British Cinema in the Fifties: Gender, Genre and the 'New Look'* (London: Routledge, 2000), pp. 188–190; Neil Rattigan, 'The Last Gasp of the Middle Class: British War Films in the 1950s', in W. W. Dixon (ed.), *Re-viewing British Cinema, 1900–1992* (Albany, NY: University of New York Press, 1994), p. 150.
19 Ralph R. Donald, 'From "Knockout Punch" to "Home Run": Masculinity's "Dirty Dozen" Sports Metaphors in American Combat Films', *Film and History*, 35/1 (2005), p. 20.
20 Dilys Powell, 'Cool Customers', *The Sunday Times*, 30 July 1950. Nicholas Cull has developed this viewpoint and suggested that POW films proved so popular because they harked back to the English tradition of public school stories from the nineteenth century. Cull, 'Great Escapes', p. 287. Interestingly, however, Gill Plain has discerned more of the borstal than the boarding school in *The Wooden Horse*. For Plain, the 'public school vision really began with *The Colditz Story*'. Gill Plain, 'Before the Colditz Myth: Telling POW Stories in Postwar British Cinema', *Journal of Culture Studies*, 7/3 (2014), p. 273. Of course, as Evelyn Waugh wryly observed in *Decline and Fall*, 'anyone who has been to an English public school will always feel comparatively at home in prison'. So perhaps Powell and Plain are not so far apart after all. Evelyn Waugh, *Decline and Fall* (London: Chapman and Hall, 1928), p. 221.
21 *The Wooden Horse*, dir. Jack Lee, 1950.
22 *Sunday Despatch*, 30 July 1950. The regimental magazine of the East Kent Regiment, The Buffs, would seem to confirm British POWs' obsession with sporting activity. Page after page is devoted to sporting news from various camps, with separate reports for rugby, hockey, football and cricket. See *The Dragon*, 359 (December 1943), pp. 270, 538 (September 1944), pp. 140–141.

23 S. P. MacKenzie, *The Colditz Myth: British and Commonwealth Prisoners of War in Nazi Germany* (Oxford: Oxford University Press, 2004), p. 1.
24 In many ways, the film's likening of the camp to a games-obsessed public school reflects the spirit of Pat Reid's memoir of the same name, upon which the screenplay was based. In the introduction, Reid compared arriving at Colditz to the first few days at a new boarding school and described his own escape as a 'sporting thrill'. Pat Reid, *The Colditz Story* (London: Hodder & Stoughton, 1952), p. iii.
25 *The Colditz Story*, dir. Guy Hamilton, 1955.
26 MacKenzie, *The Colditz Myth*, p. 2.
27 Some of the key films in this golden age were: *The Captive Heart*, dir. Basil Dearden, 1946; *The Wooden Horse*, dir. Jack Lee, 1950; *Albert RN*, dir. Lewis Gilbert, 1953; *The Colditz Story*, dir. Guy Hamilton, 1955; *Reach for the Sky*, dir. Lewis Gilbert, 1957; *Danger Within*, dir. Don Chaffey, 1959; and *The Password Is Courage*, dir. Andrew L. Stone, 1962.
28 Cull, 'Great Escapes', p. 287.
29 The film was loosely based on the mass escape from Stalag Luft III in 1944, with Squadron Leader Roger Bushell serving as the inspiration for Richard Attenborough's character, Roger "Big X" Bartlett. See Paul Brickhill, *The Great Escape* (New York: Norton, 1950).
30 *The Financial Times*, 4 September 1981. *Stalag 17* was a 1953 American comedy-drama based on Donald Bevan's and Edmund Trzcinski's hit Broadway play of the same name. William Holden, in the lead role, won an Oscar for his portrayal of a cynical prisoner wrongly accused of being an informant. *Stalag 17*, dir. Billy Wilder, 1953.
31 *Escape to Victory*, dir. John Huston, 1981.
32 Ramsden, 'England Versus Germany', pp. 580, 589.
33 *Sunday Telegraph*, 6 September 1981.
34 Ramsden, 'England Versus Germany', p. 589. See also John Ramsden, *Don't Mention the War: The British and Germans Since 1890* (London: Little, Brown, 2006).
35 *The Sunday Times*, 4 April 1982. For the full details of Fisher's speech, see *Hansard* HC Deb. Vol. 21 col. 644, 3 April 1982. [Online]. www.parliament.uk/ [accessed 31 July 2019]. Argentina were, of course, the current holders of the World Cup having won the competition for the first time on home soil in 1978.
36 *Daily Mail*, 12 May 1982. FIFA had lined up Sweden, Portugal and Rumania to take the places of the home nations. The concern was that Scotland could meet Argentina as soon as the second round, although a quick glance at Scotland's record in World Cups should have been enough to allay any fears in this regard. On 2 May Argentina lost 323 men when the *ARA Belgrano* was sunk and two days later 20 crew members of *HMS Sheffield* died when the destroyer was struck by an Exocet missile.
37 *The Times*, 25 May 1982. For full details of the debate, see *Hansard* HC Deb. Vol. 24 cols. 344–345, 30 May 1982. [Online]. www.parliament.uk/ [accessed 31 July 2019]. In fact, the Conservative government was not only concerned that withdrawing the home nations would be unfair but that it would present Argentina with 'a moral victory over the UK'. *Guardian*, 30 April 1982.
38 *The Times*, 18 May 1982. Similar logic was used by the army in 1991 when dismissing calls to boycott a triangular football tournament involving Belgium. The Belgium government, as part of its stance against the war in the Gulf, had refused to fulfil a munitions contract with Britain. General Sir James Wilson explained the Army FA's decision to compete nonetheless by noting, 'We do not feel there is any difference in the attitude of the Belgium army towards us and, after all, we all have stupid governments from time to time.' *The Times*, 29 January 1991.
39 This was long before the presence of overseas players in English top-flight football became the norm. In fact, Villa and Ardiles were the first of just a handful of international stars to arrive in Britain when the Football League lifted the effective ban on non-British professionals in 1978. Matthew Taylor, *The Association Game: A History of British Football* (London: Pearson Educational Ltd., 2008), p. 307.

40 *Guardian*, 22 May 1982. In the event, Samuel was to be disappointed. With public passions running high as a land invasion of the Falklands by British troops appeared imminent, Villa asked to be withdrawn from the Tottenham squad.
41 *Daily Mirror*, 6 April 1982; *Sun*, 5 April 1982.
42 *Daily Express*, 7 April 1982.
43 The opening match of the World Cup took place on 13 June, the day before hostilities ceased in the Falklands. Indeed, the sense that events in Spain and the Falklands were somehow connected was buttressed further by the fact that it fell to the sports commentator, David Coleman, during the build-up to the USSR versus Brazil match, to break the news of the ceasefire on 14 June.
44 Justin Wren-Lewis and Alan Clarke have noted that this 'conflation of Argentina the enemy nation and Argentina the rival football team' was quickly abandoned when the ceasefire was announced on 14 June. Argentina's comfortable 4–1 win victory over Hungary on 18 June distanced the defeated army on the Falklands from the victorious football team in Spain and allowed ITV and BBC to focus exclusively on the country's rich footballing heritage. Justin Wren-Lewis and Alan Clarke, 'The World Cup – A Political Football', *Theory, Culture and Society*, 3/1 (1983), pp. 128–129.
45 *The Times*, 22 April 1982.
46 *The Sunday Times*, 2 May 1982.
47 *The Sunday Times*, 4 April 1982. In the aftermath of England's quarter-final defeat of Argentina during a bad-tempered match at Wembley in 1966, Alf Ramsey refused to allow his players to swap shirts with the opposition, claiming the Argentinians had played like 'animals'. Matt Dickinson, *Bobby Moore: The Man in Full* (London: Yellow Jersey Press, 2014), pp. 116–118.
48 *The Times*, 6 May 1982.
49 *Daily Express*, 15 June 1982. Argentina lost their opening match of the World Cup 1–0 to Belgium.
50 *The Times*, 29 April 1982.
51 Peter Beck, 'To Play or Not to Play: That Is the Anglo-Argentine Question', *Contemporary Review*, 245 (August 1984), p. 74. England had been due to play Argentina in a tournament in Brazil in June 1984 and before that in a tour of South America in the summer of 1983.
52 Quoted in James Aulich, 'Wildlife in the South Atlantic: Graphic Satire, Patriotism and the Fourth Estate', in James Aulich (ed.), *Framing the Falklands: Nationhood, Culture and Identity* (Maidenhead: Open University Press, 1991), p. 91. On 29 May 1985, 39 people were crushed to death when a wall collapsed after Liverpool fans charged Juventus supporters before the start of the European Cup Final at the Heysel Stadium in Brussels.
53 Nick Perry, *Arrivederci Millwall* (London: Faber & Faber, 1985). The play was first performed at The Albany Empire in Deptford in 1985 and was turned into a film, directed by Charles McDougall, in 1990.
54 D. George Boyce, *The Falklands War* (London: Macmillan Publishing Ltd., 2005), p. 180.
55 Paul Greengrass, 'Foreword', in Aulich (ed.), *Framing the Falklands*, p. x. The connection between the Falklands and football is again made in Steve Barron's *Mike Bassett: England Manager* (2001). With Bassett's England due to face Argentina in the World Cup semi-final, British broadcasters are shown cranking up the tension by playing video montages of the 1982 conflict. This has the effect of pushing the already volatile England captain over the edge, and, as he heads out for the game, he punches a hole in the wall of the changing room while yelling, 'Let's fucking kill 'em'. See Alexander Ross, 'The Falklands War and the Media: Popular and Elite Understanding of the Conflict' (unpublished MA diss., University of Birmingham, 2014), p. 63. Interestingly, the *Sun* saw combat as the antidote to, rather than the cause of, hooliganism.

After 95 England fans had been arrested for rioting before an international against Turkey in Sunderland in April 2003, the paper's headline called for the government to 'Send Soccer Scum to Iraq for a Real Fight'. *Sun*, 8 April 2003.
56 Raymond Jackson [Jak], no title, *Daily Express*, 19 June 1982.
57 *Guardian*, 12 May 1982.
58 *Daily Mail*, 14 June 1982.
59 *Observer*, 20 January 1991.
60 *The Times*, 26 January 1991.
61 *The Times*, 24 March 2003.
62 *The Times*, 27 March 1999.
63 *The Times*, 17 March 2003. Simon Jenkins was of much the same opinion. The day after the invasion of Iraq had been launched, he noted that other news stories struggled to get 'a look-in. Only the ultimate anaesthetic, football, was permitted to supplant bombs as a fit subject for public interest'. *The Times*, 21 March 2003.
64 The *Sun*, in particular, delighted in attacking Pires. Not only were his anti-war protests anathema to everything the paper believed in but he also served as a handy proxy for the French nation as a whole, which, much to the paper's disgust, resolutely opposed the Coalition's actions.
65 *Guardian*, 25 March 2003.
66 *The Times*, 20 May 1982.
67 *Observer*, 20 January 1991. Wales had played England in the Five Nations Championships on 19 July.
68 *Sun*, 15 April 2003. Inverness Caledonian Thistle had beaten Celtic in the quarter-finals of the Scottish Cup. Unfortunately for Bobby Mann, and Kenny, they lost to Dundee 1–0 in the semi-final.
69 *Daily Mirror*, 4 February 1991.
70 *The Times*, 13 December 2003. The *Daily Mirror* had also run with a feature on 'Gulf Golf' in 1991. However, the piece appeared to serve more as a vehicle for obvious puns than a commentary on military qualities. Thus, one RAF pilot who, we are told, had been attacking surface-to-air missile sites the day before is, inevitably, quoted as saying, '"I Thought We Were Having a Day off from Bunkers"', *Daily Mirror*, 28 January 1991.
71 *The Times*, 30 April 2003.
72 *Daily Star*, 4 April 2003.
73 *Sun*, 4 April 2003.
74 See, for example, the *Daily Mirror*'s 'Gulf War Special Issue', 18 January 1991 or the *Yorkshire Evening Post*'s 'Land War: Sunday Colour Special', 24 February 1991. The latter, just to underline the comparison with sporting specials, had been advertised in Friday's edition of the *Post* between announcements for 'Big Fight Special' and 'City Match Report'. *Yorkshire Evening Post*, 22 February 1991. More recently tabloid readers have been encouraged to watch the 'highlights' of battle through online links. See the *Sun*, 28 March 2011.
75 See, for example, the *Sun*'s interview with Lieutenant-Colonel Swan on 9 April 2003 and the *Mirror*'s feature on Rear Admiral Sandy Woodward on 26 April 1982. For more on the 'War Traitors Dartboard', see Chris York, 'The *Sun* criticised for deleting "Traitor's [sic] Dartboard" in wake of Chilcot Report', *Huffington Post* online, 7 July 2016, <www.huffingtonpost.co.uk/entry/the-sun-iraq_uk_577e2de3e4b074297db287a6?guccounter=1&guce_referrer=aHR0cHM6Ly93d3cuZ29vZ2xlLmNvLnVrLw&guce_referrer_sig=AQAAABBVokZwB-WRn9s7tncLYqYkmXnt2_z7C0bF3sXYOtec2Ovw0EZmGNwLlIhPtxB-GMFI0QzgDDPTnlh9bQl_REqKngvVBsANIPCy2m8FcbOP65Fd185hUiz0MgFVPHPXWqI6DCX-Lc3bSe13IRcc8r7W14_2JRZk-81maoEyfAlg> [accessed 26 April 2019].
76 *Guardian*, 10 March 2003.

150 *War in the nuclear age, 1945 to present*

77 Steven Baxter, 'War Is Sport, Sport Is War', *New Statesman* online, 21 March 2011, <www.newstatesman.com/blogs/steven-baxter/2011/03/football-score-sport-war> [accessed 26 April 2019]. The Libyan leader, Colonel Muammar Gaddafi, was nicknamed in the British media' Mad Dog'. The term gained popular currency after Ronald Reagan had dubbed Gaddafi 'the mad dog of the Middle East' in the aftermath of the bombing of a Berlin nightclub, in which two American servicemen died.

78 *Guardian*, 28 March 2003. Iain St John and Jimmy Greaves fronted a popular television football programme, *Saint and Greavsie*, between 1985 and 1992. The second Gulf War was the first major conflict involving British troops to be covered by the BBC's 24-hour news channel. However, it was the first Gulf War in 1991, with CNN's rolling coverage, that really underlined television's pre-eminence in breaking news. Philip M. Taylor, *Munitions of the Mind: A History of Propaganda from the Ancient World to the Present Day* (Manchester: Manchester University Press, 1995), pp. 285–302.

79 Colin McInnes, *Spectator-Sport War*, pp. 149–150.

80 Greg Philo, *The British Media and the Gulf War* (Glasgow: Glasgow University Media Research Group, 1993), p. 7. The newscasters themselves could sometimes become caught up in this sense that they were overseeing a great sporting occasion. The BBC's Martyn Lewis, recalling the adrenalin-rush as he broke the news of the first Gulf War in 1991, said it felt like having 'a ring-side seat to history'. *Daily Mirror*, 18 January 1991.

81 *Guardian*, 30 March 1991. Peter Stothard, who spent a month 'embedded' with Tony Blair and his advisers in the lead up to the second Gulf War in 2003, commented on a similar atmosphere within 10 Downing Street. 'Pulling out my notebooks of life with the Prime Minister at that time', Stothard observed, '[was] like reading the transcript of a Radio 5 Live phone-in – irregular news bulletins, interspersed with disallowed penalties, desperate substitutions and the masochistic fatalism of the touchline'. *The Times*, 13 March 2008. See also Peter Stothard, *30 Days: A Month at the Heart of Blair's War* (New York: HarperCollins, 2003).

82 *Daily Star*, 19 March 2003.

83 *Guardian*, 25 March 2003.

84 *Guardian*, 26 March 2003.

85 *Independent*, 29 March 2003. Martin Shaw and Roy Carr-Hill, in a study reviewing the media's coverage of the first Gulf War, made a similar point about the broadcast news's tendency to sanitise war. The 'spectator-sport' approach to war reporting, they argued, served to 'screen off the actual violence'. Martin Shaw and Roy Carr-Hill, 'Mass media and Attitudes to the Gulf War in Britain', *Electronic Journal of Communication*, 2/1 (1991), <www.cios.org/EJCPUBLIC/002/1/00212.HTML> [accessed 29 April 2019].

86 Bob Deans, 'Sanitized Lexicon of Modern War', *Newspaper Research Journal*, 12/1 (Winter 1991), pp. 11–12.

87 *Daily Mail*, 21 April 2003.

88 *The Times*, 22 March 2003.

89 *Guardian*, 11 April 2003. Torrie Clarke, a US defence spokeswoman, had infamously responded to a question about civilian casualties during an unsuccessful targeted attack on a restaurant in which Saddam Hussein had been believed to have been eating, with a dismissive remark: 'I don't think that matters very much. I'm not losing sleep trying to figure out if he was in there.' Private Jessica Lynch was rescued from Iraqi captivity by US Special Operations Forces on 1 April 2003. As Barnes predicted, Lynch's story was indeed turned into a film, though not a Hollywood one. *Saving Jessica Lynch*, directed by Peter Markle, was released as a TV movie in November 2003.

90 See pp. 7–10.

91 *Daily Mirror*, 26 April 1982.

92 *Daily Express*, 26 April 1982.

93　*Daily Mail*, 27 April 1982. In fact, Woodward later claimed that he had been misquoted and that he had actually said, '[F]rankly, I'd really rather be given a walkover.' Lawrence Freedman, *Official History of the Falklands Campaign, Vol. 2: War and Diplomacy* (London: Routledge, 2005), p. 346.
94　*Daily Express*, 17 June 1982. Thompson commanded 3 Commando Brigade and orchestrated the landings at San Carlos Water on 21 May 1982. In 1991, Lieutenant-General Sir Peter de la Billière, the commander of the British forces in the Gulf, followed Moore's lead and named General Norman Schwarzkopf as his 'Gulf War's man of the match'. *Daily Mirror*, 1 March 1991.
95　Kenneth Mahood, no title, *Daily Mail*, 31 May 1982. Kenneth Mahood, who had previously worked for *The Times* and the *Evening Standard*, joined the Mail at the beginning of 1982 to draw its topical pocket-cartoon as well as supply sports cartoons. 'Kenneth Mahood' (21 March 2016), University of Kent British Cartoon Archive, <www.cartoons.ac.uk/cartoonist-biographies/m-n/KennethMahood.html> [accessed 24 July 2017].
96　*The Times*, 3 April 1982.
97　Matthew Nadelhaft, 'Metawar: Sports and the Persian Gulf War', *Journal of American Culture* 16/4 (Winter 1993), p. 28.
98　See, for example, *Daily Mirror*, 24 January 1991; *The Times*, 21 March 2003.
99　John Mueller, 'American Public Opinion and the Gulf War', in Stanley Renshon (ed.), *The Political Psychology of the Gulf War* (Pittsburgh: University of Pittsburgh Press, 1993), p. 220.
100　*Daily Mirror*, 28 March 2003. Indeed, the referencing of American football by senior commanders was so persistent that it prompted a scholarly response in the *Armed Forces Journal*. In an article published in November 2003, Joel Cassman, a foreign service officer with the US Department of State, and David Lai, a professor of international security at the US Air War College, argued that soccer, not American football, offered a better model against the unconventional threats posed by the War on Terror because the game relied on 'finesse, surprise attack and patience instead of power and force'. Joel F. Cassman and David Lai, 'Football v Soccer: American Warfare in an Era of Unconventional Threats', *Armed Forces Journal* (November 2003), pp. 49–54, 50.
101　*Daily Mirror*, 18 January 1991. The Mirror had already used a boxing metaphor in the lead-up to the war. On the eve of hostilities, the paper's military expert, Lord Bramall, who had been chief of the General Staff during the Falklands campaign, had explained in the first of his 'daily briefings' that 'the Allied soldiers were like boxers before a world title fight – anxious to forget the build-up and get going'. *Daily Mirror*, 17 January 1991.
102　*Sun*, 27 March 2003; *Daily Mirror*, 19 March 2003. Carl Sempel has argued that 'popular masculinist sport' such as boxing were among the key 'cultural institutions that functioned to buttress support for the Iraqi War'. Carl Sempel, 'Televised Sports: Masculinist Moral Capital and Support for the US Invasion of Iraq', *Journal of Sport and Social Issues*, 30/1 (February 2006), p. 82.
103　*Daily Star*, 21 March 2003.
104　*Daily Mirror*, 24 March 2003.
105　*Sun*, 21 March 2011.
106　Nadelhaft, 'Metawar', p. 28.
107　Riikka Kuusisto, 'Framing the Wars in the Gulf and in Bosnia: The Rhetorical Definitions of the Western Power Leaders in Action', *Journal of Peace Research*, 35/5 (September 1998), p. 615.
108　Jansen and Sabo, 'The Sport/War Metaphor', p. 8.
109　For example, 'We Got Him: The Beast's Pit', *Sun*, 15 December 2003; 'Rat in a Trap', *Daily Mirror*, 15 December 2003; 'Secrets of Bin Laden's Lair', *Daily Mail*, 13 May 2011; 'Bullet for the Beast', *Sun*, 4 May 2011; 'A Mad Dog in Life but a Cowering Rat in His Last Brutal Moments', *Metro*, 21 October 2011.

War in the nuclear age, 1945 to present

110 *Observer*, 22 June 2003; *Guardian*, 22 June 2003. The reconfiguration of military operations as hunts was buttressed by stories of coalition soldiers seizing 'trophies' from, or having pictures taken with, the enemy dead. See, for example, 'German Skull Row Troops Suspended' (15 November 2015), BBC online news channel, <http://news.bbc.co.uk/1/hi/world/europe/6106546.stm> [accessed 11 February 2019].

111 *The Times*, 4 May 2011. For example, a week later the paper ran a lengthy article exploring the 'assault on bin Laden's lair'. *The Times*, 11 May 2011.

112 Deborah Wills and Erin Steuter, 'The Soldier as Hunter: Pursuit, Prey and Display in the War on Terror', *Journal of War and Culture Studies*, 2/2 (2009), p. 203.

113 Kelly, 'The Paradox of Militaristic Remembrance', p. 1, 9; Roger Penn and Damon Berridge, 'Football and the Military in Contemporary Britain: An Exploration of Invisible Nationalism', *Armed Forces Journal*, 44/1 (2018), p. 134. In fact, Penn and Berridge trace the genesis of this shift as far back as the Falklands War but, nonetheless, cite the post-9/11 campaigns as really bringing it to the fore.

114 '"Courageous" Soldier Mark Ward to present FA Cup' (12 May 2011), BBC online news channel, <www.bbc.co.uk/news/uk-13373884> [accessed 2 May 2019]; 'FA Cup final duties for Service Personnel' (19 May 2014), UK Government online news channel, <www.gov.uk/government/news/fa-cup-final-duties-for-service-personnel> [accessed 2 May 2019]; 'FA Cup Duties for Armed Forces Personnel' (1 June 2015), Armed Forces Day online news, <www.armedforcesday.org.uk/fa-cup-final-duties-for-armed-forces-personnel/> [accessed 2 May 2019].

115 John Kelly, 'Popular Culture, Sport and the "Hero"-fication of British Militarism', *Sociology*, 47/4 (2012), p. 731; Penn and Berridge, 'Football and the Military', p. 131.

116 Penn and Berridge, 'Football and the Military', pp. 123–124. Penn and Berridge have called this unacknowledged presence 'invisible nationalism'.

117 Help for Heroes was set up in 2007 by Bryn and Emma Parry in 2007, and the Invictus Games Foundation was launched by Prince Harry in 2014. Other recent military charities include: Healing the Wounds (2009), Care for Casualties (2009), Tickets for Troops (2009), Walking with the Wounded (2009) and Coming Home (2011).

118 'Family Affair Becomes £50 Million Charity' (12 June 2010), BBC online news channel, <www.bbc.co.uk/news/10296858> [accessed 3 May 2019]; *Independent*, 6 March 2014.

119 The Invictus Games' mission statement cites as one of the organisation's main aims the generation of 'a wider understanding and respect for those who serve their country', while Parry has asserted that one of the core functions of Help for Heroes was to 'tap into pent-up public sentiment in support of British troops in Iraq and Afghanistan'. 'Invictus Games Foundation' (2016), Invictus Games Foundation website, <www.invictusgamesfoundation.org/foundation> [accessed 3 May 2019]; 'Family Affair', BBC News online. Of course, the use of terms such as 'Heroes' and 'Invictus' (undefeated) confers heroic status and, consequently, implies support for any actions.

120 'Footie Clubs Unite for Heroes' (2 March 2010), *Sun* online, <www.thesun.co.uk/sol/homepage/news/campaigns/our_boys/2874672/footie-clubs-unite-for-heroes.html> [accessed 3 May 2019].

121 Kelly, 'Western Militarism', p. 288.

122 2010 was the first time all premiership clubs agreed to have poppies on their shirts.

123 The initiative was not just associated with the wars in Iraq and Afghanistan. Manchester United's Nemanja Matic refused to wear the poppy in November 2018 claiming it 'reminded him of the NATO-led bombing of his home town of Vrelo during the 1999 Yugoslav wars'. 'Poppy is reminder of NATO-led bombing of my village, say Nemanja Matic', *The Times*, online, 5 November 2011, <www.thetimes.co.uk/article/memory-of-bombing-raid-is-why-ive-stopped-wearing-poppy-says-matic-zqch809b3> [accessed 3 May 2019].

124 *Sunday Mail*, 9 November 2008; *Daily Record*, 10 November 2009; 'Red-faced Celtic Apologise After Supporters Launch Shameful "Bloodstained" Poppy Protest', *Daily Mail* online, 9 November 2010, <www.dailymail.co.uk/sport/football/article-1327712/Celtic-apologise-fans-bloodstained-poppy-protest.html> accessed 3 May 2019.
125 For example, an editorial in the *Daily Record* in 2009 claimed the demonstrators were part of Celtic's 'Green Brigade', while Jim Traynor, in an opinion piece for the paper on the same day, angrily suggested that 'this spiteful minority . . . should scramble over the wall, or catch the next ferry from Stranraer and leave us all alone'. *Daily Record*, 9 November 2011.
126 Kelly, 'Popular Culture', p. 722.
127 Barrie's was the fourteenth such death in 2012. There had been just one the year before and three the year before that. *Herald*, 29 November 2012.
128 For a more detailed deconstruction of the painting, see King, 'Sport, War and Commemoration', pp. 221–224.
129 Bob Chaudry, 'Before the Dawn – Arabella Dorman', *Huffington Post* online, 3 November 2014, <www.huffingtonpost,co,uk/bob-chaudry/Arabella-Dorman-Before-the-Dawn.html> [accessed 4 May 2019]. In fact, Dorman considered the message of *Wazha-pa-Wazha* to be, ultimately, an uplifting one. 'It showed', she claimed, 'a renewed trust in the human spirit, and how the courage to trust the Afghan again after such a devastating low-hand attack triumphs violence and deceit'. Chaudry, 'Before the Dawn',

Conclusion

In August 1941, with the nation's fate still hanging in the balance, the in-house cartoonist of *The Dragon*, the regimental magazine of the Buffs, presented an affectionate portrait of the typical company commander. Resplendent in football kit and cricket pads, and carrying a hockey stick with a golf bag over his shoulder and a tennis racket under his arm, the officer was shown nonchalantly reassuring a bemused sergeant-major: 'I play only one game at a time!'[1] The suggestion that games and sporting endeavour, despite the grave military situation, continued to feature high on the army's list of priorities was further underlined by the cartoon's placement within page after page of inter-battalion sports reports. The Buffs, of course, were by no means exceptional. From the Crimean campaign onwards, British troops on active service sought out, and engaged in, a wide range of sporting activities with a level of intensity and enthusiasm that was, to the domestic press, admirable and, to the international press, astonishing. It was generally assumed by those in authority that from this passion for physical exercise accrued both physical and psychological benefits. Not only, did the thinking go, would participation in games hone the men's fitness but it would also boost their morale and sense of regimental esprit de corps. For the conscript troops of the two total wars of the twentieth century, sport in the frontline was believed to have the additional advantage of mitigating the dislocation of service in the combat zone by acting as a conduit with the temporarily abandoned civilian world.[2]

More contentious, however, was the conviction that sport prepared men for war by developing the moral qualities, what late Victorians termed character, which would sustain them in battle. In times of crises particularly this assumption came under heightened pressure as calls were made for the military's amateur sporting ethos to be abandoned in favour of a more 'scientific' professional approach. Thus, the debacle of the Crimean War, the shock of the Indian Rebellion and the attritional slog of the struggle against the Boer Republics all led to protracted discussions about the failings of a sports-obsessed army. As the nation's very existence came under threat during the two world wars, the questioning of sport intensified. Indeed, in the national emergencies of the summer of 1940, June 1941 and February 1942, the significance in wartime life of sporting culture itself was challenged. Yet, the conviction that the playing-field could function as a training ground for the battlefield proved remarkably enduring. As late as 2005, with

British troops bogged down in a vicious counter-insurgency campaign against the forces of Al-Qaeda in the aftermath of the invasion of Iraq, *The Times*' columnist Ben McIntyre still felt able to turn Orwell's famous dictum on its head and suggest that 'war is serious sport, plus the shooting'.[3] 'Orwell', he informed the paper's readers in a lengthy opinion piece on the Coalition's operational tactics,

> was speaking as one who had spent miserable hours on muddy playing fields, and ascribed the worst possible motives to sports fanaticism: 'It is bound up with hatred, jealousy, boastfulness, disregard of all the rules and a sadistic pleasure in witnessing violence.' In fact, sport has often influenced soldiers in positive ways, instilling self-discipline, comradeship and an awareness that the team can lose a game but win the championship; lose a battle, but win the war.[4]

Equally resilient was the belief that public attitudes towards sport served as a litmus test of the nation's martial spirit. To regard sport as a vehicle for passive entertainment rather than a means to keep fit was, in particular, frequently frowned on and cited as evidence of national degeneration. In December 1899, with the early defeats of the South African War still fresh in the memory, the *Daily Mail* feared that the Dominions, who 'pride themselves in healthy exercises', would soon outstrip the mother country where 'our young men are content to assemble once or twice a week, not by the thousands but by the hundreds of thousands . . . to watch a handful of their fellows, who personally gain much healthy amusement, and occasionally a good deal of money, by playing football and cricket'.[5] Just over 50 years later, two drawn matches against the Australians in the 1953 Test series were enough to prompt a reader of the same paper to arrive at a similar conclusion: 'We are becoming a nation of sports-watchers', Mr. C. G. Corfield, from the cricketing heartland of Edgbaston, complained in a letter to the *Mail*'s editor,

> and as all our major championships pass to foreign competitors all we seem content to do is to watch and comment. Decline of physical exercise has been the chief cause of the decay of preceding civilisations. It will not be the nation with the most deadly weapons which will survive another war but the nation with the fittest men. The only 'ashes' we are likely to gain are the 'ashes' of a 'C3' race.[6]

And even professional participants were not immune to accusations that they no longer lived up to the standards of manliness established by amateur sportsmen of earlier ages. The decision of six senior Chelsea players to miss the club's UEFA cup tie with Hapoel Tel Aviv in Israel because of on-going security fears in the aftermath of 9/11 did not go down well with one correspondent to the *Daily Express*. 'If Waterloo is said to have been won on the playing fields of Eton', he grumbled, 'then the Afghan war is unlikely to be won on the playing fields of Chelsea.'[7]

The centrality of sport in Britain's wartime culture was also evident in the mass media's persistent use of sporting language and imagery as it hastened to satisfy a domestic public eager for frontline news. With the wars of colonial expansion during Victoria's reign taking place far enough from home to pose no threat to the nation's stability or prosperity, accounts of heroic charges and gallant last stands could be presented to a rapidly expanding newspaper readership as differing little from particularly exciting cup ties or test matches. In the wake of the Second World War, Britain's military once again found itself engaged in limited campaigns in remote regions. Television coverage followed the lead of the printed press and packaged these conflicts as sporting entertainments. Although, as had been the case in the nineteenth century, some dissenting voices were heard, for the most part these were kept to the margins. *The Times* spoke for many when, in an editorial published shortly after the launch of Operation Desert Storm during the Gulf War of 1991, it argued that 'War will always draw on language from other areas of life, especially sport. . . . Bathos apart, simile and metaphor are appropriate tools to describe the horror of war as well as the relief of victory. If the resulting impact offends some, the failure to convey impact may offend others.'[8] Indeed, for many commentators after 1945, the use of the language and imagery of the battlefield in sports reporting was of greater concern than any attempt by the media to parcel war as sport.

The sport that lent itself most readily as a metaphor for war was hunting. Time and again during the small wars of the second-half of the nineteenth century, military operations were depicted as grouse-shoots or fox-hunts, with enemy warriors labelled beasts or prey and their leaders' headquarters lairs or dens. Although the Boers' Anglo-Saxon roots largely precluded the ascribing of sub-human appellations, this did not stop the terminology of the hunt being used to describe the campaigning in South Africa between 1899 and 1902.[9] In particular, 'bag' was regularly employed by both those in authority and the press when reporting on the killing or taking of enemy combatants in the long-drawn-out guerrilla endgame. The nature of the two total wars of the twentieth century, the immobility of the first and the scale of the second, largely militated against the use of hunting metaphors as a frame of reference. However, with a return to localised warfare in distant regions towards the end of the twentieth century, army commanders and war correspondents fell back on the terminology of blood sports to define operations. This practice did have significant repercussions. By demonising enemy combatants as quarry and refashioning military campaigns as hunts, wider political and humanitarian concerns tended to become obscured by the imperatives of the chase. Certainly, in the coverage of operations against rebel sepoys in 1857 and Taliban insurgents in 2001, thrilling accounts of 'bags' and 'kills' frequently masked more considered reportage.[10]

However, the yoking together of the sporting and military worlds was not a feature exclusive to periods of limited warfare. Even during the two world wars, as the country fought for survival, sporting language and imagery continued to be used as a tool for reimagining the fighting. Between 1914 and 1918, reconfiguring the horrors of the industrial battlefield as a sporting encounter helped to normalise events for both combatant and non-combatant. Sporting metaphors not only made understandable the confusion of trench warfare but also imbued the fighting with

Conclusion 157

a sense of fair play. And here the symbolism of cricket was especially important. Uniquely English, the game was thought to embody all that was good about the country and her armed forces. A nation with a passion for cricket, it was assumed, could be guaranteed to wage war courageously, self-sacrificingly and, critically, honourably. By contrast, the non-sporting German soldier's perceived failure to play by the rules of the 'game' enabled the press to cast him as brute who posed a threat to the very existence of Western civilisation. Although, as Eliza Riedi and Tony Mason correctly pointed out, the experience of the Great War meant that, for the new generation of officers who assumed command after 1939, 'the analogy between sport and war [was] replaced by a soberer sense of the concrete benefits sport could bring to the army', this did little to deter journalists and popular authors from continuing to couch warfare in sporting terms.[11] The tabloid press's use of the cricket scoreboard to trace the fortunes of RAF pilots during the Battle of Britain was simply the most egregious of many examples. And, just as had been the case between 1914 and 1918, reimagining the war as a game, be it a cricket match or a football fixture, allowed commentators to draw a clear distinction between the honourable British warrior-athlete and the decidedly unsporting and, hence, ignoble German stormtrooper. Indeed, so significant did sport become as a cultural signifier during the Second World War that it was even held up as a symbol of the freedoms for which the war was being waged.

There was, of course, some criticism of the sport/war nexus during the two total wars just as there had been during the imperial wars of the nineteenth century. This was most marked in the summer of 1940 as the furore surrounding Charles Gardner's 'live' radio broadcast of an aerial dogfight was played out in the pages of the national press. However, as a BBC Listener Research Report noted, even those who were repulsed by Gardner's sporting tone were prepared to concede that 'War is in bad taste anyway, and if you must fight you cannot be over-squeamish.' And such views were, in any case, in the minority. From the 'vast majority' of people, the same report concluded, there was 'widespread appreciation of the item and no criticism'.[12] In many ways, this easy acceptance of Gardner's reconfiguration of the battlefield as a playing-field should have come as no surprise. From 1850 onwards, through a wide variety of visual and literary sources, the British public had been repeatedly exposed to romanticised images of sporting warriors engaged in the 'greater game' of war. The BBC was, therefore, simply building on a long tradition in which combat and sport had been equated.

That the link between sport and war became firmly embedded in the British cultural landscape over the century and a half following the accession of Victoria would appear, therefore, to be undeniable; less clear-cut, however, is the impact this connection had on popular attitudes to warfare. Jonathan Charteris-Black suggested that it effectively legitimised warfare. When people came to regard military conflicts 'as if they were "only" sporting contests', he argued in a critical study of the function of metaphor in language, this had the effect of 'minimis[ing] resistance to war'.[13] Certainly, the conflation of war and sport and the attendant militarisation of sporting rituals and ceremonies during the War on Terror would seem to give some substance to this viewpoint. Yet, of course, throughout the period covered by this study, critical voices were raised, albeit frequently on the margins, against not only war itself but the packaging of war as a sporting entertainment. Perhaps, then, when it comes to evaluating what John Kelly called the sporting '"hero"-ification of war', closer to the mark is the more nuanced judgement of Martin Bell, the former BBC foreign affairs newsman, who experienced the frontline as both a correspondent and a casualty. This 'prettifying of war', he contended, has helped to normalise combat and 'make it an acceptable option for settling disputes'.[14]

Notes

1. *The Dragon*, 501 August 1941, p. 220.
2. For more on the enduring civilian bonds of the Great War soldier, see, John Bourne, 'The British Working Man in Arms', in Hugh P. Cecil and Peter Liddle (eds.), *Facing Armageddon: The First World War Experienced* (London: Leo Cooper, 1996), pp. 336–352.
3. Orwell, in an essay published in the *Tribune* in December 1945, had famously written that sport was 'war minus the shooting'. George Orwell, 'The Sporting Spirit', *Tribune*, 14 December 1945.
4. *The Times*, 1 January 2005.
5. *Daily Mail*, 25 December 1899.
6. *Daily Mail*, 9 July 1953. In fact, England did manage to sneak a 1–0 series victory with an eight-wicket win in the final Test at The Oval, but whether this would have been enough to satisfy Mr Corfield seems doubtful.
7. *Daily Express*, 24 October 1901.
8. *The Times*, 26 January 1991.
9. For more on the racialised depiction of the Boers in the lead up to, and during, the South African War, see, M. van Wyk Smith, 'The Boers and the Anglo-Boer War (1899–1902) in the Twentieth Century Moral Imaginary', *Victorian Literature and Culture*, 31/2 (2003), pp. 429–446.
10. Hunting terminology has continued to be used in the coverage of the campaign against ISIS. Thus, in March 2018, the *Daily Star* ran a story on an 'ISIS underground lair where jihadis are born', while, the following year, *The Times* reported that the ISIL commander, Al-Baghdadi, was 'believed to be lying low in a secret desert lair'. *The Daily Star* online, 4 March 2018, <www.dailystar.co.uk/news/latest-news/686206/MI5-bosses-ISIS-jihadi-bio-weapons-secret-UK-terror-labs> [accessed 13 August 2019]; *The Times* online, 24 March 2019, <www.thetimes.co.uk/article/caliphate-falls-but-its-crocodile-cells-plot-to-maul-the-west-hlphg6rgq> [accessed 13 August 2019].
11. Riedi and Mason, *Sport and the Military*, p. 257.
12. 'Listener Research Report: Air Battle Commentary by Charles Gardner', (1940), BBC online archives, <www.bbc.co.uk/archive/battleofbritain/11432.shtml?page=1> [accessed 19 April 2019].
13. Jonathan Charteris-Black, *Corpus Approaches to Critical Metaphor Analysis* (Basingstoke: Palgrave Macmillan, 2004), p. 114.
14. John Kelly, 'Popular Culture, Sport and the "Hero"-fication of British Militarism', *Sociology*, 47/4 (2012), p. 731; Bell quoted in Paris, *Warrior Nation*, p. 260. Martin Bell was injured by shrapnel from a mortar blast while working as a foreign correspondent in Sarajevo during the Bosnian War in 1992. See the *Independent*, 28 August 1992.

Bibliography

Primary unpublished material

Canterbury, Templeman Library Special Collections, U327, The Buffs Golfing Society Record Album, volume 1
Mass Observation, FR113 'Space Distribution in the Press 1937, 1939, 1940', 16 May 1940
Mass Observation, FR126 'Report on Press', May 1940
Mass Observation, FR261 'Air Propaganda', 12 July 1940
Mass Observation, FR279 'Charles Gardner Broadcast', 16 July 1940
Mass Observation, FR 1149 'Some Thoughts on Greyhounds and National Unity', March 1942
Mass Observation, FR1229 'Attitudes to the Continuance of Organised Sport in Wartime: April 1942', 26 April 1942

Journals and newspapers

Bell's Life in London and Sporting Chronicle
Blackwood's Edinburgh Magazine
Bucks Herald
Contemporary Review
Cornhill Magazine
Country Gentleman, Sporting Gazette and Agricultural Journal
Daily Express
Daily Graphic
Daily Mail
Daily Mirror
Daily Record
Daily Star
Daily Telegraph
Derby Mercury
Edinburgh Review
Evening News
Evening Standard
Field Magazine
Fraser's Magazine for Town and Country
Fun
Graphic

160 *Bibliography*

Guardian
Hansard
Herald
Huffington Post
Illustrated London News
Independent
Langtonian
Lloyd's Weekly Newspaper
Manchester Guardian
Metro
New Statesman
News of the World
Nottinghamshire Guardian
Observer
Punch
Spectator
Sporting Life
Sun
Sunday Despatch
Sunday Express
Sunday Mail
Sunday Telegraph
Sunderland Daily Echo
The Dragon
The Financial Times
The Sunday Times
The Times
Tribune
Vanity Fair
Western Gazette
Western Mail
Yorkshire Evening Post
Young England

Primary published material

Anonymous, *A Handbook of the Boer War* (London and Aldershot: Gale and Polden Ltd., 1910)

Alderson, E. A. H., *Pink and Scarlet or Hunting as a School for Soldiering* (London: William Heinemann, 1900)

Alderson, E. A. H., *With the Mounted Infantry and the Mashonaland Field Force, 1896* (London: Methuen & Co., 1898)

Almond, H. H., 'The Breed of Man', *The Nineteenth Century*, 48 (October 1900)

Amery, Leopold, *The Times History of the War in South Africa, Volume II* (London: Sampson Low, 1902)

Anson, Harcourt S., *With H. M. 9th Lancers During the Indian Mutiny: The Letters of Brevet-Major O. H. S. G. Anson* (London: W. H. Allen, 1896)

Baden-Powell, R. S. S., *The Matabele Campaign 1896: Being a Narrative of the Campaign in Suppressing the Native Rising in Matabeleland and Mashonaland* (London: Methuen & Co., 1897)

Bibliography 161

Baden-Powell, R. S. S., *Pigsticking; or Hoghunting: A Complete Account for Sportsmen, and Others* (London: Harrison and Sons, 1889)

Baily's Magazine of Sports and Pastimes, Volume 78 July–December 1902 (London: Vinton and Co., 1902)

Ball, Charles, *History of the Indian Mutiny* (London: London Printing and Publishing Company, 1859)

Barclay Lloyd, J., *One Thousand Miles with the C. I. V.* (London: Methuen & Co., 1901)

Brittain, Vera, *England's Hour: An Autobiography 1939–41* (London: Palgrave Macmillan, 1941)

Brontë, Charlotte, *Jane Eyre* (London: Smith, Elder, and Co., 1847)

Cairns, William Elliott, *An Absent-Minded War: Being Some Reflections on Our Reverses and the Causes Which Have Led to Them* (London: John Milne, 1900)

Cairns, William Elliott, *Social Life in the British Army* (London: Harper and Brothers, 1899)

Chisholm, Hugh (ed.), *The Encyclopaedia Britannica, Volume XX* (New York: The Encyclopaedia Britannica Company, 1911)

Churchill, Winston, *My Early Life: A Roving Commission* (London: Odhams Press Ltd., 1930)

Colquhoun, John, *The Moor and the Loch* (Edinburgh: William Blackwood and Sons, 1840)

Conan Doyle, Arthur, *The Great Boer War* (London: Smith Elder and Co, 1900)

Conan Doyle, Arthur, *The German War: Some Sidelights and Reflections* (London: Hodder & Stoughton, 1914)

Connell, J., *The Truth About the Game Laws: A Record of Cruelty, Selfishness and Oppression* (London: William Reeves, 1898)

Corelli, Marie, *My 'Little Bit'* (New York: George H. Doran Company, 1919)

Douglas, Keith, *Alamein to Zem Zem* (London: Editions Poetry London, 1946)

Grant, General Sir Hope, *Incidents in the Sepoy War, 1857–58* (London: William Blackwood and Sons, 1873)

Graves, Robert, *Goodbye to All That* (London: Jonathan Cape, 1929)

Harmsworth, Alfred, *Lord Northcliffe's War Book: With Chapters on America at War* (New York: George H. Doran Company, 1917)

Harrisson, Tom and Charles Madge, *War Begins at Home by Mass Observation* (London: Chatto & Windus, 1940)

Henty, G. A., *At the Point of a Bayonet: A Tale of the Mahratta War* (London: Blackie and Son Ltd., 1902)

Henty, G. A., *The Dash for Khartoum: A Tale of the Nile Expedition* (New York: Charles Scribner's Sons, 1902)

Henty, G. A., *Through Sikh Wars: A Tale of the Conquest of the Punjaub* (New York: Charles Scribner's Sons, 1902)

Henty, G. A., *With Clive in India: Or the Beginnings of an Empire* (New York: Charles Scribner's Sons, 1894)

Henty, G. A., *By Sheer Pluck: A Tale of the Ashanti War* (London: Blackie and Son Ltd., 1883)

Henty, G. A., *For Name and Fame: Or, Through Afghan Passes* (New York: Scribner and Welford, 1880)

Henty, G. A., *Jack Archer: A Tale of the Crimea* (New York: Mershon Company, 1880)

Hobson, J. A., *Imperialism: A Study* (London: George Allen and Unwin Ltd., 1902)

Hornung, E. W., *Mr. Justice Raffles* (New York: Charles Scribner's Sons, 1909)

Jones, Paul, *War Letters of a Public-School Boy* (London: Cassell and Co. Ltd., 1918)

162 Bibliography

Kernot, C. F., *British Public School War Memorials* (London: Roberts and Newton Ltd., 1927)

Kinglake, A. W., *The Invasion of the Crimea: Its Origin, and an Account of Its Progress Down to the Death of Lord Raglan Volume III* (Edinburgh: William Blackwood and Sons, 1874)

Lawton, Tommy, *My Twenty Years in Soccer* (Norwich: Heirloom, 1955)

Longmate, Norman, *How We Lived Then: A History of Everyday Life During the Second World War* (London: Hutchinson & Co. Ltd., 1971)

Lowther, Lieutenant-Colonel H. C., *From Pillar to Post* (London: Edward Arnold, 1912)

Luk-Oie, Ole, [Ernest Swinton], *The Great Tab Dope and Other Stories* (London: William Blackwood and Sons, 1915)

MacCarthy, R. and R. O'Moore, *The Romance of the Boer War: Humours and Chivalry of the Campaign* (London: Elliot Stock, 1901)

Madge, Charles and Tom Harrisson (eds.), *Mass Observation: First Year's Work 1937–1938* (London: L. Drummond, 1938)

Mais, S. P. D., *The Public School in War Time* (London: John Murray, 1916)

Malcolm, Sir Neill, *The Science of War: A Collection of Essays and Lectures 1892–1903 by the Late Colonel G. F. R. Henderson CB* (London: Longmans, Green and Co., 1912)

Malim, F. B., 'Athletics', in A. C. Benson (ed.), *Cambridge Essays in Education* (Cambridge: Cambridge University Press, 1917)

Meynell, Wilfred, 'The Life and Work of Lady Butler (Miss Elizabeth Thompson)', *The Art Annual* (London: The Art Journal Office, 1898)

Minutes of Evidence Taken Before the Royal Commission on the War in South Africa (Volume II) (London: Eyre and Spottiswoode, 1903)

Mr Punch's History of the Great War (London: Cassell and Co., 1919)

Newbolt, Henry, *Tales of the Great War* (London: Longman's, Green and Co., 1916)

Newbolt, Henry, *The Book of the Happy Warrior* (London: Longman's, Green and Co., 1917)

Newbolt, Henry, *The Island Race* (London: Elkin Mathews, 1898)

Newbolt, Henry, *Admirals All and Other Verses* (London: Elkin Mathews, 1897)

Osborn, E. B., *The New Elizabethans: A First Selection of the Lives of Young Men Who Have Fallen in the Great War* (New York: John Lane Co., 1919)

Osborn, E. B. (ed.), *The Muse in Arms: A Collection of War Poems, for the Most Part Written in the Field of Action, by Seamen, Soldiers, and Flying Men Who Are Serving, or Have Served, in the Great War* (London: John Murray, 1917)

Perry, Nick, *Arrivederci Millwall* (London: Faber & Faber, 1985)

Ralph, Julian, *An American with Lord Roberts* (New York: Frederick A. Stokes Co., 1901)

Ralph, Julian, *Towards Pretoria: A Record of the War Between Briton and Boer to the Hoisting of the British flag in Bloemfontein* (London: C. Arthur Pearson Ltd., 1900)

Raymond, Ernest, *Tell England: A Study in a Generation* (New York: George H. Doran, 1922)

Reid, Pat, *The Colditz Story* (London: Hodder & Stoughton, 1952)

Roberts, Field Marshal Lord Frederick, *Forty-One Years in India: From Subaltern to Commander-in-Chief, Volume 1* (London: Richard Bentley and Son, 1898)

Ross, P. T., *A Yeoman's Letters* (London: Simpkin, Marshall, Hamilton, Kent, 1901)

Sherriff, R. C., *Journey's End* (London: Victor Gollancz Ltd., 1929)

Smiles, Samuel, *Self-Help: With Illustrations of Character and Conduct* (London: John Murray, 1859)

Strickland Constable, Henry, *Something about Horses: Sport and War* (London: Eden, Remington and Co., 1891)
Surtees, Robert Smith, *Handley Cross or, the Spa Hunt. A Sporting Tale* (London: Henry Colburn, 1843)
Temple, William, *Mens Creatrix: An Essay* (London: Palgrave Macmillan and Co., 1917)
Thackeray, William Makepeace, *Vanity Fair: A Novel Without a Hero* (London: Bradbury and Evans, 1848)
War Illustrated Volume 2 (London: London Amalgamated Press Ltd., 1915)
War Illustrated Volume 7 (London: London Amalgamated Press Ltd., 1917)
War Illustrated Volume 8 (London: London Amalgamated Press Ltd., 1917)
Ward, Fred W., *The 23rd (Service) Battalion Royal Fusiliers (First Sportsman's): A Record of Its Services in the Great War, 1914–1919* (London: Sidgwick and Jackson Ltd., 1920)
Waugh, Alec, *The Loom of Youth* (London: Methuen Ltd., 1917)
Waugh, Evelyn, *Decline and Fall* (London: Chapman and Hall, 1928)
Wellum, Geoffrey, *First Light* (London: Viking, 2002)
Wilson, H. W. (ed.), *The Great War: the Standard History of the All-Europe Conflict, Volume 8* (London: Amalgamated Press, 1917)
Wilson, H. W., *With the Flag to Pretoria: A History of the Boer War of 1899–1900 Volume I* (London: Harmsworth Bros., 1900)
Wilson, H. W., *With the Flag to Pretoria: A History of the Boer War of 1899–1900 Volume II* (London: Harmsworth Bros., 1901)
Wingfield-Stratford, Ésme, *Before the Lamps Went Out* (London: Hodder & Stoughton, 1945)
Winton, A., *A History of the Zulu War* (London: Richardson and Best, 1880)

Primary sources: films

Albert RN, dir. Lewis Gilbert, 1953
Arrivederci Millwall, dir. Charles McDougall, 1990
The Captive Heart, dir. Basil Dearden, 1946
The Colditz Story, dir. Guy Hamilton, 1955
Danger Within, dir. Don Chaffey, 1959
The Lion Has Wings, dir. Alexander Korda, Michael Powell, Brian Hurst, Adrian Brunel, 1939
Mike Bassett: England Manager, dir. Steve Barron, 2001
The Password is Courage, dir. Andrew L. Stone, 1962
Reach for the Sky, dir. Lewis Gilbert, 1957
San Demetrio London, dir. Charles Frend, 1943
Saving Jessica Lynch, dir. Peter Markle, 2003
Stalag 17, dir. Billy Wilder, 1953
The Wooden Horse, dir. Jack Lee, 1950

Primary sources: newsreels

British Gaumont News, 682, 'Roving Camera Reports: Eton v Harrow Cricket Match: Harrow Gun Presented for Scrap Iron', 18 July 1940
British Gaumont News, 1130, '1941 FA Cup Final at Wembley', 15 May 1941
British Movietone News, 537A, 'No Black-Out for Football', 21 September 1939

British Movietone News, 676A, 'King and Queen See Services Cup Final', 21 May 1942
British Movietone News, 693A, 'The King's Fourth Classic', 17 September 1942
British Movietone News, 782A, 'Whitsun 1944', 1 June 1944
British Paramount News, 1447, 'Winter Racing Starts Again After Three Years', 11 January 1945
Pathé Gazette, 38941, 'Wartime Derby at Newmarket 1941', 23 June 1941
Pathé Gazette, 39690, 'Famous Football Teams at Home, No. 1 Brentford', 2 November 1936

Secondary sources: books

Altick, Richard, *English Common Reader: A Social History of the Mass Reading Public, 1800–1900* (Chicago: University of Chicago Press, 1957)
Ash, Chris, *The if Man: Leander Starr Jameson, the Inspiration for Kipling's Masterpiece* (Solihull: Helion and Co., 2012)
Aulich, James (ed.), *Framing the Falklands: Nationhood, Culture and Identity* (Maidenhead: Open University Press, 1991)
Bairner, Alan, John Kelly and Jung Woo Lee (eds.), *The Routledge Handbook of Sport and Politics* (London: Routledge, 2017)
Bateman, Anthony, *Cricket, Literature and Culture: Symbolising the Nation, Destabilising the Empire* (Farnham: Ashgate, 2009)
Birley, Derek, *A Social History of English Cricket* (London: Arum Press Ltd., 1999)
Bogdanovic, Nikolai, *Fit to Fight: A History of the Royal Army Physical Training Corps, 1860–2012* (Oxford: Osprey Publishing, 2017)
Bowman, Tim and Mark Connelly, *The Edwardian Army: Recruiting, Training and Deploying the British Army, 1902–1914* (Oxford: Oxford University Press, 2012)
Boyce, D. George, *The Falklands War* (London: Macmillan Publishing Ltd., 2005)
Brickhill, Paul, *The Great Escape* (New York: Norton, 1950)
Brooks, Stephen (ed.), *Montgomery and the Eighth Army; a Selection from the Diaries, Correspondence and Other Papers of Field Marshal the Viscount Montgomery of Alamein, August 1942 to December 1943* (London: Bodley Head for the Army Records Society, 1991)
Bryant, Mark, *Wars of Empire in Cartoons* (London: Grub Street Publishing, 2008)
Burke, Peter and Roy Porter, *Language, Self, and Society: A Social History of Language* (Cambridge: Polity Press, 1991)
Butterworth, Michael L. (ed.), *Sport and Militarism: Contemporary Global Perspectives* (London: Routledge, 2017)
Campbell, J. D., *'The Army Isn't All Work': Physical Culture and the Evolution of the British Army, 1860–1920* (Farnham: Ashgate, 2012)
Campion, Garry, *The Good Fight: Battle of Britain Propaganda and The Few* (Basingstoke: Palgrave Macmillan, 2009)
Carrington, B. and I. McDonald (eds.), *Race, Sport and British Society* (London: Routledge, 2001)
Carruthers, Susan L., *The Media at War: Communication and Conflict in the Twentieth Century* (Basingstoke: Palgrave Macmillan, 2000)
Cecil, Hugh P. and Peter Liddle (eds.), *Facing Armageddon: The First World War Experienced* (London: Leo Cooper, 1996)
Charteris-Black, Jonathan, *Corpus Approaches to Critical Metaphor Analysis* (Basingstoke: Palgrave Macmillan, 2004)

Cocker, Mark, *Richard Meinertzhagen: Soldier, Scientist and Spy* (London: Secker and Warburg, 1989)

Coldham, James D., *Lord Harris* (Sydney: Allen & Unwin, 1983)

Collins, Tony, *Rugby League in Twentieth Century Britain: A Social and Cultural History* (Abingdon: Routledge, 2006)

Collins, Tony, *Rugby's Great Split: Class, Culture and the Origins of Rugby League Football* (London: Frank Cass Publishers, 1998)

Corse, Edward, *A Battle for Neutral Europe: British Cultural Propaganda During the Second World War* (London: Bloomsbury, 2013)

Davies, Peter and Robert Light, *Cricket and Community in England: 1800 to the Present Day* (Manchester: Manchester University Press, 2012)

Dawson, Graham, *Soldier Heroes: British Adventure, Empire and the Imagining of Masculinity* (London: Routledge, 1994)

Dennis, P. and J. Grey (eds.), *The Boer War: Army Nation and Empire* (Canberra: Army History Unit, 1999)

Dickinson, Matt, *Bobby Moore: The Man in Full* (London: Yellow Jersey Press, 2014)

Dillingham, William D., *Rudyard Kipling: Hell and Heroism* (London: Palgrave Macmillan, 2005)

Dixon, W. W. (ed.), *Re-viewing British Cinema, 1900–1992* (Albany, NY: University of New York Press, 1994)

Dunphy, Eamon, *A Strange Kind of Glory: Sir Matt Busby and Manchester United* (London: Heinemann, 1991)

Eby, Cecil B., *The Road to Armageddon: The Martial Spirit in English Popular Literature, 1870–1914* (Durham: Duke University Press, 1988)

Farwell, Byron, *Eminent Victorian Soldiers: Seekers of Glory* (New York: W. W. Norton & Co., 1985)

Fennell, Jonathan, *Fighting the People's War: The British and Commonwealth Armies in the Second World War* (Cambridge: Cambridge University Press, 2019)

Field, H. John, *Toward a Programme of Imperial Life: The British Empire at the Turn of the Century* (Oxford: Clio Press, 1982)

Freedman, Lawrence, *Official History of the Falklands Campaign, Vol. 2: War and Diplomacy* (London: Routledge, 2005)

French, David, *Military Identities: The Regimental System, the British Army, and the British People, c. 1870–2000* (Oxford: Oxford University Press, 2005)

Fuller, J. G., *Troop Morale and Popular Culture in British and Dominion Armies, 1914–1918* (Oxford: Oxford University Press, 1991)

Fussell, Paul, *Great War and Modern Memory* (Oxford: Oxford University Press, 1975)

Geraghty, G., *British Cinema in the Fifties: Gender, Genre and the 'New Look'* (London: Routledge, 2000)

Girouard, Mark, *The Return to Camelot: Chivalry and the English Gentleman* (New Haven: Yale University Press, 1991)

Grant, Peter, *Philanthropy and Voluntary Action in the First World War: Mobilizing Charity* (Abingdon: Routledge, 2014)

Greaves, Adrian, *Crossing the Buffalo: The Zulu War of 1879* (London: Weidenfeld and Nicolson, 2005)

Gregory, Adrian, *The Last Great War: British Society and the First World War* (Cambridge: Cambridge University Press, 2008)

Hartesveldt, Fred R. Van, *The Boer War: Historiography and Annotated Bibliography* (Westport, CT: Greenwood, 2000)

Bibliography

Hayes, Nick and Jeff Hill, *Millions Like Us? British Culture in the Second World War* (Liverpool: Liverpool University Press, 1999)

Hill, Jeffrey, *Sport, Leisure and Culture in Twentieth Century Britain* (Basingstoke: Palgrave Macmillan, 2002)

Hinton, J., *The Mass Observers: A History, 1937–1949* (Oxford: Oxford University Press, 2013)

Holmes, Richard, *Soldiers: Army Lives and Loyalties from Redcoats to Dusty Warriors* (London: HarperPress, 2011)

Holt, Richard, *Sport and the British: A Modern History* (Oxford: Oxford University Press, 1989)

Horne, John (ed.), *State, Society and Mobilization in Europe During the First World War*, (Cambridge: Cambridge University Press, 1997)

Huggins, Mike, *The Victorians and Sport* (London: Hambledon Continuum, 2004)

Inglis, Simon, *League Football and the Men Who Made It: The Official Centenary of the Football League, 1888–1988* (London: HarperCollins, 1989)

Jackson, Alexander (ed.), *The Greater Game: A History of Football in World War 1* (London: Shire Publications, 2014)

Jeal, Tim, *Baden-Powell: Founder of the Boy Scouts* (London: Hutchinson & Co. Ltd., 1989)

Jenkins, Roy, *Asquith* (London: William Collins Son and Co Ltd., 1964)

John, Juliet (ed.), *The Oxford Handbook of Victorian Literary Culture* (Oxford: Oxford University Press, 2016)

Kerby, Martin C., *Sir Philip Gibbs and English Journalism in War and Peace* (London: Palgrave Macmillan, 2016)

Kirkham, Pat and David Thoms, *War Culture: Social Change and Changing Experience in World War Two Britain* (London: Lawrence and Wishart Ltd., 1995)

Krebs, Paula M., *Gender, Race, and the Writing of Empire: Public Discourse and the Boer War* (Cambridge: Cambridge University Press, 1999)

Liebes, Tamar and James Curran (eds.), *Media, Ritual and Identity* (London: Routledge, 1998)

Longford, Elizabeth, *Wellington: The Years of the Sword* (London: HarperCollins Publishers Ltd., 1971)

Mackay, Robert, *Half the Battle: Civilian Morale in Britain during the Second World War* (Manchester: Manchester University Press, 2002)

Mackenzie, John M. (ed.), *Popular Imperialism and the Military, 1850–1950* (Manchester: Manchester University Press, 1992)

MacKenzie, S. P., *The Colditz Myth: British and Commonwealth Prisoners of War in Nazi Germany* (Oxford: Oxford University Press, 2004)

Mallon, Bill and Ian Buchanan, *The 1908 Olympic Games* (Jefferson, NC: McFarland & Co., 2000)

Mangan, J. A., *Manufactured Masculinity: Making Imperial Manliness, Morality and Militarism* (London: Routledge, 2012)

Mangan, J. A. (ed.), *The Cultural Bond: Sport, Empire and Society* (Abingdon: Routledge, 1992)

Mangan, J. A., *The Games Ethic and Imperialism: Aspects of Diffusion of an Ideal* (Harmondsworth: Penguin, 1986)

Mangan, J. A. and Callum C. McKenzie, *Militarism, Hunting, Imperialism: 'Blooding' the Martial Male* (London: Routledge, 2010)

Mangan, J. A. and Thierry Tenet (eds.), *Sport, Militarism and the Great War: Martial Manliness and Armageddon* (London: Routledge, 2012)

Matthews, H. C. G. and Brian Harrison (eds.), *Oxford Dictionary of National Biography* (Oxford: Oxford University Press, 2004)

Mason, Tony (ed.), *Sport in Britain: A Social History* (Cambridge: Cambridge University Press, 1989)

Mason, Tony and Eliza Riedi, *Sport and the Military: The British Armed Forces, 1880–1960* (Cambridge: Cambridge University Press, 2010)

McCarthy, Tony, *War Games: The Story of Sport in World War Two* (London: Queen Anne Press, 1989)

McInnes, Colin, *Spectator-Sport War: The West and Contemporary Conflict* (Boulder: Lynne Reimer Publishers, 2002)

McLoughlin, Kate (ed.), *The Cambridge Companion to War Writing* (Cambridge: Cambridge University Press, 2009)

Messinger, Gary S., *British Propaganda and the State in the First World War* (Manchester: Manchester University Press, 1992)

Miller, Stephen M., *Lord Methuen and the British Army: Failure and Redemption in South Africa* (Abingdon: Frank Cass Publishers, 1999)

Mosse, George, *Fallen Soldiers: Reshaping the Memory of the World War* (Oxford: Oxford University Press, 1990)

Nicholas, S., *The Echo of War: Home Front Propaganda and the Wartime BBC, 1939–45* (Manchester: Manchester University Press, 1996)

Orel, Harold, *Popular Fiction in England, 1914–1918* (Lexington: University of Kentucky Press, 1992)

Paddock, Troy R. E., *A Call to Arms: Propaganda, Public Opinion, and Newspapers in the Great War* (Westport, CT: Praeger, 2004)

Pakenham, Thomas, *The Boer War* (London: George Weidenfeld and Nicolson Ltd., 1979)

Paris, Michael, *Warrior Nation: Images of War in British Popular Culture, 1850–2000* (London: Reaktion Books Ltd., 2000)

Parker, Peter, *The Old Lie: The Great War and the Public-School Ethos* (London: Hambledon Continuum, 1987)

Pedelty, Mark, *War Stories: The Culture of Foreign Correspondents* (London: Routledge, 1995)

Philo, Greg, *The British Media and the Gulf War* (Glasgow: Glasgow University Media Research Group, 1993)

Pretorius, Fransjohan, *Historical Dictionary of the Anglo-Boer War* (Lanham: Scarecrow Press, 2009)

Ramsden, John, *Don't Mention the War: The British and Germans since 1890* (London: Little, Brown, 2006)

Redmond, Christopher, *Sherlock Holmes Handbook*, 2nd Edition (Toronto: Dundurn Press, 2009)

Renshon, Stanley (ed.), *The Political Psychology of the Gulf War* (Pittsburgh: University of Pittsburgh Press, 1993)

Richards, Jeffrey, *British Films and National Identity: From Dickens to Dad's Army* (Manchester: Manchester University Press, 1997)

Ripon, Anton, *Gas Masks for Goal Posts: Football in Britain During the Second World War* (Stroud: Sutton Publishing Ltd., 2005)

Sandford, Christopher, *The Final Over: The Cricketers of Summer 1914* (Stroud: Spellmont, 2014)

Bibliography

Sheffield, Gary, *Leadership in the Trenches: Officer-man Relations, Morale and Discipline in the British Army in the Era of the First World War* (Basingstoke: Macmillan Press Ltd., 2000)

Shrosbree, Colin, *Public Schools and Private Education: The Clarendon Commission, 1861–64, and the Public Schools Acts* (Manchester: Manchester University Press, 1988)

Sillars, Stuart, *Art and Survival in First World War Britain* (Basingstoke: Macmillan Press Ltd., 1987)

Sillars, Stuart, *Fields of Agony: British Poetry of the First World War* (Penrith: Humanities-ebook, 2007)

Simon, Brian and Ian Bradley (eds.), *The Victorian Public School: Studies in the Development of an Educational Institution* (Dublin: Gill and Macmillan, 1975)

Sissons, Ric and Brian Stoddart, *Cricket and Empire* (Sydney: Allen & Unwin, 1984)

Skelley, Alan, *The Victorian Army at Home: The Recruitment and Terms and Conditions of the British Regular, 1859–1899* (London: Croom Helm, 1977)

Smith, Adrian and Dilwyn Porter (eds.), *Amateurs and Professionals in Post-War British Sport* (London: Frank Cass, 2000)

Spiers, Edward, *The Army and Society, 1815–1914* (London: Longman, 1980)

Spiers, Edward, *The Late Victorian Army, 1868–1902* (Manchester: Manchester University Press, 1992)

Stothard, Peter, *30 Days: A Month at the Heart of Blair's War* (New York: HarperCollins, 2003)

Streets, Heather, *Martial Races: The Military, Race and Masculinity in British Imperial Culture, 1857–1914* (Manchester: Manchester University Press, 2004)

Tate, Tim, *For Team and Country: Sport on the Frontlines of the Great War* (London: John Blake Publishing Ltd., 2014)

Taylor, Matthew, *The Association Game: A History of British Football* (London: Pearson Educational Ltd., 2008)

Taylor, Philip M., *Global Communications, International Affairs and the Media since 1945* (London: Routledge, 1997)

Taylor, Philip M., *Munitions of the Mind: A History of Propaganda from the Ancient World to the Present Day* (Manchester: Manchester University Press, 1995)

Terret, Thierry and J. A. Mangan (eds.), *Sport, Militarism and the Great War: Martial Manliness and Armageddon* (London: Routledge, 2012)

Thomas, Donald, *An Underworld at War: Spivs, Deserters, Racketeers and Civilians in the Second World War* (London: John Murray, 2003)

Todman, Dan, *The Great War: Myth and Memory* (London: Hambledon Continuum, 2005)

Vat, Dan van der, *Gentlemen of War: The Amazing Story of Commander Karl von Muller and the SMS Emden* (New York: Book Sales, 1984)

Walvin, James, *The People's Game: The History of Football Revisited* (London: Allen Lane, 1975)

Warwick, Peter (ed.), *The South African War: The Anglo-Boer War, 1899–1902* (Harlow: Longman, 1980)

Wessels, Andre, *Lord Kitchener and the War in South Africa, 1899–1902* (Stroud: Sutton Publishing Ltd., 2006)

Wigglesworth, Neil, *The Evolution of English Sport* (Abingdon: Routledge, 1996)

Williams, Jack, *Cricket and England: A Cultural and Social History of the Inter-war Years* (Abingdon: Frank Cass, 1999)

Winter, Jay, *Sites of Memory, Sites of Mourning: The Great War in European Cultural History* (Cambridge: Cambridge University Press, 1995)

Secondary sources: articles and chapters

Adams, Iain, 'A Game for Christmas? The Argylls, Saxons and Football on the Western Front, December 1914', *International Journal of the History of Sport*, 32/11–12 (2015)

Adams, Iain, 'Football: A Counterpoint to the Procession of Pain on the Western Front', *Soccer and Society*, 16/2 (2015)

Adams, Iain, 'Over the Top: "A Foul; a Blurry Foul!"', *International Journal of the History of Sport*, 29/6 (2012)

Adams, Iain and John Hughson, 'The First Ever *Anti*-Football Painting? A Consideration of the Soccer Match in John Singer Sargent's *Gassed*', *Soccer and Society*, 14/4 (2013)

Aldgate, Anthony, 'British Newsreels and the Spanish Civil War', *Film and History*, 3/1 (2013)

Allen, Brooke, 'G. A. Henty and the Vision of Empire', *New Criterion* (April 2002)

Allen, Dean, 'England's "golden age": Imperial Cricket and Late Victorian Society', *Sport in Society: Cultures, Commerce, Media, Politics*, 15/2 (March 2012)

Allen, Dean, '"Bats and Bayonets": Cricket and the Anglo-Boer War, 1899–1902', *Sport in History*, 25/1 (2005)

Althaus, Scott L., 'Global News Broadcasting in the Pre-Television Era: A Cross-National Comparative Analysis in World War Two Newsreel Coverage', *Journal of Broadcasting and Electronic Media*, 62/1 (March 2018)

Arnold, A. J., '"Not Playing the Game?" Leeds City in the Great War', *International Journal of the History of Sport*, 7/1 (1990)

Aulich, James, 'Wildlife in the South Atlantic: Graphic Satire, Patriotism and the Fourth Estate', in James Aulich (ed.), *Framing the Falklands: Nationhood, Culture and Identity* (Maidenhead: Open University Press, 1991)

Badsey, Stephen, 'The Boer War (1899–1902) and British Cavalry Doctrine: A Re-evaluation', *Journal of Military History*, 71/1 (2006)

Badsey, Stephen, 'The Boer War as a Media War', in P. Dennis and J. Grey (eds.), *The Boer War: Army Nation and Empire* (Canberra: Army History Unit, 1999)

Baker, Norman, '"A More Even Playing Field?" Sport During and After the War', in Nick Hayes and Jeff Hill (eds.), *Millions Like Us? British Culture in the Second World War* (Liverpool: Liverpool University Press, 1999)

Beck, Peter, 'To Play or Not to Play: That Is the Anglo-Argentine Question', *Contemporary Review*, 245 (August 1984)

Best, Geoffrey, 'Militarism in the Victorian Public School', in Brian Simon and Ian Bradley (eds.), *Victorian Public School Studies in the Development of an Educational Institution* (Dublin: Gill and Macmillan, 1975)

Blanch, M. D., 'British Society and the War', in Peter Warwick (ed.), *The South African War. The Anglo-Boer War, 1899–1902* (Harlow: Longman, 1980)

Bourne, John, 'The British Working Man in Arms', in Hugh P. Cecil and Peter Liddle (eds.), *Facing Armageddon: The First World War Experienced* (London: Leo Cooper, 1996)

Bradley, James, 'The MCC, Society and Empire: A Portrait of Cricket's Ruling Body, 1860–1914', *International Journal of the History of Sport*, 17/1 (1990)

Burrell, Richard, *One Hundred and Fifty Years of the Oxford and Cambridge Boat Race* (London: Precision Press, 1979)

Campbell, J. D., '"Training for Sport Is Training for War": Sport and the Transformation of the British Army, 1860–1914', *International Journal of the History of Sport*, 17/4 (December 2000)

170   Bibliography

Cassman, Joel F. and David Lai, 'Football v Soccer: American Warfare in an Era of Unconventional Threats', *Armed Forces Journal* (November 2003)

Clark, Gail S., 'Imperial Stereotypes: G. A. Henty and the Boys' Own Empire', *Journal of Popular Culture*, 18/4 (Spring 1985)

Clarke, Nic, '"The Greater and Grimmer Game": Sport as an Arbiter of Military Fitness in the British Empire – The Case of "One-Eyed" Frank McGee', *International Journal of the History of Sport*, 28/3 (2011)

Collins, Tony, 'Amateurism and the Rise of Managerialism: The Case of Rugby Union, 1871–1995', *Sport in History*, 30/1 (2010)

Collins, Tony, 'English Rugby Union and the First World War', *Historical Journal*, 45/4 (2002)

Crane, Ralph and Lisa Fletcher, 'Picturing the Empire in India: Illustrating Henty', *ELT Journal*, 55/2 (2012)

Cull, Nicholas J., 'Great Escapes: "Englishness" and the Prisoner of War genre', *Film and History*, 14 (2002)

Davies, Godfrey, 'G. A. Henty and History', *Huntingdon Library Quarterly*, 18/2 (February 1955)

Deane, Bradley, 'Imperial Boyhood: Piracy and the Play Ethic', *Victorian Studies*, 53/4 (2011)

Deans, Bob, 'Sanitized Lexicon of Modern War', *Newspaper Research Journal*, 12/1 (Winter 1991)

Donald, Ralph R., 'From "Knockout Punch" to "Home Run": Masculinity's "Dirty Dozen" Sports Metaphors in American Combat Films', *Film and History*, 35/1 (2005)

Gregory, Adrian, 'A Clash of Cultures: The British Press and the Opening of the Great War', in Troy R. E. Paddock (ed.), *A Call to Arms: Propaganda, Public Opinion, and Newspapers in the Great War* (Westport, CT: Praeger, 2004)

Hampton, M., 'The Press, Patriotism and Public Discussion: C. P. Scott, the *Manchester Guardian*, and the Boer War, 1899–1902', *Historical Journal*, 44/1 (March 2001)

Hands, Robert, 'They Also Served – Re-evaluating and Reconsidering the Neglected', in Thierry Terret and J. A. Mangan (eds.), *Sport, Militarism and the Great War: Martial Manliness and Armageddon* (London: Routledge, 2012)

Hannan, Brian D. P., 'Creating the War Correspondent: How the BBC Reached the Frontline in the Second World War', *Historical Journal of Film, Radio and Television*, 28/2 (2008)

Heggie, Vanessa, 'Bodies, Sport and Science in the Nineteenth Century', *Past and Present*, 231/1 (May 2016)

Horne, John, 'Introduction: Mobilizing for Total War, 1914–1918', in John Horne (ed.), *State, Society and Mobilization in Europe During the First World War* (Cambridge: Cambridge University Press, 1997)

Huggins, Mike, '"Everybody's Going to the Dogs"? The Middle Classes and Greyhound Racing in Britain Between the Wars', *Journal of Sport History*, 34/1 (2007)

Huggins, Mike, 'Projecting the Visual: British Newsreels, Soccer and Popular Culture 1918–39', *International Journal of the History of Sport*, 24/1 (2007)

Huggins, Mike, 'Sports Gambling During the Second World War: A British Entertainment for Critical Times or a National Evil?' *International Journal of the History of Sport*, 32/5 (2015)

Jansen, Sue and Don Sabo, 'The Sport/War Metaphor: Hegemonic Masculinity, the Persian Gulf War, and the New World Order', *Sociology of Sport Journal*, 11 (1994)

John, Simon, '"A Different Kind of Test Match": Cricket, English Society and the First World War', *Sport in History*, 33/1 (2013)

Kelly, John, 'The Paradox of Militaristic Remembrance in British Sport and Popular Culture', in Michael L. Butterworth (ed.), *Sport and Militarism: Contemporary Global Perspectives* (London: Routledge, 2017)

Kelly, John, 'Western Militarism and the Political Utility of Sport', in Alan Bairner, John Kelly and Jung Woo Lee (eds.), *The Routledge Handbook of Sport and Politics* (London: Routledge, 2017)

Kelly, John, 'Popular Culture, Sport and the "Hero"-fication of British Militarism', *Sociology*, 47/4 (2012)

King, Anthony, 'Sport, War and Commemoration: Football and Remembrance in the Twentieth and Twenty-First Centuries', *European Journal of Sport and Society*, 13/3 (2016)

King, Samantha, 'Offensive Lives: Sport-State Synergy in the Era of Perpetual War', *Cultural Studies – Critical Methodologies*, 8/4 (2008)

Kriegel, Laura, 'The Strange Career of Fair Play, or, Warfare and Gamesmanship in the time of Victoria', in Juliet John (ed.), *The Oxford Handbook of Victorian Literary Culture* (Oxford: Oxford University Press, 2016)

Kuusisto, Riikka, 'Framing the Wars in the Gulf and in Bosnia: The Rhetorical Definitions of the Western Power Leaders in Action', *Journal of Peace Research*, 35/5 (September 1998)

Lanfranchi, Pierre and Matthew Taylor, 'Professional Football in World War Two Britain', in Pat Kirkham and David Thoms (eds.), *War Culture: Social Change and Changing Experience in World War Two Britain* (London: Lawrence and Wishart Ltd., 1995)

Lieven, Michael, 'A Victorian Military Genre: Military Memoirs and the Anglo-Zulu War', *Journal of the Society of Army Historical Research*, 77/310 (1999)

Livingstone, Sonia, 'Relationships Between Media and Audiences: Prospects for Audience Reception Studies', in Tamar Liebes and James Curran (eds.), *Media, Ritual and Identity* (London: Routledge, 1998)

Lowerson, John, 'Golf', in Tony Mason (ed.), *Sport in Britain: A Social History* (Cambridge: Cambridge University Press, 1989)

Luedtke, Brandon, 'Playing Fields and Battlefields: The Football Pitch, England and the First World War', *Britain and the World*, 5/1 (2012)

Mangan, J. A., 'Tragic Symbiosis: Distinctive "Anglo-Saxon" Visions and Voices', in Thierry Terret and J. A. Mangan (eds.), *Sport, Militarism and the Great War: Martial Manliness and Armageddon* (London: Routledge, 2012)

Mann, Michael, 'The Roots and Contradictions of Modern Militarism', *New Left Review*, 162 (March 1987)

Marlin, Randal, 'Media and Propaganda: The Northcliffe Press and the Corpse Factory Story of World War One', *Global Media Journal: Canadian Edition*, 3/2 (2010)

McDonald, Robert H., 'Signs from the Imperial Quarter: Illustrations in Chums, 1892–1914', *Children's Literature*, 16 (1998)

Monger, David, '"No Mere Silent Commander?" Sir Henry Horne and the Mentality of Command During the First World War', *Historical Research*, 82/216 (May 2009)

Mueller, John, 'American Public Opinion and the Gulf War', in Stanley Renshon (ed.), *The Political Psychology of the Gulf War* (Pittsburgh: University of Pittsburgh Press, 1993), p. 220

Nadelhaft, Matthew, 'Metawar: Sports and the Persian Gulf War', *Journal of American Culture*, 16/4 (Winter 1993)

Osbourne, John, '"To Keep the Life of the Nation in the Old Line": *The Athletic News* and the First World War', *Journal of Sport History*, 14/2 (Summer 1987)

Penn, Roger and Damon Berridge, 'Football and the Military in Contemporary Britain: An Exploration of Invisible Nationalism', *Armed Forces Journal*, 44/1 (2018)

Plain, Gill, 'Before the Colditz Myth: Telling POW Stories in Postwar British Cinema', *Journal of Culture Studies*, 7/3 (2014)

Pope, Steven W., 'An Army of Athletes: Playing-Fields, Battlefields, and the American Military Sporting Experience, 1890–1920', *Journal of Military History*, 59/3 (1995)

Ramsden, John, 'England Versus Germany, Soccer and War Memory: John Huston's *Escape to Victory*, (1981)', *Historical Journal of Film, Radio and Television*, 26/4 (October 2006)

Rattigan, Neil, 'The Last Gasp of the Middle Class: British War Films in the 1950s', in W. W. Dixon (ed.), *Re-viewing British Cinema, 1900–1992* (Albany, NY: University of New York Press, 1994)

Razzell, P. E., 'Social Origins of Officers in the Indian and British Home Army, 1758–1962', *British Journal of Sociology*, 14 (1963)

Richards, Jeffrey, 'Popular Imperialism and the Image of the Army in Juvenile Literature', in John M. Mackenzie (ed.), *Popular Imperialism and the Military, 1850–1950* (Manchester: Manchester University Press, 1992)

Richardson, John, 'Imagining Military Conflict During the Seven Years' War', *Studies in English Literature, 1500–1600*, 48/3 (Summer 2008)

Riedi, Eliza and Tony Mason, '"Leather" and the Fighting Spirit: Sport in the British Army in World War One', *Canadian Journal of History*, 41/3 (2006)

Roberts, James, '"The Best Football Team, The Best Platoon": The Role of Football in the Proletarianization of the BEF, 1914–1918', *Sport in History*, 26/1 (2006)

Sandiford, Keith, 'English Cricket Crowds During the Victorian Age', *Journal of Sport History*, 9/3 (1982)

Seagrove, Jenny, 'The Sports Metaphor in American Cultural Discourse', *Culture, Sport, Society*, 3/1 (Spring 2000)

Semenza, Gregory M. Colón, 'Sport, War, and Contest in Shakespeare's Henry VI', *Renaissance Quarterly*, 54/4 (Winter 2001)

Sempel, Carl, 'Televised Sports: Masculinist Moral Capital and Support for the US Invasion of Iraq', *Journal of Sport and Social Issues*, 30/1 (February 2006)

Shaw, Martin and Roy Carr-Hill, 'Mass Media and Attitudes to the Gulf War in Britain', *Electronic Journal of Communication*, 2/1 (1991)

Smith, M. van Wyk, 'The Boers and the Anglo-Boer War (1899–1902) in the Twentieth Century Moral Imaginary', *Victorian Literature and Culture*, 31/2 (2003)

Spiers, Edward, 'The British Cavalry 1902–1914', *Journal of the Society of Army Historical Research*, 57/230 (1979)

Spivey, Nigel, 'Walston, Sir Charles (1856–1927)', in H. C. G. Matthews and Brian Harrison (eds.), *Oxford Dictionary of National Biography* (Oxford, Oxford University Press, 2004)

Strachan, Hew, 'The Idea of War', in Kate McLoughlin (ed.), *The Cambridge Companion to War Writing* (Cambridge: Cambridge University Press, 2009)

Stearn, Roger T., 'War Correspondents and Colonial War, c1870–1900', in John M. Mackenzie (ed.), *Popular Imperialism and the Military, 1850–1950* (Manchester: Manchester University Press, 1992)

Stoddart, Brian, 'Sport, Cultural Imperialism, and Colonial Response in the British Empire', *Comparative Studies in Society and History*, 30/4 (October 1988)
Summers, Anne, 'Militarism in Britain Before the Great War', *History Workshop Journal*, 2 (Autumn 1976)
Taylor, Matthew, 'Sport and Civilian Morale in Second World War Britain', *Journal of Contemporary History*, 53/2 (2018)
Taylor, Matthew, 'The People's Game and the People's War: Football, Class and Nation in Wartime Britain, 1939–1945', *Historical Social Research*, 40 (2015)
Tozer, Michael, 'Cricket, School and Empire: E. W. Hornung and his Young Guard', *International Journal of the History of Sport*, 6/2 (1989)
Travers, Tim, 'The Hidden Army: Structural Problems in the British Officers Corps, 1900–1919', *Journal of Contemporary History*, 17/3 (July 1982)
Usherwood, Paul, 'Officer Material: Representations of Leadership in Late Nineteenth Century British Battle Painting', in John M. Mackenzie (ed.), *Popular Imperialism and the Military, 1850–1950* (Manchester: Manchester University Press, 1992)
Vamplew, Wray, 'Exploding the Myths of Sport and the Great War: A First Salvo', *International Journal of the History of Sport*, 31/8 (2014)
Veitch, Colin, '"Play Up! Play Up! And Win the War!" Football, the Nation and the First World War', *Journal of Contemporary History*, 20/3 (July 1985)
Wagg, Stephen, '"Time Gentlemen Please": The Decline of Amateur Captaincy in English County Cricket', in Adrian Smith and Dilwyn Porter (eds.), *Amateurs and Professionals in Post-War British Sport* (London: Frank Cass, 2000)
Wilkinson, Glenn R., '"The Blessings of War": The Depiction of Military Force in Edwardian Newspapers', *Journal of Contemporary History*, 3/1 (January 1998)
Wills, Deborah and Erin Steuter, 'The Soldier as Hunter: Pursuit, Prey and Display in the War on Terror', *Journal of War and Culture Studies*, 2/2 (2009)
Wren-Lewis, Justin and Alan Clarke, 'The World Cup – A Political Football: The International Scene: The Play's the Thing . . .', *Theory, Culture and Society*, 3/1 (1983)

Unpublished theses

Hichberger, Joan, 'Military Themes in British Painting, 1815–1914' (unpublished Ph.D. thesis, University College London, 1985)
Ross, Alexander, 'The Falklands War and the Media: Popular and Elite Understanding of the Conflict' (unpublished MA diss., University of Birmingham, 2014)
Veitch, Colin, 'Sport and War in the British Literature of the First World War' (unpublished MA diss., University of Alberta, Edmonton, 1983)
Winrow, Philip, 'The British Regular Mounted Infantry, 1880–1913: Cavalry of Poverty or Victorian Paradigm?' (unpublished D.Phil. thesis, University of Buckingham, 2014)

Websites

'"Courageous" Soldier Mark Ward to present FA Cup' (12 May 2011), BBC online news channel, <www.bbc.co.uk/news/uk-13373884> [accessed 2 May 2019]
Eastwood, Joe, 'Major E. R. (Roddy) Owen DSO The XXth The Lancashire Fusiliers' (17 October 2006), XXth Lancashire Fusiliers website, <www.lancs-fusiliers.co.uk/featre/roddyowen/RoddyOwen.htm> [accessed 17 March 2017]

'FA Cup Duties for Armed Forces Personnel' (1 June 2015), Armed Forces Day online news, <www.armedforcesday.org.uk/fa-cup-final-duties-for-armed-forces-personnel/> [accessed 2 May 2019]

'FA Cup Final Duties for Service Personnel' (19 May 2014), UK Government online news channel, <www.gov.uk/government/news/fa-cup-final-duties-for-service-personnel> [accessed 2 May 2019]

'Family Affair becomes £50 Million Charity' (12 June 2010), BBC online news channel, <www.bbc.co.uk/news/10296858> [accessed 3 May 2019]

'German Skull Row Troops Suspended' (15 November 2015), BBC online news channel, <http://news.bbc.co.uk/1/hi/world/europe/6106546.stm> [accessed 11 February 2019]

'Invictus Games Foundation' (2016), Invictus Games Foundation website, <www.invictusgamesfoundation.org/foundation> [accessed 3 May 2019]

'Joseph Lee' (21 March 2016), University of Kent British Cartoon Archive, <www.cartoons.ac.uk/cartooinst-biographies/k-l/JosephLee.html> [accessed 3 December 2018]

'Kenneth Mahood' (21 March 2016), University of Kent British Cartoon Archive, <www.cartoons.ac.uk/cartoonist-biographies/m-n/KennethMahood.html> [accessed 24 July 2017]

Levithan, Josh, 'A View-Halloo from Colwyn Phillips' (14 March 2015), A Century Back: Writing the Great War Day by Day blog, <www.acenturyback.com/tag/colwyn-philipps/> [accessed 4 October 2017]

'Listener Research Report: Air Battle Commentary by Charles Gardner' (1940), BBC online archives, <www.bbc.co.uk/archive/battleofbritain/11432.shtml?page=1> [accessed 19 April 2019]

Index

Note: Numbers in *italics* indicate figures on the corresponding page.

Absent-Minded War, An 50
Adams, I. 68, 69–70, 82
Adventures of a Subaltern, The 74
Afghanistan 144
Alderson, E. 22, 31
Allen, D. 41
Allhusen, F. E. 112
Almond, H. H. 59
Amateur Cracksman, The 45
amateurism 67–68, 95–96
Amery, L. 50
Anderson, J. 102
Argentina 8, 129–135
Army Isn't All Work, The: Physical Culture and the Evolution of the British Army, 1860–1920 4
Army Reform 19
Arnold, A. J. 86
art, sporting culture in 29–30, 144–145
Art Annual, The 29
Athletic News 80
At the Point of a Bayonet 17

Baden-Powell, R. 20, 30, 42, 43, 44, 54
Badsey, S. 40
Baily's Magazine 54
Baker, T. 29
Balcon, M. 101
Ball, C. 27
Barnes, J. 139
Barrie, W. 144
Bartlett, R. 128
Bateman, A. 66
Battle of Britain 104–105, 115
BBC 115–117, 157, 158
Beck, P. 131
Begg, S. *69*

Bell, M. 158
Bell's Life 23
Bennett, E. 28
Benson, A. C. 81
Berliner Neueste Nachrichten 48
Berridge, D. 143
Best, G. 12
Bibbs, D. 116
bin Laden, O. 142
Blackwood's Magazine 24
Book of the Happy Warrior, The 74, 81
boxing 24–26, 72
Boy's Own Paper 16
Brackenbury, H. 14
British Gaumont News 104, 108
British military, the: anti-intellectual stance in 19–20; criticisms of use of sports by 50–52, 80–82; equestrian sports and 47–48; militaristic imperialism of 14, 156; officers in 1, 22, 48–50, 95; physical fitness and games in training of 4–5, 12–13, 17–23, 40–42, 70–74, 86–87; promotion of sporting activity during the Second World War 110–111; sporting culture in 4–5, 12–13, 17–20, 29–31, 44–45, 74–75; sports-related charities for 143–144; trench warfare by 66–67, 157–158; *see also* sporting warrior, the
British Movietone News 96, 104
British Paramount News 106
Brockes, E. 138
Brontë, C. 1
Brooke, R. 66
Brown, I. 112
Brown, T. 106
Browning, F. H. 80–81

176 Index

Buchanan, R. 14
Buenos Aries Herald 130
Buller, R. 40, 41, 45
Burgoyne, J. 19
Burke, P. 6
Burkinshaw, K. 130
Burton, C. 83
Butler, F. 102, 103
By Sheer Pluck: A Tale of the Ashanti War 17

Caine, M. 128
Cairns, W. E. 30–31, 50
Call, The 83
Cambridge Essays on Education 81
Cameron, J. 59
Campbell, C. 26
Campbell, J. D. 4, 12, 65–66
Cape Argus 46
Cardwell Reforms 19
Carruthers, G. 82
Carruthers, S. 5
Carter, H. 99–100
Castell, D. 129
Cetywayo, Chief 27–28
Chamberlain, N. 114
charities, sports-related military 143–144
Charlton, J. 29
Charteris-Black, J. 110, 157
children and sporting culture 15–17
Chums 16
Clarendon Commission 12
Clark, G. 16
Clarke, A. 3
Clarke, T. 139
Clements, A. B. 100
Clifton Chapel 18
Cocker, M. 24
Colditz Story, The 127–128
Cold War era, the: British popular culture during 126–129; end of 126; Falklands War, 1982 8, 129–135; Gulf War, 1991 125–126, 135–138
Cole, D. 139
Collins, T. 86
Cologne Gazette 76, 77
Conan Doyle, A. 44, 46–47, 78
Connell, J. 28
Constable, H. S. 14
Contemporary Review 28
Cooper, J. 87, 131
Corelli, M. 81
Corfield, C. G. 155
Cornhill Magazine 20
Corrigan, P. 135

County Gentleman 26
Cox, R. 130
cricket 17–20, 68, 70; during the First World War 84–85; during the Second World War 106–107; in South Africa 43–45, 59–60
Cricket 1915 83
Cricketer, The 115
Cricketers of Flanders, The 73
Crimean War 13–16, 19, 21–22, 31, 154
Cripps, S. 98, 101
Crowdy, J. G. 73
Cull, N. 128
cult of athleticism 1, 66; centrality of amateurism in 67–68; First World War and 66, 67, 77–78; imperial power and 16, 18; public schools and 56–57, 80–81, 85–86; South African War and 40, 52; in Victorian society 7, 11, 41, 59
Curtin, D. T. 78
Curtin, J. 106
Curtis-Bennett, N. 111

Daily Express 6, 49, 58, 113, 155; coverage the Gulf War, 2003 140; on the ethics of greyhound racing 102–104; on the FIFA World Cup, 1982 130–131; on sporting in the military during World War I 68, 70
Daily Graphic 43
Daily Mail 6, 22, 30, 155; on boxers 72; coverage of South Africa in 40–42, 44, 48–50, 55, 59; coverage of the Gulf Wars 139; on fair play 75–76; on Germany in the First World War 77; on the Russian invasion of Poland 96; on sporting during the Second World War 105; on sporting in the military during World War I 68, 82, 83–84; sporting metaphors used by 115
Daily Mirror 115, 140–142
Daily Star 136, 142
Daily Telegraph 12
Dash to Khartoum, The 16, 17
Dawson, G. 5
Dean, B. 116–117
Deane, B. 30
Deans, B. 138
Derby Day 106–108
Dimbleby, D. 137
Doe, E. 84
dog racing *see* greyhound races; Mass Observation

Doherty, P. 113
Donald, R. 127
Dorman, A. 126, 144–145
Dormer, F. 46
Dragon, The 108, 110, 154
Drummond, R. C. 72
Dunn, T. N. 142

Edinburgh Review 11, 16
Edward VII 11
Elwes, R. 29
enemies, demonisation of British 26–28, 76–78, 156
Engel, M. 125
equestrian sports 47–48
Escape to Victory 128–129
Evans, T. 102, 103
Evening News 113
Evening Standard 94, 114

Falklands War, 1982 8, 129–135
Farr, W. 105
Fennell, J. 95
Field, The 21, 76
Financial Times, The 128
First Boer War 29–31
First World War 7–8, 156–157; cult of athleticism in 66, 67, 77–78, 80–81, 85–86; hunting and 71–72; newspaper coverage of Germany in 76–78; rugby football and 68–70, 72, 73, 75, 78–84; sense of fair play and 75–76; sporting culture during 66–67, 78–79; sporting events during 68–69; sports as training for soldiers of 70–74; trench warfare in 66–67, 157–158
Fisher, N. 129
Floreat Etona! 29
football: Falklands War and 129–131; during the First World War 68–70, 72, 73, 75, 78–84; during the Second World War 96–97, 104–105
Ford, W. J. 59
For Name and Fame; or, Through Afghan Passes 17
Forty-One Years in India 24
Franco, F. 114
Franco-Prussian War 19
Fraser's Magazine 14
French, D. 4, 13
From Pillar to Post 29
Fry, C. B. 58
Fuller, J. G. 67
Fun 24

Fussell, P. 66
Fyfe, H. H. 82

Gaddafi, M. 142
Gardner, C. 115, 157
Gas Masks for Goal Posts 5
German War, The 78
Germany, newspaper coverage of 76–78, 97–98, 107–109
Gilham, J. 70
Gilroy, P. 125
Girouard, M. 15
Gordon, H. 114
Grace, W. G. 72–73
Graphic 22
Great Boer War, The 47
Greater Game, The 5
Great Escape, The 128
Great War, The: The Standard History of the All-Europe Conflict 76
greyhound races 99, 100, 102–104
Guardian 6; coverage of the Gulf Wars by 125, 137–139
Gulf War, 1991 125–126, 135–138, 156
Gulf War, 2003 137–141

Haig, D. 72
Hall, J. N. 73
Hamilton, G. 127
Hamilton, I. 65
Handbook of the Boer War, A 51
Hands, C. E. 55
Hands, R. 66
Hannay, D. 81
Harington, C. H. 111
Harmsworth, A. 40
Harris, P. 99
Hawins, R. H. 115
Hayes, R. A. 99
He Fell Among Thieves 14
Henderson, G. F. R. 50–51
Henty, G. A. 16–17, 20
Heron-Maxwell, B. 75
Hichberger, J. 29
Hilbourne, W. C. 54
Hill, J. 94
Hill, R. M. 112
Hiller, F. 75
Historical Journal of Film, Radio and Television 129
History of the Indian Mutiny 27
Hitler, A. 106, 114
Hofmeyr, J. 46
Holmes, R. 4

Hope Grant, J. 23
Horne, J. 76
Hornung, E. W. 45
horse-racing 100
Huggins, M. 95, 101
Hughes, T. 15–16, 18
Hughson, J. 69–70
hunting 71–72
Hussein, S. 125, 139, 141–142
Huston, J. 128

Illustrated London News 69
imperialism, militaristic 14, 156
Independent 138
Indian Rebellion, 1857–1858 13, 19, 20, 154; boxing as metaphor for 24–26
Inge, W. R. 66
Iraq 125–126, 135–142, 144, 155
Ireland, E. 70
Islanders, The 39, 56–59, 65

Jackson, A. 5
Jamaican Revolt 13
James, W. 111
Jane, F. T. 78
Jane Eyre 1
Jansen, S. 126, 142
John, S. 60, 68
Jones, P. 78
Journal of War and Culture Studies 142

Kaye, J. 20–21
Kelly, J. 126, 143, 144, 158
Khan, A. 25
King, A. 126
King, S. 126
Kinglake, A. W. 21, 31
Kipling, R. 7, 39, 56–59, 65
Knox, W. G. 81
Korda, A. 107–108
Kriegel, L. 16
Kuusisto, R. 142

La Marseillaise 128
Lee, J. 113
Leech, J. 24–26
Le Temps 39
Lion Has Wings, The 107–108
Lloyd, J. B. 53
Lloyd's Weekly Newspaper 41
localization of war 126
Lockwood, M. 47–48
Longmate, N. 95

Loom of Youth, The 82
Lord Northcliffe's War Book 78
Low, D. 114
Lowther, H. C. 28–29
Lowther, J. W. 46
Luedtke, B. 67–68
Lyttleton, A. 52

MacFarlane, N. 129
Mackay, R. 95
MacKenzie, S. P. 127–128
Madge, C. 101
Mais, S. P. D. 80
Malim, F. B. 81
Manchester Guardian 13, 19, 22, 27; call for donations by 106; coverage of South Africa in 41–44, 46, 48, 52, 55–56; criticisms of sporting during the Second World War by 101; on the First World War 76; on football during the Second World War 97, 98, 104; on Game Laws 72; on greyhound races 99; military promotion of sporting activity in 110–111; sporting metaphors used by 115
Mangan, J. A. 3, 6, 11, 14, 17
Mann, M. 125
Mason, T. 4, 65, 67, 94, 95, 157
Mass Observation: on Air Propaganda 116; establishment of 101; on public attitudes toward racing 112; on racing sports reporting in the media 103–104; on war puritanism 117
McAllan, I. 30
McDonald, R. 16
McInnes, C. 126
McIntyre, B. 155
McKenzie, C. 3, 6
Meinertzhagen, R. 24
Mens Creatrix 80
metaphors, sporting 115, 156–157
Meynell, W. 29
militaristic imperialism 14
Mirror 6, 130
Montgomery, B. 113
Moore, J. 140
Morning Post 72
Morrison, H. 100, 113
motion pictures, Cold War-era 126–129
Mountbatten, L. 114
Muse in Arms, A 73
Mussolini, B. 114
My Early Life 23

Nadelhalft, M. 142
Napoleon III 19
Nash, A. S. 68–69
Newbolt, H. 12, 14–15, 18, 74, 81
News of the World 41
New Statesman 137
Nineteenth Century, The 59
No Black-Out for Football 96
Norman, M. 140
Nottinghamshire Guardian 30

Oberon, M. 108
Obolensky, A. 112
Observer 19, 41, 43, 48, 57, 112; on the Gulf Wars 135, 142; on sporting during the Second World War 103, 105
O'Grady, L. 143
One Thousand Miles with the C. I. V. 53–54
Operation Desert Storm 138, 156
Orwell, G. 155
Osborn, E. B. 72, 73
Osborne, G. 15
Osborne, J. H. 78
Outram, J. 20

Paris, M. 5, 6, 12, 18, 66, 95, 125, 127, 139
Parker, P. 66
Parsons, N. 112
Partridge, B. *53*
Pathé Gazette 98
Peacock, J. 138
Pemberton, M. 82
Penn, R. 143
Petersburgskiya Viedomosti 28
Philipps, C. 72
Philo, G. 137
Pigsticking 20
Pink and Scarlet 31
Pollard, A. F. 79
Pope, J. 83–84
popular militarism 7
Porter, R. 6
Powell, D. 127
Pragnell, G. 57
Preston, P. 137
prisoner-of-war (POW) films 127–129
Pronay, N. 103
Public School in War Time, The 80
public schools and cult of athleticism 56–57, 80–81, 85–86
Pulton, R. 75

Pun, D. 143
Punch 24, 53, *53*, 79; on Germany in the First World War 76, 77

Ralph, J. 49–50
Ramsden, J. 126, 129
Ramsey, A. 131
Ray, R. 84
Raymond, E. 84
Reader, W. J. 66
Richards, J. 13
Riedi, E. 4, 65, 67, 94, 95, 157
Ripon, A. 5
Roberts, F. 25
Roberts, J. 66
Roberts, Lord 24
Romance of the Boer War, The 43–44
Ross, P. T. 52
Roundell, C. S. 48
rugby *see* football
Russell, W. H. 5–6

Sabo, D. 126, 142
Sahib, N. 27
Samuel, J. 130
San Demetrio London 101–102
Schwarzkopf, N. 141
Scotsman 22
Seagrove, J. 2
Seaman, O. 77
Second Anglo-Maratha War 17
Second Boer War 81
Second Opium War 23
Second World War 8, 157; athlete volunteers in 94; Battle of Britain in 104–105, 115; BBC reports during 115–117, 157; cricket during 106–107; criticism of sporting during 99–102; Derby Day and 106–108; government attitude toward sport during 94–95, 102–103; greyhound races during 99, 100, 102–104; ideal of the sporting warrior in 95; media coverage of Germany during 107–109; newspaper coverage of 97–98; packaged in language of sport 112–117; public enjoyment of sports during 97–98; rugby football during 96–97, 104–105; sporting culture during 109–110
Self-Help 15
September 11, 2001 terrorist attacks 126, 145, 155
Shakespeare, W. 2

180 *Index*

Sheffield, G. 67, 70–71, 74
Shinwell, M. 100
Shukman, D. 137
Sillars, S. 85
Simpson, F. E. W. 113
Sisson, H. A. 111
Smiles, S. 15
Smith, G. E. 73
Smith-Dorrien, H. 74–75
Snow, W. 84
Social Life in the British Army 31
Soldier Heroes: British Adventure, Empire and the Imagining of Masculinity 5
Soldier's Pocket Book for Field Service, The 19–20
Something About Horses 14
South African War, 1899–1902 7, 154, 155, 156; civilian sporting culture and 45–46, 59–60; concerns over professionalism of British troops in 48–50, 56–57; criticisms of British military training in 50–52; equestrian sports in 47–48; literary references to sporting during 43–45, 52–57; newspaper coverage of 39–43, 49–51; populist history of early stages of 46–47; Rudyard Kipling on 56–59, 65; sporting culture prior to 39–41
Spectator, The 45, 66, 72, 79, 83–84
Spiers, E. 4, 12
Sport and the Military: The British Armed Forces 1880–1960 4
sporting culture, British 1–3; as agent of moral and physical well-being 14–15; amateurism in 67–68, 95–96; in art 29–30, 144–145; boxing in 24–26, 72; for children and young people 15–16, 18–19, 66, 68–69, 73–75, 85–86; cricket in (*see* cricket); equestrian sports in 47–48; during the First World War 66–67, 78–79; hunting in 71–72; manliness and 11–12; prior to the South African War 39–41; rugby football in (*see* football); during the Second World War 109–110; self-sacrifice and honour in 75–76; in South Africa 45–46; sports-related military charities in 143–144; trench warfare and 66–67, 156–157; *see also* cult of athleticism
Sporting Life 68, 100
Sporting Times 83
sporting warrior, the 1, 5–8, 84; contempt for others in 28; criticisms of 50–52,
80–82; fair play and 44–45, 75–76; potential of 14; Second World War and 95
Stalag 17' 128
Stanhope, H. 140
Steuter, E. 142
Stuart, H. 11–12
Sturges, J. 128
Summer, J. B. 27
Summers, A. 7
Sun 8, 136, 137, 141
Sunday Telegraph 129
Sunday Times, The 116–117, 127, 130
Surtees, R. 2–3
Sutcliffe, H. 114
Swinton, E. 83

Tales of the Great War 74
Tate, T. 87
Taylor, M. 95
Taylor, P. 5
Telegraph 6
Tell England 84
Temple, W. 80
tennis 113
Thackeray, W. 15
Third Opium War 25
Thomas, C. 131
Thomas of the Light Heart 77
Thompson, E. 29
Thompson, G. 24–26
Thompson, J. 140
Through the Sikh Wars 20
Times, The 5–7, 22, 23, 156; coverage of South Africa in 39, 40–41, 46–48, 50, 52, 56–57; coverage of the Gulf Wars 139; on cricket 84–85; criticisms of sporting during the Second World War by 100–101; on Derby Day 106–107; on the FIFA World Cup, 1982 129–131; on Germany in the First World War 76; on Military Football Season of 1914 68; military promotion of sporting activities in 111–112; portrayals of Britain's enemies in 26–28; on rugby football 79, 82, 96–97; on the Second World War 97, 105–106; on sport as training for war 70–71; on sporting culture in the First World War 75; sporting metaphors used by 114, 115; on war as greatest sporting contest of all 83
Times History of War in South Africa 50
Tom Brown's School Days 15–16, 18
Townley, E. 70

trench warfare 66–67, 156–157
Tristram, H. B. 79

'Urabi, A. 26

Vamplew, W. 66
Vanity Fair 15
Veitch, C. 67
Vernede, R. G. 83
Victorian era, the 157; Crimean War in 13–16, 19, 21–22, 31; manliness in 11–12; popularity of cricket in 17–18; sporting practices in 1–2, 11; sports and fitness in the military in 12–13; war conceptualized as sport in 3–4; wars of 5–7
Vitaï Lampada 14, 83
von Muller, K. 78

Waldstein, C. 44–45
Walter, A. 40
Walvin, J. 94
Wand-Tetley, T. H. 97
war: boxing as metaphor for 24–26; British public experience with 5–8, 23; conceptualized as sport 3–4, 21–24, 55–56, 126, 157–158; localization of 126; newspaper coverage of events of 5–7, 22–23, 26–29, 39–43, 49–51, 76–78, 97–98, 105–106; portrayals of British enemies in 26–28, 76–78, 156; prettifying of 158; *see also* First World War; Second World War; South African War, 1899–1902; sporting warrior, the
Ward, M. 143

War Illustrated 72, 78, 82, 83
Warner, P. 114–115
War on Terror 126, 141–145, 155, 157
war puritanism 117
Warrior Nation: Images of War in British Popular Culture, 1850–2000 5
Waugh, A. 82
Wavell, A. 111
Wazha-pa-Wazha 144–145
Western Mail 53
Westminster Gazette 28
White, G. 30, 54
Wigglesworth, N. 94
Wilkinson, G. 41
Williams, J. 85
Wills, D. 142
Wilson, H. W. 42, *43*
Wingfield-Stratford, É. 23
Winter, J. 7
With the Flag to Pretoria 42, *43*
With the Mounted Infantry and the Mashonaland Field Force, 1896 22
Wollen, W. 29
Wolseley, G. 19
Wood, E. 72
Wooden Horse, The 127
Woodward, S. 140
Wren-Lewis, J. 3

Yea, L. 21, 31
Ye Mingchen 23
Young England 16

Zulu War, 1879 26, 27–28

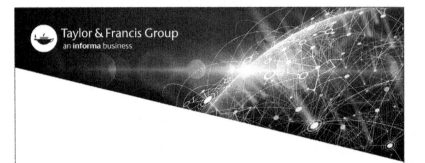